W9-DGI-041

Talent and Society

NEW PERSPECTIVES IN THE IDENTIFICATION OF TALENT

DAVID C. McCLELLAND
Professor of Psychology, Harvard University

ALFRED L. BALDWIN
Professor and Head, Department of Child Development and Family Relationships, Cornell University

URIE BRONFENBRENNER
Professor of Psychology and of Child Development and Family Relationships, Cornell University

FRED L. STRODTBECK
Associate Professor of Social Psychology University of Chicago

D. VAN NOSTRAND COMPANY, INC.

PRINCETON, NEW JERSEY

TORONTO LONDON

NEW YORK

D. VAN NOSTRAND COMPANY, INC.
120 Alexander St., Princeton, New Jersey *(Principal office)*
257 Fourth Avenue, New York 10, New York

D. VAN NOSTRAND COMPANY, LTD.
358, Kensington High Street, London, W.14, England

D. VAN NOSTRAND COMPANY (Canada), LTD.
25 Hollinger Road, Toronto 16, Canada

Published simultaneously in Canada by
D. VAN NOSTRAND COMPANY (Canada), LTD.

Library of Congress Catalogue Card No. 58-11115

First Published June 1958
Second Printing October 1959

PRINTED IN THE UNITED STATES OF AMERICA

Preface

IN 1950 the John and Mary R. Markle Foundation, which has operated with conspicuous success a program for selecting and supporting medical scholars, developed a concern for understanding better how talented young people can be identified. Its executive secretary, John Russell, stated the question this way in his Annual Report for 1950. "From the Neolithic Age to the Atomic Age man has culled his young in search of superior offspring. . . . This generation, like every other, knows that the future of the world depends on encouraging the best. But who are the best? How can they be identified at an early age? How should one go about finding the best Scout in America, the best young scientist in our high schools, the best boy to go to college, the best son of a taxi-driver, the best daughter of an automobile plant employee, or the best all-around student for deferment from military service? How can we find our future leaders at an early age?"

The Foundation came to the Social Science Research Council to see what advice was available from experts in talent identification. In December, 1950, the Council called a conference of interested sociologists and psychologists to review progress in the field and to consider whether any steps might be taken to improve the study of talent identification. The group recommended strongly the need for basic research and theory. It felt that the practical assessment devices currently available had been developed to the point of diminishing returns, and that further major developments were not likely to take place unless the whole problem was thought through again at a fundamental level. The situation in talent identification was compared to the status of cancer research, where clinical progress toward cure of the disease seems to depend ultimately on basic knowledge at the biochemical level as to just what the cancerous growth is. The participants argued that, since practical assessment research would be likely to continue anyway because of the great social need for better selection devices, a more distinctive contribution would be to encourage basic research and new thinking on problems of talent development and identification.

Accepting this point of view, the Council appointed a Committee on Identification of Talent in 1951 consisting largely of psychologists and sociologists who had not worked specifically on the problem in the past but who, it was hoped, might bring their experience in basic personality research and theory to bear on talent identification. It was recognized from the outset that the task of the committee was not to find new "gadgets" for selecting talented young people, but to plough up new ground and to develop research perspectives that in the long run might permit the construction of such tests.

The committee met regularly until 1955, reviewed previous research, called togther several conferences of experts, and with the help of a generous grant from the Markle Foundation ultimately undertook research projects of its own to fill the gaps in current knowledge of what talent is and how it develops.

The present book is our report. It reviews the problems we discovered in trying to take a broader and a fresher look at talent identification, the research we undertook in our search for solutions to those problems, and the new perspectives, both theoretical and practical, we felt we had achieved after four years of study. Much of what we have to say must necessarily be tentative, since we set out on an exploratory mission of very broad scope. Its true value can be realized only as it stimulates others to re-examine and redefine the objectives of research leading to the better identification of talented young people.

In our task we have been greatly aided by the Council and its staff—in particular by M. Brewster Smith, who served as the always efficient Council staff member in the committee. We are also much indebted to Katherine F. Bruner for editorial assistance in the final draft of the manuscript.

The Committee on Identification of Talent

Alfred L. Baldwin
Department of Child Development and Family Relationships, Cornell University

Urie Bronfenbrenner
Department of Child Development and Family Relationships, Cornell University

Leonard S. Cottrell
Social Psychologist, Russell Sage Foundation

David C. McClelland, Chairman
Professor of Psychology, Department of Social Relations, Harvard University

Fred L. Strodtbeck
Associate Professor of Social Psychology, University of Chicago

Dael Wolfle
Executive Officer, American Association for the Advancement of Science

Contents

I

Issues in the Identification of Talent

DAVID C. McCLELLAND

THE Committee on Identification of Talent did not begin its work with a careful theoretical analysis of what is meant by the phrase "identification of talent"; it hoped, indeed, in the course of its labors to clarify just such points. It did have in mind a working definition or a working analysis of the problem of talent identification—a working viewpoint which guided its early thinking and in particular led to the support of the kind of research reported in the following chapters. To recapitulate the thinking that went into our planning, even though much of it was not explicit at the time, may be helpful here. To this end, three questions should be considered: (1) What is meant by identification of talent? What is it that we decided to study? (2) What is wrong, if anything, with the way talent is identified now; why did the problem need further study? (3) In the light of the answers to these questions, what did we propose to do about the situation? How did the projects we supported meet the research needs as we had analyzed them? With these questions the present chapter is concerned.

The term *talent,* to begin with, is ambiguous. Sometimes it refers to an aptitude or ability *in* the person, and sometimes it refers to talented performance *by* the person—i.e., behavior which goes beyond the ordinary in meeting some criterion of desirability. We shall try to keep our meaning clear by using terms like *ability* or *talent potential* for the first meaning, and *talented performance* for the second. The ambiguity has, of course, some theoretical significance, as is often the case in such matters. When we say that we want to identify talent, we mean simultaneously that we want to find people who have potential talent now and who in addition will, on a subsequent occasion, turn in a talented performance. To pursue the distinction one step further, we usually measure potential talent by sampling behavior in one situation and actual talent by sampling what may be a different kind of behavior in a different situation. Yet this is not necessarily so; sometimes the two kinds of behavior may be fairly similar—as, for example, when we try to predict grades in school (talented behavior) from test grades (aptitude tests). In both these instances the same kinds of knowledge may be called for in the same kind of situation (i.e., a written examination). Here the talent measured by a test score is "actual" so far as the test is concerned but "potential" in the sense of predicting how a person will do in a similar situation of presumably greater importance. At other times the difference between test behavior and criterion behavior, as it is usually called, may be very considerable; thus we may, for example, want to know on the basis of certain test scores whether a boy is likely to be a "success in life."

The accompanying diagram may point up some of the problems involved in predicting from one situation or response to another:

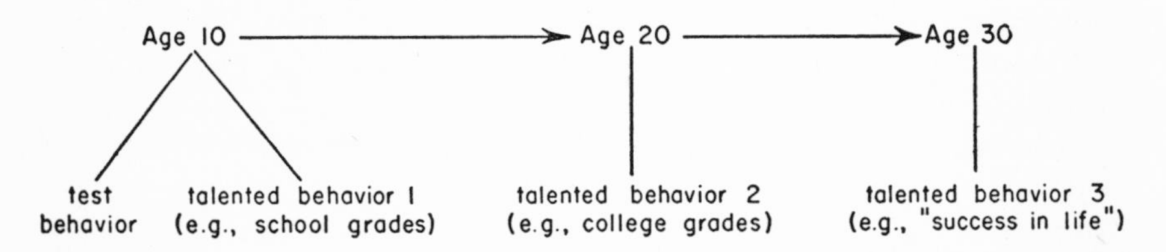

Thus, although we may be able to predict fairly well from a boy's test behavior at ten what his school grades will be at the same age, when we try to predict later criteria of talented performance—such as his college grades at twenty, or some measure of his success in life at thirty—we head for trouble.

In the first place, unless we test again, we are assuming that whatever characteristic we measure at Age 10 will not develop or change by Age 20 or 30, an assumption which for many types of traits has simply not been tested. We may test again at Age 20 and make a useful prediction as of that moment concerning the criterion, college grades; but in that case, of course, we are no longer identifying talent potential far ahead of time, which is what society demands. In the second place, we are assuming that the situation does not change, that it will remain for the individual at twenty and at thirty approximately what it was at ten. Such an assumption may not be too far off as long as a boy stays in school, but "life" may bring on a marked change in the situation, calling for quite different types of behavior. Hence he may now blossom or fade in ways which would be inexplicable in terms merely of his past behavior in school; the new situation is an added and a complicating factor. Not only may the situation be different; it may be better or worse so far as eliciting talented behavior is concerned. It is possible, of course, to study talent-evoking situations as well as talented persons; in the research covered by the present report we have not done so because our primary concern was with the person. Thus we more or less ignore variations in the environment, simply noting that we can make better predictions of talented performance from test behavior the more similar the situations in the two instances. Though we do not treat the situational variable explicitly, we call attention to it from time to time by trying to demonstrate its importance in concrete instances.

Granting that traits and situations do not remain the same over time, what can we do about the problem thus raised? Several things. First, we need studies of the constancy of various traits over time and in particular the ways in which they develop throughout childhood. That is, if we knew the laws of trait development, we could predict from a test at Age 10 what the characteristic would be at Age 20.

Second, we need to analyze the functional characteristics of various performance situations (including school, the professions, various occupations, etc.) so that, by uncovering functional identities across situations, we can better our predictions. Medicine, for example, may be, as Parsons has argued (*11*),[1] a profession which requires for various societal reasons a considerable degree of "affective neutrality" or "impulse control." It looks as if the prolonged period of training for medicine may require the same characteristic—and require it to such an extent that people who do not have it drop out. Thus one might be able to argue, on the basis of the identity of functional requirements of a long medical training and of the medical profession, that medical training provides a good, if unintentional, means of selecting individuals fit for the pro-

[1] Italic numerals in parentheses refer to bibliographical references at the end of each chapter.

fession. Performance in medical school, in short, is a good predictor of performance as a doctor. In certain respects the two "jobs" are functionally similar—i.e., the person is being tested in the same type of situation in which he will later have to perform. This is a hypothetical argument, needless to say, introduced simply to illustrate the potential value of functional analyses of situations to discover their identities.

Third, we need research which will shed at least indirect light on relationships over time by testing different individuals at different stages of development. Consider Table 1, for example, which has been constructed without reference to the time line we have just been discussing. Here we say that (A) certain antecedent conditions produce (B) a person with certain characteristics who interacts with (C) a situation having certain characteristics, to produce performance with (D) desired outcomes. The four classes of variables thus listed provide an abstract scheme for representing various types of talent research, but the variables are seldom, if ever, studied by following the same individuals through various developmental stages indicated by going from left to right across the table. Instead, different pairs of variables are often considered successively at different age levels. For example, the relationship between A (authoritarian family structure) and B (authoritarian attitudes as represented by F-scale scores) and D (leadership) in a certain situation C (a military setting) may be investigated at Age 20. Suppose it is found that soldiers with high F-scale scores make poor military leaders, as seems to be the case (7). From linked studies of this sort conclusions may be drawn about, for example, the relationship between a personal characteristic at time 1 (say, low F-score at Age 10) and talented performance at time 2 (superior leadership behavior in a military setting at Age 20). That is, it may seem reasonable to conclude, in our hypothetical example, that authoritarian family structure tends to produce individuals who make poor leaders in a military setting or that boys who score high in authoritarian attitudes at Age 10 tend to make poor military leaders (have low potential talent for military leadership) and should perhaps not be selected for specialized military training.

But note the assumptions that have to be made just in the second instance:

(1) Boys who score high on the F-scale early will also score high later.

(2) Boys who score high on the F-scale early are neither more nor less susceptible to specialized military training; in short, though

TABLE 1. ILLUSTRATIVE ANALYSIS OF THE DETERMINANTS OF PERFORMANCE CONSIDERED "TALENTED" IN TERMS OF ITS DESIRED EFFECTS

A *Antecedent conditions* produce →	B *A person with certain characteristics* who interacts with →	C *A situation with certain characteristics* to produce performance with →	D *Desired outcomes*
Heredity	Abilities	Working conditions Skills required Values required Motives required Stability required	Work efficiency
Cultural values	Emotional Stability		Occupational rank
Family structure	Values		School grades
Socio-economic status	Motives		Salary earned
Parent attitudes	Characteristic modes of response (traits)	Type of persons in the situation	Community service
			Good morale
			Successful leadership
			Social effectiveness
			Inclusion in *American Men of Science*

conclusion (1) might be correct for ordinary civilian schooling, it might be incorrect, or even reversed, if the boys were given military training.

(3) Even supposing that (1) and (2) were correct, the demands of the military setting must remain substantially the same while the boys are growing up or talent will have been identified for the wrong criterion.

Despite the hazards of such linked studies, they are often the only ones that can give leads as to how to identify talent potential in a short period of time. And sometimes the situation is not so difficult as in the hypothetical example cited. Abilities at Age 10 (Column B), which tend to remain fairly constant, may be related to successive related criteria, for example, to school grades at Age 10 (Column D) which in turn may be related to school grades at Age 20 (still Column D) and subsequently to salary earned (still Column D). Here too, however, the table ignores the time dimension and succeeds only in listing the types of variables frequently interrelated. Such a listing has nevertheless its function in classifying various types of talent research and in showing how links may be established across time by successive studies of different pairs of variables at different age levels.

So far we have accomplished two things. (1) We have shown that the identification of talent implies predicting from one sample of behavior to another; that this ordinarily, but not always, involves a prediction of future behavior, which in turn requires a knowledge of developmental sequences (only approximated by linked studies on different subjects) and of trait and situational constancies. (2) We have listed in Table 1 some of the major variables to be considered in talent studies. Our next problem is to describe the current state of talent assessment in terms of our analysis. For simplicity in exposition, it may be helpful to set up a straw man, an oversimplified version of the way traditional assessment procedures fit into our analytical scheme. Then we shall be in a better position to show how, in terms of that analysis, such procedures might be expanded.

Suppose we want to know who will make a good surgeon. Ordinarily we begin in Column D on the right-hand side of Table 1 by trying to state objectively the criterion or outcome in which we are interested. In this case the problem is not too difficult, at least at a crude level. The minimum outcome in which we are interested is "passing the Surgical Boards or Examinations." We are striving, in other words, to predict which people, when faced by their final examinations, can pass them and be approved by the established medical authorities. This criterion implies a set of earlier criteria—graduating from medical school, being admitted to medical school, doing good enough work in college to warrant recommendation for medical school, etc. All these criteria involve, among other things, a working situation (Column C in Table 1) which requires certain problem-solving, examination-taking skills. If the person is to pass these hurdles, he must have certain abilities (Column B in Table 1), and these fortunately we are in a pretty good position to assess by means of standardized intelligence and medical aptitude tests. If we inquire further as to what the antecedent conditions are which produce these abilities (Column A in Table 1), we know in a general way that heredity is important, as well as an exposure, at home and in school, to the kind of education which will bring to fruition that hereditary potential.

Usually, however, we need not push the inquiry even this far. All we need do for selection purposes is correlate aptitude test scores with certain intermediate or final criteria (such as graduating from college or medical school), and we find that the correlations are substantial. We can, in short, predict pretty well on the basis of test scores who the people are who will do sufficiently able academic work to become surgeons. The reason seems to be that the major characteristic involved (intelligence) and the major situation involved (school) both remain relatively constant over time. Psychological research has been stalled at this level for some time, partly because it has been so successful in predicting academic performance and partly because it has not seen how to improve very much on this approach.

But it is precisely here that the Committee felt more work should be done—a more thorough and complete analysis of this process of becoming a good surgeon. The task is not too difficult. We can, for example, begin expanding the criteria in column D in which we are interested. Plainly we are concerned not only with those persons who can pass their Surgical Board examinations but also with those who subsequently turn out to be skillful surgeons. We suspect that being a good surgeon requires many more things than certain basic skills and knowledge. It probably involves the kind of motivation that will keep a man working hard for a distant goal over a long period of time, and which will make him want to go on learning new surgical techniques even after he has been approved. It involves enough emotional stability so that, when he knows what to do, he is not prevented from doing it by an attack of "nerves" if a crisis arises during an operation. In all likelihood it involves certain values, such as a belief that postponing ordinary gratifications for a prolonged period of medical training is worth the sacrifices necessary, and a belief that the individual is worthy of respect and should not be cut up at the whim of a particular surgeon or a particular government which may demand an operation for its own ulterior ends.

Technically what we are doing here is performing a criterion analysis—trying to state our desired outcomes in more detail (column D) and analyzing the working requirements of the student and professional roles until we can specify what values, motives, and the like we want to measure in the individual (column B). Even a crude analysis like this demonstrates the need for expanding the number of variables taken into account in columns B, C, and D beyond the measure of ability and performance in academic situations with which psychologists have ordinarily been concerned.

Thus it is not difficult to expand the number of variables to be considered in selecting and developing good surgeons, using the analytical scheme presented in Table 1. To expand them for other outcomes, like becoming a leader—where hereditary abilities probably play less of a role than they do for professions like surgery—would be even easier. But should the analysis be expanded? Just because it *can* be done is no reason why it *should* be done unless there is something to be gained from doing it. Perhaps it would be rewarding to take a look at some of the practical reasons which have forced a re-examination of the talent-selection process along the lines just described. The very listing of these puzzles and the difficulties which arise with present methods will serve to focus attention on the variables which ought to be considered if we are to understand the problem better.

Current Problems in Identifying Potential Talent

Lack of Fit Between Performance in School and in Later Life

Nothing is so frustrating to the talent scout as the "late bloomer," the boy who looked so unpromising in school, or who perhaps dropped out of college, but who later went on to be president of a large company or perhaps even President of the United States or Justice of the Supreme Court. As if that riddle were not enough, the talent scout has also to contend with the "morning glory," the boy who looks marvelous in school, who is a natural leader, on the Honor Roll, and the darling of his associates and teachers; yet who, despite this excessive display of promise, fades away into obscurity. These two types, as they are frequently exemplified in the flesh, are a reminder to the talent selectors that they are not yet nearly proficient enough at their jobs. If one is to believe the examples featured so frequently in the newspapers, it seems that "late bloomers" are particularly likely to occur among leaders of men, among statesmen and politicians. Who, for instance, would have guessed from Franklin D. Roosevelt's record at Harvard that he had such potential for outstanding leadership? There is some evidence that "late bloomers" appear even among professional men, for whom formal school preparation would seem much more relevant. For example, not every one of the top-flight scientists studied by Roe (*12*) had exceptionally good school records. To plead that, on the average, talent selection on the basis of school performance is fairly effective is not an adequate defense; we simply cannot afford to miss out on even a few of the top-flight men we are considering here. And some college admission requirements, both on aptitude test scores and secondary school records, are so strict that it is doubtful whether some of our leading citizens could get into these schools or colleges now.

The error here lies in assuming that school and life require *identical* abilities or character traits. What the "late bloomer" and "morning glory" show is not so much that individual characteristics wax and wane, but that different situations call for different types of talented performance. There was probably no demand at Harvard to bring out in Roosevelt the characteristics of leadership he displayed later, though he may have had them even then. Life did demand them of him.

Since it is life performance that we normally want to predict, it would be a serious error to judge exclusively in terms of the less important immediate criterion of aptitude for academic performance. True, a man has to go to school to become a pilot, a doctor, or a statesman; but it is not safe to use school aptitude alone as a means of weeding out the unfit—unless one is certain that scholastic aptitude is requiring the same thing of a man as the job itself will require. The fact of the matter is that in many cases we do not know enough about what the job requires to answer such a question. If we did, we might even want to change the school until it would rank individuals more in line with their future performance in life situations. It is this lack of fit between school and life—the constant reminder of the "late bloomers" and the "morning glories" —that forces us, perhaps more than any other single factor, to scrutinize the whole problem of talent.

Some Problems in Predictive Efficiency

Psychological tests are commonly designed to reflect sensitively differences in criterion groups (e.g., the talented and the untalented) so that scores on the test can be used to predict in which of the groups a person is most likely to belong. It is obvious, for instance, that psychotics cannot display most types of talented performance. Psychologists have tried to capitalize on this fact by producing various personal adjustment tests which can be scored to show the extent to which a person answers the items the way neurotics or psychotics do; the assumption is, of course, that the more he reacts as they do, the less potential talent will he have. Often positive, though small, validity coefficients are reported to show that high scorers on a neuroticism inventory are in fact less likely to be successful.

While the logic of this approach seems straightforward enough, it runs into a number of difficulties that are frequently ignored in practice. In the first place, as Meehl and Rosen (9) have pointed out, use of tests as selectors, even if fairly valid, may be less efficient than simply relying on the base rates where "the base rates of the criterion classification deviate greatly from a 50 per cent split." For example, the base rate of serious maladjustment among leaders must be fairly low—5 to 10 per cent. So if no selection at all is made on the basis of potential neuroticism, 5 to 10 per cent of the candidates who are "passed" will subsequently turn out to be poorly adjusted. And it would be hard to reduce this small number of "mistakes" even by using a neuroticism test with fairly high validity as a selecting device, because the test is imperfect and misclassifies individuals. Moreover, it screens out a number of people who would have done all right, and of course fails to screen out some people who will not do all right.

A second difficulty in predicting from tests of this sort arises from the fact that the reactions of individuals are commonly obtained after they are already members of one of the criterion groups—after, for example, they have turned out to be psychotic or normal. Such differences in reactions are then taken as a basis for scoring the responses of individuals who are not yet members of either group—to find out if they are potentially psychotic. The fact is, of course, that there is no certainty about whether psychotics in their pre-psychotic stage would have answered the items the way they do now as psychotics. The same point is made in a quite different connection by Whyte (*20*), who claims that successful executives do not answer personality schedules the way they "should" (according to the scoring key). Presumably, having "arrived," they feel they can be more honest. Such an argument does not necessarily prove the inventories invalid, of course, since the successful executives *might* have answered the way they "should" if they were being considered for a job. But the main point is well taken: easy assumptions about the similarity of meaning of test responses given under different "sets" or at different points in a person's development should not be made without being tested.

A third difficulty arises from assuming, often without checking, that a positive validity coefficient proves the relationship between the test and criterion to be linear throughout the entire range. For example, it seems possible, even probable, that personal maladjustment is some kind of threshold phenomenon. Once it gets above a certain point, it seriously interferes with work; below that point, it may have no correlation whatsoever with success. If the whole range of maladjustment is included, there should be a positive correlation with success; but to use anything but extreme scores for selection purposes would be to ignore the fact that over most of the range the correlation is zero. Recent tests like the Minnesota Multiphasic Psychological Inventory call attention to this fact by establishing fairly wide "normal" limits. But the argument can theoretically be pushed one step further: it is at least possible that the large majority of *moderately* able men may answer certain inventories as they should—their future success may, in fact, be the basis of the inventory's validity—while the very few really exceptional men may actually be penalized by the inventory for "exceptional" thinking. The relationship between test and criterion, in short, may in some instances be curvilinear, so that validity holds only for moderate ranges of success. Such illustrations point up the necessity of studying test and criterion relationships carefully for nonlinear trends.

These three difficulties do not apply with the same force to ability testing. While neuroticism tests are used to screen out rare cases of unfit persons, ability tests are used to "screen in" rare cases of persons who deserve special treatment. Predicting from base rates alone, therefore, has opposite practical effects in the two cases. If we want to select the top 5 per cent in academic competence, we *could* use no selective device and let everyone enter graduate school; but the base rate would be working against us, and we would include 95 per cent of the people we did not want. But if, on the other hand, we want to screen out the 5 per cent who will be neurotic, we can use no selective device, pass everybody, and still include only 5 per cent of the people we did not want. Consequently, selecting graduate students on the basis of almost any test with validity in the intelligence area is an improvement over waiting for selection to take place in terms of the base rate in the general population.

There are, however, base rates for different segments of the population which, if used for comparison, make it more difficult for tests to show any improvement in predictive efficiency. Perhaps an example from weather forecasting will make the point clearer. One "base rate"—the most general one—is to assume that the weather tomorrow is as likely to be one kind as another. Against this "chance" base line, the forecaster does pretty well. We say he predicts "better than chance." But suppose we establish as a base line the prediction that tomorrow's weather will be like today's. The weather man has a much harder time beating this simple prediction. The situation is analogous in the field of predicting talented performance from tests. If we make the most general base-line assumption—that any boy is as likely to do well as any other—then our tests do pretty well in increasing our predictive efficiency. But suppose we make another base-line assumption—that a child will achieve the same level of success as his father. It is much more difficult to demonstrate that a testing program will do a more efficient job of forecasting eventual success than will this simple assumption. (See Chapter 3.) It is probably fortunate that the value of tests must be measured not only against sheer predicting efficiency but also against the democratic belief that each individual deserves the opportunity to demonstrate what he can do.

In intelligence testing there is no problem of possible differences in test responses of potential and actual members of criterion groups, since ability test scores are not readily influenced by changes in a person's attitude toward the test. But the question of the linearity of the relationship of intelligence test scores to even so simple a criterion as school performance has not been studied as it deserves. Let us admit that morons cannot do good school work. But what evidence is there that intelligence is not a threshold type of variable; that once a person has a certain minimal level of intelligence, his performance beyond that point is uncorrelated with his ability? Several studies suggest that if such a minimal level is set fairly high, ability may no longer play a crucial role in success. Anne Roe in her study of eminent scientists has reported intelligence test data showing a wide range from the highest to the lowest person tested. It is true that the *average* score was very high, but it is equally true that there were several scientists whose tested intelligence was only moderately above average. In other words, given a certain moderately high level of intelligence, it is possible to be one of the world's greatest living scientists.

Terman and Oden's follow-up study of gifted children (*16*) is even more interesting. Among their subjects, all of whom had had high I.Q.'s as children, they were able to distinguish a conspicuously successful group and another group relatively less successful. The difference in the average intelligence between these two groups was slight. *At this high level,* the correlation between ability and achievement practically disappears. Naturally this is to a considererable extent simply the result of restriction in the range of test scores, since Terman worked with only a small percentage of cases at the top of his I.Q. distribution. Yet it suggests the desirability of plotting carefully the relationship of ability test scores to performance criteria *over the entire range,* in order to check for threshold, deceleration, or other curvilinear relationships. At the very least, it suggests the wisdom in such cases of presenting test data in gross units of measurement (e.g., deciles rather than percentiles), thus forcing judges to make discriminations in terms of some other variables known to be influential at high levels of intelligence.

What some of these other variables are is also shown by Terman and Oden. The factors which really differentiated the successful and less successful groups at a high level of intelligence were, they found, socio-economic in nature. That is, subjects who came from better backgrounds (professional homes, with more books in the home, etc.) did better in life, were more successful, than equally intelligent subjects from less advantaged homes. A similar finding emerges from data reported by Wolfle and Smith (22) which show that post-high-school education is a more important determinant of future success (measured by income) than intelligence is. Indeed, if I.Q. score is held constant, post-high-school education makes a considerable difference in income level; but if post-high-school education is held constant, I.Q. makes a smaller difference in income level. So the advantage of a better education, presumably also associated with socio-economic status, is greater than the advantage of higher intelligence, at least so far as this measure of success is concerned.

Stimulated by such findings, Brim surveyed for the Committee studies of the relationship between ability and achievement to see whether factors associated with socio-economic status (SES) had been taken into account. I.Q. and SES are related *both* to such criteria as school grades and to each other. A partial correlation would doubtless show that I.Q. continues to be related to school grades, after the influence of SES is removed; but the relationship may not be linear across the whole range of I.Q., SES, or school level. Brim could find no evidence that the problem had been investigated thoroughly—possibly because it falls somewhere between psychology and sociology. He could, in short, find no good example of a study which compared the school performance of two groups of subjects differing on the average in intelligence but matched on socio-economic status at upper-, middle-, and lower-class levels. The presumption would be, of course, that even though the groups were matched for background factors, the average difference in intelligence should make a large difference in their school performance. At the lower end of the intelligence scale, it certainly would, if the comparison were between feeble-minded and normal children, whatever their backgrounds. The fact of the matter is that, for normal levels of intelligence and above, the definitive study has apparently not been made. Yet it becomes especially important to attempt it because of the findings by Terman and Oden (*16*) and by Wolfle and Smith (*22*) that, with intelligence held constant, background factors do make a large difference in future success. Since probably no other single assumption is so widely held among both scientists and laymen as that intelligence, as such, regardless of background, is linearly associated with success both in school and in life, the importance of clarifying the whole issue is crucial. It should be accorded high priority in any set of research projects undertaken to improve the predictive efficiency of test scores.

The Meaning of Good Performance

Talented performance was defined above as an exceptional display of desired or desirable behavior in a given situation. But a lot of problems lie concealed in such phrases as "desirable behavior" or "a good performance." Already we have raised certain questions as to whether good performance in school is necessarily the same thing, or involves the same characteristics, as good performance in life. But a little further reflection raises other difficulties. To put the point somewhat crudely for the sake of clarity, is it possible to develop a test score which would predict equally well success in *any* environment—for example, in Communist China, Fascist Germany, or the democratic United States? Is potential talent, in other words, solely a property of the person? Obviously not; yet sometimes psychologists seem to act as if they thought it were. Will the Stanford-Binet (or its translation) predict equally well how a child will do in an American school, a Nazi school, or a Communist school? It will so far as the school situation is identical in the three cases. But if one school system defines good performance by memory skill, another by unquestioning loyalty to pat formulas, and still another by social charm or athletic ability, it will not. If our primary aim is the prediction of talented performance, we must first define that commodity; only then can we find suitable test variables to predict it—not begin the other way around with a test variable which we trust to predict performance under any conditions. The fact is that even such an apparently clear-cut criterion as school performance contains more or less "hidden" characteristics whereby the child is judged over and beyond his sheer problem-solving skills—characteristics which become obvious enough when we make comparisons across school systems in different countries. If we are to do a better job of predicting from test scores, we must know what the full meaning of talented performance is, even in the school situation; we must, for instance, measure those variables other than sheer ability (values, motives, etc.) which also lead to kinds of behavior in terms of which the pupil is finally to be judged.

The problem resolves itself, as we have seen in Table 1, into a more complete analysis of what outcomes we are interested in, of what characteristics, for example, a vocation really requires the point of view of social structure—including what values, what motives, or what ability to withstand stress. People nowadays want to know about more than the actual performance of the job in question; they want to know about such things as skill in human relations, community responsibility, and social sensitivity (or the ability to know what others are thinking, feeling, and wanting). Studies of such aspects of good performance as these are clearly needed if we are to make a real improvement in identifying talent potential.

Loss of Potential Talent

A fundamental assumption of democracy is that young people should have a chance. We believe that no one should be denied the opportunity to go as far as his abilities will allow. Yet we know that many students do not even graduate from high school, among them many even of above average intelligence. Certainly a high school education is a prerequisite for the development of most types of talent; for many, even a college education. So there has been a natural concern with the loss of talent, the seepage out of the school system of potentially able people for whatever reason. Wolfle (*21*) and Berdie (*1*) have published extensive studies of this problem. Here we need give illustrative figures only.

As just one concrete example, in New Haven, Connecticut, a city of around 200,000 people, Davie (*3*) reports that in a year shortly after World War II over 1,000 sixteen- and seventeen-year-olds, or approximately 28 per cent of the total population of this age group, left school after sixteen, the legal minimum age of required school attendance. Though naturally the figures vary from city to city and state to state, it may be safely estimated that only around 60 per cent of American young men and women graduate from high school and that of these graduates about 35 per cent enter and 21 per cent graduate from college (*21*, p. 313). Numerically, then, a large number of young people are lost at an early age out of the normal line of development toward a high-level career.

Most of these students, we know, have poor school records and are less intelligent, on the whole, than their fellows who continue in school (*21*, p. 313); but this does not mean that they include no persons of high ability. And it is about these that we are concerned. For example, Stouffer (*15*) has reported data from another choice point—namely, the point at which a person decides to go on to college or not. In a medium-sized school system near Boston, he located 236 individuals who were classified as falling in the top 20 per cent of I.Q. test scores. These represent the "intellectual elite" who are certainly potentially capable of doing college work. Of these 236 students, 102 (or around 43 per cent) did not go to college. These figures agree well with those from larger studies which have shown that only about 50 per cent of students in the upper 10 to 20 per cent of the ability range are in college (*1*, p. 14; *21*, p. 150). So it is not low I.Q. alone which explains why people drop out of school. Nor is it low grades. In Stouffer's group of 102 subjects with high I.Q.'s who did not go to college, 46 had consistently good academic records throughout all their schooling. The fact that the other 56 did not have good grades demonstrates, incidentally, that other factors must have been at work even earlier to turn these people's interests away from the normal line of school achievement.

But still 45 per cent did have good records. Why didn't they go to college?

What about finances, as a first possibility? Perhaps they had not enough money to go to college. To some extent, the figures bear this out. The father's occupation was known in 89 of the 102 cases cited above, and, of these 54 (or 60 per cent) were classified as Working Class. Out of the 54 high I.Q. students from relatively poor homes, 23 had good enough academic records to be admitted to college.

Would liberal scholarships have saved these 23 students for college and presumably for a more important career in life? Berdie (*1*) after an extensive study of Minnesota high school students thought not, for the reason that they would not have applied for the scholarships. There was a very low correlation (of the order of .10), he found, between economic status and college plans; he concluded that "making additional funds available through scholarship programs . . . will have little effect other than to make it easier for those students now attending college, or planning to enter, to obtain higher education" (*1*, p. 81).

Mulligan (*10*) has reported data which bear on this point directly. He compared the proportion of students at the University of Indiana having fathers in a given occupational category with the proportion employed in that category in the State of Indiana (see Table 2). Normally sons from the upper end of the socio-economic scale are present at the University in considerably greater propor-

TABLE 2. PERCENTAGES OF VETERAN AND NONVETERAN STUDENTS ENROLLED IN THE UNIVERSITY OF INDIANA IN 1947 HAVING FATHERS IN DIFFERENT OCCUPATIONAL CATEGORIES COMPARED WITH PERCENTAGES EMPLOYED IN THOSE CATEGORIES IN THE STATE OF INDIANA (AFTER MULLIGAN (*10*), P. 193)

Father's Occupation	State of Indiana %	Students at the Univ. of Indiana		
		Nonveterans %	Veterans %	Gain or Loss
Professional men	4.2	17.4	14.0	—3.4
Farmers	14.2	12.9	7.8	—5.1
Proprietors	8.3	27.5	23.0	—4.5
Clerical workers	11.9	16.4	18.1	1.7
Skilled workers	16.4	11.1	18.9	7.8
Semi-skilled workers	19.4	3.5	6.7	3.2
Unskilled workers	24.3	4.9	6.7	1.8
Unknown	1.2	6.3	4.8	—

tion than one would expect from the state employment figures; compare the first two columns in Table 2. The reverse is true of the lower end of the socio-economic scale, from which sons appear less than one fifth as often as on a chance basis they should. The influence of making generous scholarship money available through G.I. benefits can be observed by comparing the veteran with the nonveteran figures. Obviously financial aid has increased the proportion of students from economically underprivileged groups going to college. Just as obviously, the increase comes nowhere near wiping out the underrepresentation from lower income groups; nor is the increase equally marked in all initially underrepresented groups; nor is the change greater, the greater the degree of economic deprivation. Whereas the greatest absolute increase is for the sons of skilled workers, there is a very slight increase for the sons of unskilled workers, and an actual decrease for the sons of farmers, even though they too were initially underrepresented. Clearly, factors other than financial ones are influencing the effect of scholarship aid on the decision to go to college.

One of these other factors is almost certainly motivation. Some of these students may not want to get ahead, to pursue high-level careers. Rosen has data (*13*) that bear out this supposition, at least in part. He finds that a motive for high achievement is present much less often among lower-class high school students than among middle-class ones. But this is not the whole story. Even among his high school students with motivation for high achievement, most of those from the lowest socio-economic group did not plan or want to go to college. Although they had high motivation, they did not intend to go on with school. What this fact strongly suggests is another important factor in the loss of talent potential: the value placed by the family group on education and on high-level careers as compared with certain other values, such as making money, supporting and helping the family, and so on. The whole pattern of family interests, Berdie concludes, is a crucial factor in determining the college plans of the high school students he studied; "any program of action must be directed toward the parents of high school students" (*1*, p. 79) who often are just not interested in higher education for their children.

Even such a brief illustrative analysis shows that potential talent is "lost" in a variety of ways—any one of which, or any combination of which, may be sufficient to prevent a person from developing into a talented performer: low intelligence, low school record (which may itself be a result of other factors), lack of financial help, lack of motivation, or simply lack of a set of values which would push one toward a high-level career. Certainly we need to know more about all these factors and how they interact if we are to improve our present imperfect rate of talent development.

Cultural Differences in Occupational Achievement

One of the striking features of the American scene is the disparity in occupational achievement shown by certain groups as a whole; for example, Jews tend to be high-achievers, whereas certain other groups, such as the Catholics, are in comparison with other groups low-achievers. There has been a natural reluctance to pay much attention to such facts, because minority groups have so often and so recently been the target of persecution and prejudice that it often seems preferable not to make them conspicuous in any way. Yet it may be that a study of group differences in achievement would help us understand which values lead to talent development and which do not. It could; that is, unless, as some social scientists argue, group differences in achievement are all to be attributed to prejudice. The difficulty with that argument is that it is often used both ways. It is used to explain why Negroes or Catholics do less well occupationally: prejudice has kept them from rising on the American scene. The next moment, it is used to explain the conspicuous achievement of the Jews: prejudice has had the opposite effect; it has stimulated them to greater effort. Such reasoning, at the very least, suggests that a more thorough analysis of additional factors contributing to the response to prejudice is highly desirable.

Others may question whether there are large enough group differences in achievement to make it worth studying the characteristics of over- and under-achieving groups. To take the best-documented instance, there is ample evidence from a variety of sources to show that Jews are conspicuous over-achievers. They do better in school than one would expect on the basis of I.Q. alone (*2, 16*); a larger percentage of them go to college (*14*); in a New England city they have been reported to have risen more rapidly in the class system than other immigrants arriving about the same time and facing the same disadvantages (*18*); among those with high I.Q. in Terman and Oden's study (*16*) the Jews were strikingly more often in the successful category than in the unsuccessful one; according to Havemann and West's study (*6*) of over 9,000 college graduates, they make more money, on the average, than either Catholics or Protestants. Perhaps the single most striking finding is Strodtbeck's estimate (Appendix A) that, whereas in the United

States urban population as a whole approximately 35 to 40 per cent of the gainfully employed persons may be classified as belonging in upper-level occupations (e.g., clerks, managers, professionals), 80 to 85 per cent of the gainfully employed urban Jews are in these same high-status occupations. Possibly other groups, like the Presbyterians, Quakers, and Mormons, have performed equally well, but the data are not available for exact comparisons.

Easy explanations for such differences, such as prejudice or racial inheritance, are clearly inadequate. Even differences in the kind of schooling children receive, an explanation correctly used to explain why many Negroes are under-achievers, is not in all cases a sufficient explanation. It will not explain why Jews do so much better than other students attending the same schools. It will not explain why Negroes who have lived for several generations in Ontario where there is minimal prejudice (certainly less than that directed against Jews in many locations where they have succeeded) and attending the same schools as whites, still continue as a group to be under-achievers (*17*, pp. 292-296). The facts point clearly to the necessity for a study of the value-orientations of different cultural groups. Negroes may still carry with them for generations the dependent values and motives developed under slavery (cf. Dollard, *4*), whereas Jews may have opposite values leading to upward mobility based on a long tradition of literacy and respect for learning.

Although behavioral scientists have been slow to follow its lead, there is ample historical support for the study of value differences. Max Weber argued over fifty years ago (*19*) that the religious ideology of Protestantism seemed to be closely tied up with the development of capitalism. He noted that Protestants were more drawn than Catholics to entrepreneurial occupations, for example, and tended to be more successful in business. The same tendency appears in occupational choices even today, as Table 3 shows. The religious groups listed in this table started off about equal: they were all college graduates and all had about the same financial backing, to the extent that backing can be estimated by the fact that approximately equal percentages were on scholarship in college. Yet the Protestant college graduates end up significantly more often in managerial occupations than do the Catholics, as Weber had observed in Germany many years ago. The table also illustrates the over-achievement of Jews mentioned earlier.

To cite just one other example, Knapp and Goodrich (*8*) have reported that scientists are much more likely to come from Protes-

TABLE 3. OCCUPATIONAL ACHIEVEMENT OF JEWISH, PROTESTANT, AND CATHOLIC COLLEGE GRADUATES AS OF 1947-48. (N=9,064) (FROM HAVEMANN AND WEST (6))

Occupational Achievement	Jews %	Protestants %	Catholics %
Proprietors, managers, executives	33	34	26
Nonteaching professionals	45	34	32
Teachers	6	12	13
All types of white collar and manual workers and farmers	16	20	29
Per cent earning $7,500 and over a year	27	21	15

tant than Catholic colleges, and that lawyers are more likely to come from Catholic colleges. It would be impossible to take the time here to go into a thorough analysis of the reasons for such cultural differences. They have been stressed even in this much detail because it has appeared that one of the major weaknesses with current talent research is its neglect of those cultural or value factors which may predispose some persons toward occupational achievement or toward a certain type of occupation. A study of cultural differences among differentially achieving groups should yield a rich return in discovering which values are likely to be associated with talent development.

The "Moving" Criterion

Much talent research to date has been what is technically called "criterion specific." In other words, a pool of items is developed to predict whether a person will pass a specific criterion, such as graduating from school or passing a test of flying proficiency. One may even go further, as Gough has done (5), and develop questionnaire items which will predict different specific school criteria, such as doing well in high school, doing well in college, and doing well in graduate school. The items which will predict different school criteria are, as Gough has shown, different—a fact which suggests that we need to analyze much more carefully what is required of a student in different types of school situations.

Although "criterion specific" research is often valuable for immediately practical ends, it may have serious drawbacks when the criterion moves around. Consider the following three items, for example, which come from Gough's scales for predicting academic performance in high school, college, and graduate school.

High School	*College*	*Graduate School*
I wake up fresh and rested most mornings. (True)	The trouble with many people is that they don't take things seriously enough. (False)	We ought to pay our elected officials better than we do. (True)

The answers in parentheses are the ones correlated with academic success. No one of the three items is useful at any of the other levels of academic performance, although a few other items do appear in more than one scale (e.g., "I liked 'Alice in Wonderland' by Lewis Carroll"). Whatever is being measured at the high school level is either not important for success in college and graduate school, or it is being measured by different types of items. If it is not important, then it may be dangerous to identify talent potential at the high school level with such an instrument, since it may exclude some people who will do well in college. If it is measured in a different way, we have no clear idea what "it" is, since the items themselves at different levels cannot easily be classified as tapping similar attitudes, values, or interests. The most serious problem is that in attempting to maximize correlations of particular items with specific criteria like this, little attention is given to such basic questions as what is being measured, how it happens to be related to the criterion, and how it might be related to subsequent long-range criteria.

Why, for example, should successful graduate students feel that our elected officials should be better paid? If we don't know the answer, then when the criterion changes (to success in a profession, for example) or the background for the item changes (perhaps when elected officials raise their salaries), it is hard to know what to do next other than to start over again by throwing out our test. The correlation disappears, and we have no information on which to build a new one. In other words, just as in the case of some animal species in evolution, specialization has its immediate advantages, but it is not well adapted to coping with change.

It may be objected that criterion specific research is not intended to cope with change but to select talent potential for a specific objective. If the goal can be achieved without interfering with long-range objectives, no complaint is in order. Often, however, selecting on the basis of an immediate objective may exclude some people who would perform better in terms of long-range (and sometimes more important) objectives. We may pick men for admission to graduate school on the basis of academic aptitude, only to discover that subsequently some of them will have to become scientific administrators or that the creative ones among them were not necessarily the ones with the highest grades. True, screening will continue throughout life, sifting out the creative scientists and the administrators; but it would be unfortunate if our means of selecting for academic aptitude were so efficient as to exclude individuals who could be distinguished by such subsequent criteria. In a mobile society like ours, where it is difficult to predict what values, abilities, and motives may be required of a man, it might be better strategy to develop measures which relate moderately well to several criteria. At the least, it might be wise to set only minimum levels of characteristics needed for specific criteria, so that above those levels talent potential can be assessed in terms of other measures and broader criteria, and in particular in terms of the theoretical understanding of the relationships among successive criteria and the measures that predict them. For, with relationships thus genuinely understood, it becomes possible to make decisions about what to do when the basis for the test changes, or when attention shifts from one particular criterion to another, or indeed to several criteria to be predicted at once.

The Educational Problem

There are those who doubt the wisdom of trying to identify potential talent at all. They say in effect: Suppose we could locate the "comers"; what would we do about it? The following paragraph from the *New Yorker Magazine* for December 4, 1954, illustrates the point nicely: *

> Field Marshal Viscount Montgomery, visiting here, put in a plug for the "élite" system of education. He said our schools should try to pick a few comers among the students and give them the works, leaving the dullards to plod along. It is a nice theory and an old one. The catch seems to be how to determine which are the comers. So often it happens that the sleepy boy in the back of the room, fumbling with his jack-knife and gazing out of the window, turns out 20 years later to be Robert Frost. On the whole, an intellectual élite has little more to be said for it than a social élite or a racial élite. An élite system today would be a proper mess anyway; everybody of any consequence would be under investigation, and all the brightest boys and girls would be getting cautionary letters from their congressmen, advising them not to open their traps, lest their remarks be used against them in later life.

Though we laugh at such descriptions and rush to the defense of psychology by pointing out the great advantages that could be provided for promising boys and girls if we were only more certain who they were, we cannot dismiss the question so easily. Suppose we could locate that sleepy boy in the back row, the potential poet; what would we do for him? Would we offer him a liberal scholarship to one of our better private schools? Would we "enrich" his curriculum with special readings in poetry, or in the Greek classics? Or would we perhaps excuse him from school requirements altogether on the ground that he would do better as a self-educated man? Or would we supply him with a vocational counselor who would help him find his real niche in life? These are not silly questions. The plain fact of the matter is that we do not know what we would do; we do not know enough about what goes into the making of a poet. We may know somewhat more about what goes into the making of a scientist or a professor (based on I.Q. tests and academic training); but we still know far too little to be confident about how to develop talented performance out of talent potential.

At the present stage of our knowledge, to identify the real "comers" is only the preliminary step to understanding *why* they are promising. Suppose, for example, by a series of really massive explorations of test items correlated with various criteria, we were able to construct a test which inevitably pointed to the promising young person. And suppose further, as is often the case with contemporary psychological tests, it would be extremely difficult to understand why a given item on the test had the connection it did with the future success. Suppose, in short, that the instrument worked, but that we had no idea as to why or how it worked, or what the problem of talent development really involved—in other words, that we had no theory. We would be able to identify talent potential without understanding its nature or the process by which it develops.

What advantage would such an instrument be to us? What should be done with the gifted students it identified? Certainly there would be no lack of advice. Perhaps it would not be their congressmen writing to the "comers" telling them to keep their mouths shut, but it would certainly be somebody—if only the psychologists and educators—telling them what to do. The chances are, however, that any special educational ventures would spoil some of the talent potential, since in our hypothetical example it would have been identified from validity coefficients based on allowing students to develop normally in the previous generation. If careful control experiments were performed to uncover just what educational procedures *decreased* the validity coefficients of the tests, we might, after generations, begin to learn something about the kinds of education which favor the development of talent.

But the whole orientation of such an approach is wrong. It places far more emphasis on talent potential as a fixed attribute of a few people than we have any reason to suppose is true. Rather, talent potential may be fairly widespread, a characteristic which can be transformed into actually talented performance of various sorts by the right kinds of education. If so, the emphasis should shift from identifying talent potential to *studying the process by which talent becomes actual,* by which it develops. Such a focus requires above all a knowledge of theory—an understanding of what we are measuring, how it develops under different circumstances, and how it is related to the ultimate criteria of talented performance which we want to predict. Until we achieve these goals, our ignorance of the process by which talented performance develops will remain an outstanding gap in current talent research.

The Committee's Plan of Attack

Although there are doubtless other reasons why talent research needs to be opened up and pushed vigorously today, the seven issues just discussed provide a sufficient indication of the challenges and conundrums that await the investigator. Unconventional issues and methods of attack have been stressed, not because previous approaches have failed to bear fruit (quite the contrary, they have made very important contributions); but because our task as a Committee was to explore new areas of research with an eye to finding what variables and what problems had been traditionally neglected. Certainly we uncovered a great many. Although not all of them were obvious in the beginning when the Committee decided on its research projects, the general picture was sufficiently clear to aid the planning of research in three main areas.

(1) *Non-academic types of talented behavior.* Among the many gaps in current research just reviewed, a general ignorance of any criteria of talented performance other than the strictly academic ones was something frequently noticed. It came up in discussions of the lack of "fit" between school and life, in discussions of the meaning of good performance, and in discussions of the changing criterion. Since accomplishment is easy to measure in school and since adequate school performance is a prerequisite to many types of further talented behavior, it is small wonder that research scientists have concentrated on prediction of academic success. But one of our first objectives was to break new ground by investigating other types of talented behavior. Two problems were selected for

study—social sensitivity and subjective standards for success in life. The first project was undertaken by Bronfenbrenner and the second by McClelland. Their reports appear in Chapters 2 and 3, respectively.

(2) *Non-intellectual determinants of achievement.* Another problem repeatedly mentioned in our introductory survey was the need to know more about non-intellectual determinants of achievement. The question came up in connection with socio-economic determinants of success at high levels of intelligence, in connection with reasons for the loss of talent potential from the school system, and in connection with differences in occupational achievement among various cultural sub-groups. Some patterns of values, motives, and interests seem unmistakably to favor the development of talent potential more than others. To shed light on this problem, Strodtbeck undertook a project comparing the values, family interaction patterns, motives, and achievements of Jewish and Italian groups. His report, which appears in Chapter 4, contains also some useful information on the problem of talent development, since he was able to study not only children but their parents, and the relationships between the two generations.

(3) *Theoretical analysis of the nature of talent.* As a group, the Committee felt that there was nothing the field of talent research needed quite so much as a better theoretical understanding of its variables and their interrelationships. To some extent all members of the Committee took the responsibility for trying to develop theory, but the most formal move in this direction was undertaken by Baldwin, who attempted to fit the "talent identification and development" way of thinking about things into a general theory of behavior. His report appears in Chapter 5.

In addition to the research it sponsored in these three main areas, the Committee decided (a) to review the major problems in the field (as summarized above), (b) to consult with other major research groups working on talent problems, (c) to hold meetings of interest to talent research workers in order to clarify points at issue and to share insights, and (d) to issue a general summary of its findings. The present report is aimed at fulfilling the last objective, although more detailed publications on specific research projects have already appeared and will doubtless continue to appear in the future. The chapters to follow present selected findings from the studies sponsored by the Committee; and the final chapter provides a brief summing up both of research findings and of some of their practical implications for the better identification of talent.

References

1. Berdie, R. F. *After High School, What?* Minneapolis: Univ. Minn. Press, 1954.
2. Clark, E. L. Motivation of Jewish students. *J. soc. Psychol.*, 1949, *29*, 113-117.
3. Davie, J. S. Social class factors and school attendance. *Harv. educ. Rev.* 1953, *23*, 175-185.
4. Dollard, J. *Caste and Class in a Southern Town.* New Haven: Yale Univ. Press, 1937.
5. Gough, H. Some theoretical problems in the construction of practical assessment devices for the early identification of high-level talent. Paper given at SSRC conference on "Non-intellective determinants of achievement," Princeton, N. J., 1953.
6. Havemann, E., and West, P. S. *They Went to College.* New York: Harcourt, Brace, 1952.
7. Hollander, E. P. Authoritarianism and leadership choice in a military setting. *J. abnorm. soc. Psychol.*, 1954, *49*, 365-370.
8. Knapp, R. H., and Goodrich, H. B. *Origins of American Scientists.* Chicago: Univ. of Chicago Press, 1952.
9. Meehl, P. E., and Rosen, A. Antecedent probability and the efficiency psychometric signs, patterns, or cutting scores. *Psychol. Bull.*, 1955, *52*, 194-216.
10. Mulligan, R. A. Socio-economic background and college enrollment. *Amer. sociol. Rev.*, 1951, *16*, 188-196.
11. Parsons, T. Illness and the role of the physician. *Amer. J. Orthopsychiatry,* 1951, *21*, 452-460.
12. Roe, A. *The Making of a Scientist.* New York: Dodd, Mead, 1953.
13. Rosen, B. The achievement syndrome. *Amer. social. Rev.*, 1956, *21*, 203-211.

14. Seligmann, B. B. The American Jew: some demographic features. In *American Jewish Yearbook 1950, 51,* 3-52. Philadelphia: Jewish Publication Society of America.
15. Stouffer, S. A. Social mobility of boys in the Boston Metropolitan Area. Paper given at SSRC conference on "Non-intellective determinants of achievement," Princeton, N. J., 1953.
16. Terman, L. M., and Oden, M. H. *The Gifted Child Grows Up.* Stanford: Stanford Univ. Press, 1947.
17. Tyler, L. E. *The Psychology of Human Differences.* (2nd edition). New York: Appleton-Century-Crofts, 1956.
18. Warner, W. L., and Srole, L. *The Social Systems of American Ethnic Groups.* New Haven: Yale Univ. Press, 1945.
19. Weber, M. *The Protestant Ethnic and the Spirit of Capitalism.* (Translated by Talcott Parsons). New York: Scribner, 1930.
20. Whyte, W. H. The fallacies of "personality" testing. *Fortune,* 1954, *50,* No. 3, 117-121; 204-210.
21. Wolfle, D. *America's Resources of Specialized Talent.* New York: Harper, 1954.
22. Wolfle, D., and Smith, J. G. The occupational value of education for superior high school graduates. *J. higher Educ.,* 1956, *27,* 201-213.

II

The Measurement of Skill in Social Perception[1]

URIE BRONFENBRENNER, JOHN HARDING and MARY GALLWEY

---

1. INTRODUCTION

IT IS now seven years since L. S. Cottrell (*12*), in his presidential address to the American Sociological Society, reproached his fellow social psychologists for "ignoring almost completely . . . one of the most challenging as well as one of the most critical" problems confronting the behavioral scientist—"empathic ability" or the capacity to "take the role of the other." The problem was of crucial significance, he argued, not only on theoretical but also on practical grounds, for "empathic responsiveness" was probably essential for the solution of many problems in human relations and for the successful performance of "various

[1] We wish to acknowledge the participation of Dr. C. R. Henderson, who served as statistical consultant to the project; Richard Lesser, Dorothy Hartman, and Montserrat Zayas, who were in charge of machine computations; and Joan Bechhofer, Edward C. Devereux, Paul F. Dempsey, Mary K. Girshick, Jacqueline Goodchilds, Julie Gray, Muriel Hewitt, Jan Howard, Doris M. Kells, William W. Lambert, Lloyd Lovell, Howard Shevrin, and Fay Suchman, all of whom contributed significantly to various phases of the research. We are grateful to Lee J. Cronbach, N. L. Gage, and their associates at the University of Illinois for their courtesy in exchanging ideas in connection with our somewhat similar analyses of the components of the accuracy score.

The research on which this chapter is based was carried on as part of a long-range program of research sponsored by the Department of Child Development and Family Relationships in the N. Y. State College of Home Economics at Cornell University under the title Cornell Studies in Social Growth. Finally, we are grateful to the Center for Advanced Study in the Behavioral Sciences for providing an opportunity for completing the final phases of the analysis and preparation of the manuscript.

roles called for in our society." In short, Cottrell saw in empathic ability an important form of social talent. Calling on social psychologists to devote "vigorous effort" to investigation in this area, he suggested that exploratory work by himself and his student, Dymond (*13, 17, 18, 19, 20*) might indicate a promising approach.

To judge from the sheer number of papers published on this problem since 1950, Cottrell's call has not gone unheeded. More than sixty studies have appeared in sociological and psychological publications, and the list grows with succeeding issues. Most of these investigations, moreover, have followed the method adopted by Cottrell and Dymond for measuring "empathy" or "the ability to take the role of the other." According to this method, success in anticipating the behavior of another is evaluated, logically enough it would seem, by asking a "judge" to predict the responses of another person, or group of persons, on a questionnaire or rating scale.

In view of the optimism, productivity, and uniformity of technique which have characterized research in this area, it seems appropriate, now after seven years, to take stock of the scientific endeavor not simply in terms of the empirical results—a task which has been performed ably elsewhere (*8, 51*)—but rather in the broader perspectives of theory and method. What seems called for is a critical review, in the light of research experience, of the nature and validity of the assumptions underlying what might be called "the prediction approach" to the study of social perception; an examination of the logical—and psychological—implications of the virtually standard procedures employed for measurement in this area; and a consideration of the consequences of these implications both for the interpretation of research results obtained in the past and for the planning of scientific work in the future.

In the present chapter, we undertake this type of critical appraisal. Since our analysis developed primarily from our own attempt to apply conventional methods of measurement in our research on skills in social perception, most of the issues are raised in the context of these data. Readers familiar with the literature, however, will readily recognize that the problems examined have direct implication for virtually all of the empirical investigations of ability or skill in social perception and social judgment carried on, not only since 1950, but for many years earlier.

The last phrase calls attention to the fact that the present boom in research on "emphatic ability" and related skills is not without its antecedents, both theoretical and empirical. Today's emphasis on the emphatic concept reflects the convergence of two streams of scientific thought. The first stems from a theoretical concern with problems of socialization and personality development on the part of sociologists like Cooley (*9, 10*), Angell (*3*), and Mead (*41*), and psychologists such as Freud (*23, 24, 25*), McDougall (*40*), and Sullivan (*50*). All these theorists gave central emphasis to the recognition by the individual of other peoples' feelings toward him and the eventual incorporation of these attitudes into his own self-image. The process of sensing or responding to other people's thought and feelings is often referred to in this theoretical tradition as *empathy*. The capacity for empathy is regarded as essential for socialization.

The second stream of thought of crucial importance for research in this area is more exclusively psychological; it is concerned with the general problem of one person's ability to "understand" another. This tradition has its origin in the theories of intuition and inference of Klages (*34, 35*) and the phenomenological analyses of social perception by Lipps (*39*), Köhler (*36*), and especially Scheler (*47*). To describe certain aspects of the processes through which one person becomes aware of the thoughts, feelings, and motives of another, these writers frequently used the term *Einfühlung*, which was translated as "empathy." In the context of American psychology, with its emphasis on measurement and its concern with individual differences, interest in the processes involved in judging others gave way to the problem of measuring ability in this area.[2]

It is these two lines of thought—the concern with social-psychological theories of socialization on the one hand, and, on the other, the investigation of ability in understanding others—which have converged in the work of Cottrell and Dymond (*11, 12, 13, 17, 18, 19, 20*). In their research the psychologist's interest in measurement was combined with a theoretical rationale which made this problem of central importance for the study of social relations. Thus it became possible to argue that the ability to "empathize" or "take the

[2] Two important exceptions to this general trend in American research on interpersonal perception are G. W. Allport and H. A. Murray. While these psychologists were among the first to focus attention on the problem of individual differences in ability and their measurement, they have continued to be concerned with the processes of social perception and their theoretical and phenomenological analysis. Allport has done much, both in his teaching and writing (*1, 2*), to sensitize Americans to the contributions of German phenomenologists. Murray (*43*), by his introduction of such concepts as "recipathy," has anticipated the current "interactive" approach to the theoretical analysis of social perception (*32, 33, 44, 45*).

role of the other" was essential to a wide range of basic processes, knowledges, and skills in the area of social behavior and development. Cottrell, for example, asserted that empathic ability is basic "in such phenomena as the development of a conception of self, in acquiring a role, in the emergence of insight, in communication, in the integration of a group, in the internalization of social norms" (*12*, p. 706). Similarly, Dymond proposed that the analysis of empathic ability will lead to a better understanding of such diverse questions as "how the self emerges and the child becomes socialized, how individual behavior can be predicted more efficiently, the reasons groups become or fail to become integrated" (*18*, pp. 11-12). She suggested further that empathic ability is required for success in a variety of occupations including "clinical work, psychiatric work, interviewing, field work, social work, arbitration, and so forth." In like manner, Bender and Hastorf take the position that "the ability to judge people" represents an important social talent (*5*, p. 556):

> In everyday situations, we depend necessarily on our capacity to perceive and predict the behavior, thoughts, and feelings of the other person. . . . Our socialization is reared on this foundation of perception of persons in terms of prediction. The credit manager forecasts the ability and willingness of the customer to pay his bills. The diplomat forecasts the readiness of his vis-à-vis to accept or reject propositions. The therapist makes not only a diagnosis but a prognosis of his client. All the subtle interchanges of love and friendship rest, howsoever insecurely, on this tenuous skill in perception and prediction.

Trend toward Operationalism in the Definition of Empathy and Related Concepts

The preceding quotations are typical of many that occur in the present-day literature of social psychology. They reflect the importance currently accorded the notion of a generalized ability to recognize or predict the behavior, feelings, or motives of other people. Yet, paradoxically enough, the exact nature of this ability has not been subjected to careful theoretical scrutiny. This is perhaps because American scientists, unlike their European counterparts, are not so likely to feel a compulsion to subject an idea to *a priori* conceptual analysis or to search the literature for earlier or related formulations. Instead, American researchers, having customarily resorted to what we are only now beginning to recognize as a naive operationalism, have tacitly defined their variable in terms of the procedure employed for its measurement. This procedure has typically involved asking a "judge" to predict the responses of another on a questionnaire, and then comparing the prediction with the response. The discrepancy (commonly an absolute difference in rating) between predicted and actual response provides the basis for computing an *accuracy score*, which then constitutes the measure of empathy, understanding, ability to judge—or whatever term the investigator prefers.

Such a technique has a number of advantages. It is easy to administer. It is "objective": it requires no subjective judgment by the experimenter, the results can be expressed in quantitative terms, and, above all, it all has a kind of literal "face validity" which it seems almost presumptuous to question. We are interested in A's ability to predict the responses of B; what can be a more appropriate index of this ability than the error which A makes when asked to estimate a series of responses by B? Virtually every investigator, whether he speaks in terms of "empathy," "social insight," "understanding," or "ability to 'judge'" proposes this same operational definition. With this almost universal agreement on measurement, problems of theoretical assumptions and possible conceptual distinctions have receded into the background. The obvious task has been to gather data and analyze the results.

2. A Review of Reviews

This task has been performed with a will. In the two most recent reviews of research in this field—one by Bruner and Tagiuri (*3*) and the other by Taft (*51*)—there are references to probably fifty different studies of what is perhaps most properly called "predictive accuracy." At least another score have appeared in psychological and sociological journals since then. What is the outcome of this imposing array of data? Does the evidence support the notion of a generalized ability to understand others and to predict their behavior? Does such an ability tend to make for overall social effectiveness, as hypothesized by Cottrell, Dymond, and others? An examination of the painstaking summaries by Taft and by Bruner and Tagiuri does not permit an unequivocal answer to these questions.

Taft's Evaluation of the "Ability to Judge People"

Taft classifies the research results under five different headings: (1) perception of emotional expression in photographs, drawings, models, and moving pictures; (2) rating and ranking traits; (3)

personality descriptions; (4) personality matchings; and (5) prediction of behavior and life history data. Investigations of what we have called predictive accuracy are included under this last heading. Taft also examines the studies in terms of another and independent classification which he regards as particularly important—namely, whether they require *analytic* or *non-analytic* judgments. This distinction he draws as follows (*51*, p. 1):

In analytic judgments, the judge (J) is required to conceptualize, and often to quantify, specific characteristics of the subject (S) in terms of a given frame of reference. This mainly involves the process of inference, typical performances of J being rating traits, writing personality descriptions, and predicting the percentage of a group making a given response. In non-analytic judgments, J responds in a global fashion as in matching persons with personality descriptions and making predictions of behavior.

Some studies of predictive accuracy Taft classifies as belonging in the first category, others in the second. For example, Dymond's empathy test (*18, 19*), which requires the judge to estimate ratings made on six personality traits by a series of others, is classed as non-analytic, while Kerr and Speroff's "mass empathy test" (*48*), in which the judge predicts the combined responses of a group of people, is called analytic.[3]

Using this twofold system of classification, Taft poses his first basic question: "Is there a general ability to judge others?" Although he finds many contradictions in the research findings, he is inclined to make his reply "yes." He summarizes his conclusions this way (*51*, p. 20):

The ability to judge others has been considered as a personality trait. . . . Five different methods of measuring this ability have been described and it was suggested that the results of the studies quoted may vary according to the operational definition used. This would seem to apply particularly to the distinction between analytic and non-analytic techniques, although, when we review the findings on the correlates of the ability to judge, we find that few reveal a definite difference between these two types of techniques.

The contradictions found between studies may be due partly to the low reliability of the measures used, and partly to the effect of specific factors such as the type of judgment required, the traits being judged, and the Ss used. This problem of specificity arises with all traits, but it seems to be particularly marked in the case of the ability to judge others; nevertheless, there does seem

[3] The basis for this distinction does not seem altogether clear, since Dymond's procedure certainly requires the judge "to conceptualize, and often [in fact invariably] to quantify specific characteristics of the subject in terms of a given frame of reference." Taft states as the basis for his decision the belief that "the mass empathy test for prediction is more likely to be tackled analytically than is the empathy test, as it does not lend itself so readily to empathizing with any particular person."

to be sufficient generality in this ability to justify describing at least some judges as "good" or "poor."

Artifacts in the Measurement of Accuracy and Its Correlates

The second basic question proposed by Taft concerns the correlates of the ability to judge, and here he sounds a note of caution. He points out that although accuracy measures have shown "a consistent positive relationship with measures of social skill such as leadership, salesmanship, and popularity," this may well be a spurious relation resulting from a chance similarity between the judge's predictions and the criterion against which they are being validated. This caution regarding the interpretation of accuracy scores, first proposed by Hastorf and Bender (*30*), has been developed systematically by Cronbach and Gage and their associates (*14, 15, 16, 26, 27, 28*). Its importance in evaluating research and its relevance to our own work make it essential to understand the relationships involved. It is now a well-documented fact (*21, 22*) that in making estimates of how others will respond to a questionnaire, most people tend to "assume similarity"; that is, they attribute to others the same response they would make themselves. It follows that the judge who will be most accurate is the one whose own responses most closely resemble the criterion in terms of which accuracy is determined. Hence, it is not surprising that significant positive relationships are frequently reported (*8*) between the judge's ability to predict and his similarity to the group being judged. "The best judge of others is the one who resembles others" becomes under such circumstances a somewhat circular statement.

Another correlation based upon artifact is the often-cited high positive relationship between accuracy in judging others and self-insight, or accuracy in judging one's self (*8, 51*). Taft describes the possibly spurious nature of such results (*51*, p. 15):

> In many studies it has been found that the J's tend to rate themselves high on admirable traits and low on reprehensible ones. Consequently, those who are *actually* high on admirable or low on reprehensible traits will tend to be scored higher than others on self-insight. This same artifact operates in all studies of self-insight, no matter how measured, and could affect the relationship found between self-insight and ability to judge others.

Such a statement can indeed be broadened to include any situation in which a judge is asked to estimate how others evaluate him. Since most people tend to expect favorable evaluations, those who actually receive such evaluations will turn out to be right. Hence we have the large number of studies reporting positive relationships between ability to judge others and leadership, social skill, popularity, and the like. There is no doubt, of course, about the positive relationships; the real question is whether there is anything in them which was not foreordained by the measurement used. Taft, in summarizing the evidence on the correlates of ability to judge, chooses (somewhat questionably, in our opinion) to present such relationships at their face value; among the characteristics "fairly consistently found to be positively correlated with the ability to judge" he includes "insight into one's status," "social skill," and "good emotional adjustment and integration."

A Résumé of Bruner and Tagiuri

These reviewers also give considerable attention to difficulties in the interpretation of accuracy and its correlations with other variables. Indeed, in their final evaluation they are inclined to weigh such difficulties more heavily than Taft, with the result that their conclusions regarding our present state of knowledge are more guarded (8, p. 646):

> Studies of "accuracy" of judging others have not progressed to a point at which firm substantive conclusions can be brought to bear upon a theory of judgment. The criteria employed have too often been of a consensual kind: accuracy is mostly defined as agreement with others regarding a person's characteristics. Given systematic biases of judgment . . . these studies may mean simply that a particular judge shares the most common bias to be found among his fellow judges. Taken from the point of a theory of judgment, relatively few firm conclusions can be drawn.

On the matter of the generalizability of a capacity to judge others, Bruner and Tagiuri, though again somewhat more cautious than Taft, end up at essentially the same position (8, pp. 645-6):

> The preceding discussion assumes that "accuracy" in social perception is a generalized ability. An evaluation of this assumption would carry us far into problems of statistical analysis. There is evidence for both specificity and generality of accuracy. . . . We are inclined to agree with G. W. Allport's claim that it would be more erroneous to "consider the ability entirely specific than to consider it entirely general."

This same quotation from Allport is cited and endorsed by Taft, who concludes that the experimental evidence, on the whole, supports Allport's contention. It is of particular interest that these two recent comprehensive reviews should concur in supporting a single generalized ability to judge other people, for this conclusion is in direct opposition to the principal hypothesis that has guided our own research and our major findings.

3. Background and Aims of the Present Research

A Distinction between Two Major Types of Ability in Social Perception

The general hypothesis guiding the present research emerged somewhat slowly and painfully during a period of exploration in which we experimented with a variety of approaches. They ranged from clinical evaluation of "empathy" (subjectively defined) in role-playing to a detailed statistical analysis of accuracy scores obtained by eight strangers who had interviewed each other in pairs and then predicted each other's ratings on a questionnaire of twenty-four items. In the course of this exploratory work, we developed the notion of two contrasting types of ability in social perception.

The first type, which we called *sensitivity to the generalized other,* involves an awareness of the social norm or the typical response of a large class or group. Thus it is *sensitivity to the generalized other* that is being tapped when a judge is asked to predict such phenomena as community attitudes, the results of public opinion polls, or the "typical response" for some special class of people, say college students, on a series of items in a personality questionnaire.[4] In each of these instances, the person is asked to identify characteristics which people have in common and is not required to discriminate individual departures from the norm.

Right there we come to the second type of ability in social perception—recognition of the ways in which one person may differ from another (or from the "average") in his behavior, feelings, or motives. We have referred to this ability as *sensitivity to individual differences* or *interpersonal sensitivity.* It is altogether possible, we felt, for a person to excel in one of these skills but not the other. A union leader, for example, may correctly appraise the general sentiments of the membership, yet be blind to differences in opinion among individual members. Or a department-store manager may be a good predictor of which items will sell, but a poor judge of which customers will buy. Conversely, a teacher may be keenly aware of individual differences among her pupils and yet completely overestimate, say, what an average fourth-grader can do. Or, to cite a more striking example, the paranoid schizophrenic may be-

[4] The term "generalized other" is borrowed from G. H. Mead (*41*). In the present context, it is used in a broad sense to include any collection of persons to which a perceiver attributes common characteristics. Certain further distinctions regarding the type of group or collective being perceived will be introduced at a subsequent point in the discussion (see Section 4).

lieve quite mistakenly that everyone is plotting against him and yet exhibit an almost uncanny sensitivity to real but subtle differences in attitude toward him among doctors or fellow patients.

As the preceding examples indicate, it is possible for a judge to have excellent interpersonal sensitivity, to know very well how a person differs from others, and still make quite inaccurate judgments about that person. Thus our teacher may be correct in thinking that Johnny Jones is her most able student, and at the same time be shocked when Johnny, along with all the others, falls far below the grade norms on a standardized test. In other words, *accurate* judgment of a particular other calls for both types of skill. One must be able to recognize both the characteristics that the other shares with his fellow men and also those which are uniquely his own. A person with sensitivity to the generalized other might be able to do the former, but not necessarily the latter. It was our impression, developed in the course of exploratory work, that this situation might indeed be the rule rather than the exception. In other words, we began to suspect that interpersonal sensitivity and sensitivity to the generalized other might represent quite different skills, related in the general population only slightly. This means, in turn, that persons possessing one or the other of these abilities might exhibit quite different personality and behavioral characteristics.

Finally, turning from theoretical to practical questions, we felt that the two types of skill might find somewhat different applicability in various walks of life. Thus a person with sensitivity to the generalized other, even if he does not excel in interpersonal sensitivity, may be able to function quite effectively in fields requiring accurate appraisal of public opinion and response, as in advertising, merchandising, show business, journalism, finance, or public administration. Certain other occupations, on the contrary, would seem to call for sensitivity to individual differences as well; for instance, clinical medicine, personnel selection, play direction, labor mediation, or face-to-face diplomatic negotiation.

An Analysis of the Accuracy Score in Terms of Component Skills

The two forms of sensitivity we have described above are both represented in the conventional accuracy score. Such a score, although it does not distinguish between interpersonal sensitivity and sensitivity to the generalized other, reflects both, with far greater weight on the latter than on the former. Let us see how this comes about. We may take as an example Dymond's pioneering study of "empathic ability" (*18, 19*), which has set the pattern for much subsequent research. Dymond asked her judges (all of them college students) to predict the rating responses of each one of seven (sometimes six) classmates on a series of personality traits. The ratings and predictions for each trait were expressed on a five-point scale. An accuracy score was then computed for each judge, taking the sum of the absolute differences between his predictions and the actual responses made by the fellow members of his group. The accuracy score is thus equal to the sum of all the errors made by the judge. As in golf, a low score indicates good performance.

Let us consider the situation of a particular judge estimating the self-ratings of six or seven others. Presumably, the more sensitive he is to individual differences among his associates, the better able he will be to minimize his errors of prediction. From this point of view the accuracy score reflects, at least in part, the judge's ability in interpersonal sensitivity. But it is also possible for the judge to make accurate predictions without being at all aware of individual differences. Indeed, he does not even have to see the people whose responses he predicts. An ingenious demonstration of this fact is reported by Gage (*26*). He first asked judges to predict the questionnaire responses of subjects whom they had never seen (but who were identified as college students); and then subsequently secured a new set of predictions following a period of direct observation. Paradoxically, his judges did somewhat more poorly after "exposure" than before.

> The difference between mean scores before vs. after observation is significant at the 1 per cent level . . . but is opposite in direction from the common-sense expectation. That is, it seemed reasonable to expect that the predictions of the knowledge merely of the cultural subgroup to which the strangers belonged would be *less* accurate than those made not only after this knowledge but also after observations of the strangers' expressive behavior. But these results suggest that the clues to personality which the expressive behavior should have provided either did not appear or were misused by the judges.

Employing our terminology, we would conclude that, at least in this situation, the interpersonal sensitivity of the judges (or perhaps lack of it) interfered with their comparatively accurate sensitivity to the generalized other. Gage refers to a judge's success in estimating the average response of a group as "stereotype accuracy." Although there are some minor differences in the applicability of the terms (see Section 4), this concept is substantially identical with our notion of sensitivity to the generalized order.

Whatever it may be called, such awareness of the typical response of a group is reflected to a considerable degree in conventional accuracy scores of the sort employed by Dymond. Indeed, when we recall that the judge's score in her study was based on success in estimating six or seven different subjects, it seems probable that over-all accuracy was determined primarily by the judge's ability to predict the modal pattern of response for the group rather than by his sensitivity to individual differences. Striking confirmation for this hypothesis is presented in a critique of Dymond's study by Lindgren and Robinson (38). These investigators repeated Dymond's procedure with minor revisions, but added a "normative empathy" score based on the difference between the judge's estimate and the average response of 100 college students. The correlation between this "normative empathy" score and the original empathy score was .74. Pointing out that this correlation is of the same order as the reliability of the empathy test itself ($r = .69$), Lindgren and Robinson conclude:

> This raises the question of whether the test measures the tendency of individuals to respond to an interpersonal situation in terms of cultural norms rather than emphatic promptings. It is suggested that both factors may operate.

If both factors do operate and if, as we have proposed, the two abilities are relatively independent, then this fact may contribute to the contradictory character of research results in this area. Moreover, to the extent that consistencies are present, they may well be a function of the preponderance in the accuracy score of the component reflecting what we have called sensitivity to the generalized other.

The preceding discussion of the accuracy score highlights the fact that if we are to investigate hypotheses regarding the existence of different types of skill in social perception and their correlates, we must solve a number of prior and complex methodological problems. First, we must devise a measure of interpersonal sensitivity, which, unlike the conventional accuracy score, is independent of the judge's awareness of the group norm. Analogously, we must find a measure of sensitivity to the generalized other which is unaffected by awareness of individual differences. In a sense, the solution to this last problem is already in hand in the procedures employed by Gage and others of computing an accuracy score based on the judge's predictions not of particular individuals but of the typical pattern of response for the group as a whole.

But this solution brings with it new problems. There is the question of the degree to which such an accuracy score reflects genuine recognition by the judge of the characteristics of the group, or simply a high degree of similarity between the judge and the group in the manner in which they respond to questionnaire items. This question, in turn, poses two new problems. On the one hand, there is the task of developing a "pure" measure of sensitivity to the generalized other, or at least of estimating the degree to which conventional accuracy scores reflect *bona fide* awareness of properties of the group. On the other hand, we may argue that the ability to predict accurately is important in its own right, irrespective of whether it is the result of objective perception or simply of an appropriate type of judgmental bias. If the latter, then it becomes desirable to specify the nature of the bias and the circumstances under which it may lead to accurate prediction.

Principal Research Objectives

The research to be presented in the remainder of this chapter emphasizes six major aims:

1. The formulation of a conceptual framework for the analysis of skills in social perception.
2. The development of methods for measuring skill in interpersonal sensitivity and sensitivity to the generalized other, which are (a) operationally independent; and (b) uninfluenced by the degree of similarity between the judge and the person or group being judged; or, lacking this, accompanied by an estimate of the degree to which the measure reflects—over and above such similarity—*bona fide* recognition of properties of the "other."
3. Investigation of the general hypothesis that interpersonal sensitivity and sensitivity to the generalized other represent different abilities or skills (*i.e.*, their intercorrelation is low).
4. Investigation of the general hypothesis that persons scoring high on interpersonal sensitivity will exhibit different personality and behavioral characteristics from those scoring high on sensitivity to the generalized other.
5. Analysis of the personal biases affecting judgment of others and the conditions under which such biases may lead to accurate prediction.
6. A re-evaluation, in the light of 1 to 5 above, of the problem of measuring skills in social perception, with recommendations of strategy for future research.

4. A Conceptual Framework for the Analysis of Social Sensitivity

While the differentiation between interpersonal sensitivity and sensitivity to the generalized other is of first importance in the present research, it is not the only distinction we wish to make with respect to skill in social perception. We have selected these two variables for investigation because they represent two highly contrasting types in a several-fold classification of different forms of social sensitivity (see Fig. 1).

Variation in Social Object

The principal basis for this system of classification is the *social object,* a category describing *the person or group being judged.* We have already become familiar with two of the three major types of object: namely, the *generalized other* and the *particular other.* The third class of objects—intermediate between the other two—is the *face-to-face group.*

Before proceeding to a discussion of the face-to-face group, however, it may be helpful to clarify our usage of the term "generalized other" and to specify the range of phenomena which its subsumes and excludes. The concept is borrowed from G. H. Mead (*41*), who defines the generalized other as "the attitude of the whole community," using the term "community" loosely to encompass virtually any social group of which the individual is a member. Thus Mead cites as an example a baseball team, which serves as "the generalized other in so far as it enters—as an organized process or social activity—into the experience of any one of the individual members of it."

Our own usage of the term is in one respect broader but in another more restricted. It is broader in that the concept includes any large group or class which is recognized as such by the person, irrespective of whether or not he himself is a member of that group or class. Thus we may ask a judge who is a college student to estimate the attitudes of his fellow students, of Americans in general, of wage earners, employers, minority groups, etc. In each instance our interest is in the judge's ability to recognize attitudes or actions which are in some sense typical for the group under consideration.[5] This means, of course, that there are many different generalized

[5] Certain important problems arise regarding what is meant by "typical" both from the viewpoint of the judge's perceptions and in relation to the criterion in terms of which the validity of these perceptions is to be evaluated. For a discussion of these problems see Section 8.

others, some more inclusive than others. Accordingly, in speaking of sensitivity to the generalized other, it is always necessary to specify the class or classes of persons being judged.

For certain purposes also it may be useful to distinguish different types of sensitivity to the generalized other. For example, we may wish to study separately the person's awareness of the norm in the classes or segments of society with which he affiliates himself, what Merton and Kitt (*42*) have referred to as "reference groups." This reference-group sensitivity may be quite unrelated to the person's knowledge of typical responses in other cultures, classes, or social groups outside the judge's own sphere of associations. Finally, there is the possibility of an analogue at the group level of what we have called interpersonal sensitivity; i.e., there is the question of the person's ability to recognize how various classes or segments of society differ from each other. Such *sensitivity to interclass differences* may have special importance in such fields as political analysis or public administration.

As the preceding discussion indicates, there are many important distinctions and restrictions that can be applied to the notion of sensitivity to the generalized other. Largely for reasons of simplicity of presentation, we have chosen to introduce only one such restriction in our formal conceptual scheme. This is the exclusion from the concept of those groups which are sufficiently small to permit observation of all their members in face-to-face contact. The distinction is similar to that commonly made between "primary" and "secondary" groups, save that we wish to avoid the connotations of intimacy and long duration ordinarily associated with the former term. A face-to-face group may be a family, or it may be a short-lived committee or military detail with only perfunctory duties.

There are several reasons for selecting the face-to-face group for special consideration in an analysis of social sensitivity. First, there is a growing body of research which indicates that such "small groups" have their own special laws of behavior, which are in a number of important ways independent both of the individual and the larger social context (*49*). Second, the role of sensitivity in the face-to-face group is of especial social importance, since it is in this context that the skill is particularly likely to influence decision-making.

Finally, the distinction between sensitivity to the face-to-face group and sensitivity to the generalized other illustrates in their clearest form the theoretical and methodological problems which arise in attempting to differentiate the types of groups to which a person may be sensitive. Let us begin with a concrete example. When we speak of sensitivity to face-to-face groups, we are concerned with such phenomena as an officer's capacity to evaluate *esprit de corps* in different units of his command, or a teacher's ability to gauge the level of difficulty of materials for a particular class (as against the norm, say, for sixth-graders in general). In other words, in order to judge a face-to-face group, it is necessary to have knowledge of the group as a separate unit in its own right. Analogous to the situation previously described for the particular other, the judge must recognize both the characteristics which the group members share with the general population of which they are a part (the generalized other) and the unique features which distinguish the particular face-to-face group from such a norm.

This raises the question of still another and possibly independent skill in social perception—namely, *sensitivity to group differences.* While such a possibility exists, it seems to us more likely that this type of sensitivity represents, not a skill in its own right, but rather a combination of sensitivity to the generalized other, on the one hand, and to individual differences, on the other. The question remains to be settled by research. If sensitivity to group differences does represent a separate ability, then it would enter into judgments of a particular other when this other was being observed as a member of a face-to-face group. This possibility has been indicated in the left-hand column of Fig. 1; that is, for each social object we have shown the abilities presumably involved in making an accurate judgment.

The three general types of objects could each be further differentiated in terms of variations in sex, age, social role, and so on. For example, some people may be able to recognize individual differences among men but not among women. Others may be sensitive with children's groups but not with adults. One person may be well informed about a variety of generalized others (e.g., the attitudes of labor vs. management, the shifting balance of forces in French public opinion, the Catholic reaction to the late Senator McCarthy, etc.), while another is familiar with nothing but his own "reference group" (e.g., the Babbitt who knows only his own kind). These, together with many other possible distinctions, seem to us more properly hypotheses for research than bases for a system of classification. In differentiating abilities that might be required for judging different types of social objects, we have therefore confined ourselves to the three variables we feel most likely to show consistent variation in research results. Even here, we have had suffi-

SOCIAL OBJECT (with presumed requisite abilities)	REFERENT			
	Non-personal Sensitivity	First-person Sensitivity	Second-person Sensitivity	Third-person Sensitivity
Generalized Other (1) Sensitivity to the generalized other	How does the community feel about "released time" for religious education?	Is my stock rising in this community?	Do the teachers think they are doing a good job?	Whom will the city elect to the School Board this fall to replace Mr. Jones?
Face-to-Face Group (1) Sensitivity to the generalized other (2) Sensitivity to group differences	What tax rate will the board approve for next year?	Was I too informal in my talk at the PTA last night?	Does the Student Council have any confidence in its own abilities?	Will our team be able to win the county championship?
Particular Other (1) Sensitivity to the generalized other (2) Sensitivity to group differences (3) Sensitivity to individual differences (interpersonal sensitivity)	How much does the new school principal know about problems of school financing?	What will my wife think of me when I tell her I have to go out again tonight?	Is Miss Smith getting close to another nervous breakdown?	What does the President of the School Board think of the new principal?

Fig. 1. A Schematic Representation of Different Forms of Social Sensitivity (with hypothetical illustrations from the life of a school superintendent)

cient confidence to state a differential hypothesis only with respect to the two most contrasting types, i.e., interpersonal sensitivity versus sensitivity to the generalized other.

Variation in Terms of Content

Somewhat similar considerations apply to variation in the content to which the judge is asked to respond. We may, for instance, require him to be sensitive to physical characteristics, abilities, overt behavior, internal emotional states, attitudes and beliefs, etc. It is possible that some people may be able to recognize certain of these phenomena better than others can; but, as before, we are inclined to regard this as a question for research rather than as a foundation for a theoretical schema.

There is one aspect of the content, however, which we feel does merit formal conceptual distinction. This is the person or group to whom the content refers, or the *referent.* To illustrate this concept, let us consider judge A's sensitivity to a single other person, B. Now, if we think of A as ego, we may be interested in A's sensitivity to what B thinks of him; here the referent is A or ego. We call this *first-person sensitivity,* the recognition by ego of how others feel toward him. In contrast, we may be concerned with A's awareness of how B feels about B; this is *second-person sensitivity.* In analogous fashion, *third-person sensitivity* deals with A's recognition of B's feelings toward still another person, C. Finally, there is *non-personal sensitivity* such as that represented by A's recognition of B's feelings about certain physical objects or abstract ideas which have no reference to particular individuals or groups.

Classification of sensitivity simultaneously in terms of *object* and *referent* gives rise to the twelve-fold schema shown in Fig. 1. To clarify these several distinctions, we have illustrated each by a fictitious example taken from the life of one person, a school superintendent in a large city. The role of school superintendent is particularly well suited for our purpose for, as Gross and his colleagues have emphasized (29), this position requires a high degree of social sensitivity in a wide range of areas. Taking Gross' descriptive account as a point of departure, we have attempted to illustrate each form of sensitivity called for by our conceptual framework with a hypothetical question which a typical school superintendent might ask himself in the course of the day's (and night's) work. As these examples indicate, the lines between classifications are not hard and fast. As with virtually all conceptual schemata in the behavioral sciences, the categories merge one into the other—representing, at best, shifts along a gradient rather than discrete, mutually exclusive classes.

Variation through Time

We may now add a third and last dimension to our conceptual structure—namely, a time axis. With this addition, we recognize that a judge may be sensitive not only to differences *among* social objects (individuals, groups, etc.), but also to variation *within* a particular object through time—for example, changes in the emotional state of an individual, in group atmosphere, or in public opinion. Such variation may be the result of purely internal processes (e.g., individual maturation, the development of intra-group attachments or antagonisms), or of changes in the external situation, or of interactions between the two. To permit schematic representation of such temporal variations, we may think of Fig. 1 as extending in three dimensions with a time axis lying perpendicular to the plane of the page. This extension allows for the possibility of recognizing, predicting, or postdicting variations for each object-referent combination at different periods and under varying situational conditions.

The manifold distinctions represented in our conceptual schema pose a host of problems for theory and research in social perception. To mention but a few: What is the relationship among various forms of sensitivity? Is the person who knows his own status in a group (first-person sensitivity) likely to be a better judge of the status of others (third-person sensitivity)? Can the person who recognizes differences among individuals at a particular point in time (interpersonal sensitivity) also sense changes within the same person over time (intrapersonal sensitivity)? What is the effect of different situational conditions on various forms of social sensitivity? Are there certain situations in which, for example, interpersonal sensitivity is enhanced, and others in which it is impaired? What is the relative difficulty of various types of sensitivity: is it easier to estimate others' opinions on non-personal matters (non-personal sensitivity) than their feelings toward people (first- through third-person sensitivity)? Are errors more likely to occur when one is judging feelings toward the self? Which is easier to predict—the reaction of an individual or of a group? What are the personality and behavioral correlates of different forms of sensitivity? Does the person who excels in interpersonal sensitivity make an unusually good therapist? Does the good judge of face-to-face groups function more effectively than others as a chairman? Finally, to what extent are the contradictions in existing studies of the social and psychological correlates of accuracy a function of failure to differentiate among various forms of sensitivity?

In the present research we have obviously had to limit ourselves to only a few of these questions; even with these, we have merely scratched the surface. Our data are essentially confined to second-person indices of interpersonal sensitivity and sensitivity to the generalized other, with scattered information about a few other types. We turn now to a consideration of methods and results in relation to the first of these variables—interpersonal sensitivity.

5. The Measurement of Interpersonal Sensitivity

The Method of Differential Comparison

One of our first steps was to devise a measure of interpersonal sensitivity which would be independent of sensitivity to the generalized other and of similarity between the judge and the person being judged. Such a measure was essential in order to test hypotheses regarding its relationship to other variables. In the course of our pilot investigations we had developed a general strategy for meeting these requirements; namely, forcing the judge to discriminate individual differences among two or more subjects in their responses to the same stimulus situation. For example, we would ask an applicant who had been interviewed by several prospective employers to rank these employers in terms of their probable willingness to hire him for the job. We may refer to this general approach as "the method of differential comparison."

In the context of the conventional research situation involving questionnaire ratings and predictions, the approach calls for a measure of the judge's ability to estimate correctly the *relative position* of ratings made by a series of others on a particular item. In the case of a single item, such a measure is provided by the correlation coefficient between the ratings made by the several subjects and the judge's corresponding estimates of these ratings. In the usual questionnaire situation, when many items are used, the measure of correlation must still be one which reflects variation *within* but not *among* items. Otherwise the index is substantially influenced by the correspondence between the judge's estimates and the average response of the several subjects; in other words, the measure once again reflects primarily the judge's sensitivity to the group norm.

These extraneous components can be avoided, however, by computing the correlation coefficient on a within-item basis; that is, by expressing each estimate as a deviation (x_i) from the mean of the estimates made by the judge for all subjects on that item, each rating as a deviation (y_i) from the mean rating given by all subjects for that item, and then computing the simple correlation ($r_{x_iy_i}$) between x_i and y_i over all items and subjects for the particular judge.[6] The resulting coefficient provides an index of the judge's ability to recognize individual differences among subjects in their responses to each item. Since both the criterion ratings for evaluating the accuracy of predictions and the predictions themselves are expressed as deviations from the respective means for all the members of the group, the measure is independent of the judge's similarity and sensitivity to the generalized other (or to the face-to-face group where one exists). His tendency to "assume similarity" cannot affect his score, for the latter is based on the variation among his estimates for the several subjects rather than on the absolute value for any one subject. It is our belief that the only way in which a judge can obtain a high score (i.e., a high correlation) with this type of index—except, of course, through errors of measurement—is by being aware of objective differences among the persons he is asked to judge. If this is indeed so, we have succeeded in satisfying the requirements for a "pure" measure of interpersonal sensitivity,[7] and

[6] This index corresponds to the "average within-group correlation" in conventional analysis of covariance (see, for example, Snedecor, G., *Statistical Methods*, Fourth Edition, pp. 318-329). The measure can be treated in exactly the same way as the ordinary correlation coefficient (it is algebraically equivalent), except for the fact that the usual methods for evaluating statistical significance of r cannot be applied directly. This is because successive paired values are not always independent, due to intercorrelations among items. As a result, the exact number of degrees of freedom associated with r is not known. (One can only be certain that this number is not less than $N-3$, where N is the number of different subjects being judged.)

The selection of the "average within-item correlation" as the measure of interpersonal sensitivity was based on a mathematical and statistical analysis of accuracy scores from a pilot study involving eight subjects. The purpose of the analysis was to search for components of the accuracy score which might meet the requirements for "pure" measures of various types of social sensitivity. The results of this statistical inquiry are not reported here, since a similar but more detailed and penetrating analysis, employing data from this same pilot study, has been carried out by Cronbach (*14*). We are extremely grateful to Cronbach for this independent confirmation and further development of ideas very similar to our own.

[7] The present index provides a measure of Judge A's sensitivity in recognizing individual differences among a series of others (B, C, D, etc.). Using an adaptation of the correlational method described above, it would also be possible to develop a "pure" measure of Judge A's interpersonal sensitivity to a particular other B; or, more precisely, an index of A's ability to specify in what respects B differs from a series of others. If such a measure can be made sufficiently reliable, it can be used to in-

we are now ready to turn to an experiment in which this index has been employed.

The Statler Experiment

In order to obtain measures of interpersonal sensitivity on a substantial number of subjects under controlled experimental conditions, we invited 72 Cornell students to dinner at the Statler Inn on the Cornell campus.[8] The students were all volunteers from two large English courses in American and European fiction, selected because each drew from a broad cross-section of undergraduates at the University. Upon arrival at the Inn, the students were divided into twelve discussion groups. Except for certain specified conditions, assignment to groups was made at random. Thus each group was to consist of three men and three women, and the members of any one group were to be strangers to each other. The latter condition was set in order to eliminate the influence of previous acquaintance as a factor affecting sensitivity. Each group participated in two discussions, one before dinner and the other immediately after. The first involved reaching a group decision concerning three courses that should be required of every Cornell student; the second entailed reaching consensus on three things one would wish to have along if marooned on a desert island. Six of the groups, selected at random, discussed the first task before dinner, while the other six began with the second.

After thus being together throughout dinner and two discussion periods—in all, a total of about four hours—the group members rated themselves and each other on two sets of adjectives, one selected from a list previously judged by 190 college students as representing

---

vestigate questions of dyadic relationship hitherto beclouded by spurious effects. To cite but a few examples: Is A more likely to be sensitive to B's idiosyncrasies if he likes him or if he dislikes him? Conversely, do we tend to be more sensitive to the idiosyncrasies of people who like us? If two persons are similar, are they more likely to be sensitive to each other's unique qualities? Are there dyadic effects in interpersonal sensitivity, so that if A is sensitive to B, B is also likely to be sensitive to A? Such questions are not only of theoretical interest, but, depending on the behavior correlates of interpersonal sensitivity, may also be of practical importance in such problems as placing a man under the right supervisor, choosing an appropriate therapist, selecting room mates, assistants, co-workers, etc.

[8] We wish to acknowledge the major contribution of Paul F. Dempsey in the planning and carrying-out of the experimental procedures employed in the Statler experiment. We are also indebted to Mr. William Conner, manager of the Statler Inn, for his generous cooperation and patient understanding of the somewhat peculiar requirements of an "experimentally controlled" dinner and discussion—randomized and fixed seating arrangements, only six persons to a table, no communication between tables, separate rooms for each discussion group, etc.

"desirable" qualities, the other from a list of "undesirable."[9] The instructions for rating were: "Describe yourself and every other group member with respect to the way in which each of you reacted during the particular discussion in which you have just participated." After making his ratings, the student was asked to predict how the other five students had rated him (first-person referent) and themselves (second-person referent) on each adjective.

Both ratings and predictions were made on a six-point scale. It was therefore possible to compute our "within-item" correlational measures for both first- and second-person sensitivity. Our first attempt at constructing an index of first-person sensitivity was based on the correlation between the five ratings received by a judge on each item from the other members of his group and the five estimates he made of how these group members would rate him.[10] An analogous index of second-person sensitivity was constructed in terms of the correlation between the five self-ratings on each item made by the other members of the group and the judge's estimates of these self-ratings.

A Statistical Analysis of Interpersonal Sensitivity Scores

Since the scores yielded by our procedure take the form of correlation coefficients, before subjecting them to statistical manupulation, we transformed them into Fisher's z's. Across-item reliabilities for each index were computed from two alternate forms of the test, each form containing six items (three favorable and three unfavorable). To consider the more successful measure first, the reliability of the index of second-person sensitivity is .67 (corrected by the Spearman-Brown formula). The average value of z for the 72 cases was .17, which corresponds to an r also of .17. Mean scores for men and women were virtually identical. The standard deviation for the distribution of z-scores is .20 with a total range corresponding to r's from —.30 to .61. An analysis of variance of these data revealed that the mean value differed significantly from zero ($P < .01$), and that, in terms of the reliability of the test, the judges differed significantly from each other ($P < .05$). There was also marked variation

[9] The "desirable" or "favorable" adjectives were helpful, influential, interesting, observant, reasonable, and warm; the "unfavorable" items were domineering, immature, shy, submissive, unimaginative, and worried.

[10] In this initial attempt to develop indices of interpersonal sensitivity we gave little thought to the fact that the persons being judged included both men and women. Failure to consider the implications of this circumstance had serious consequences which will become apparent later.

($P < .01$) in sensitivity score from one group of six to another, a variation which could not be explained by the differences among individuals within groups.[11] There were no signficant differences in the order or content of the discussion task.

A contrasting picture is presented by the data for first-person sensitivity—the judge's ability to recognize how others differed in their ratings of him. The measure showed a reliability of zero, a mean of essentially zero and, as might be expected, no significant differences among scores for individuals or groups. Apparently the task was so difficult that our subjects could do no better than chance, perhaps because judging the feelings of others toward the self mobilizes defenses which prevent accurate discrimination. There is a more plausible explanation, however, in terms of the different sorts of cues available to the judge for making each type of prediction. The subjects had started the evening as complete strangers, and the period of active social interaction was comparatively short —not more than an hour and a half. (The rest of the time was spent in registering and filling out forms.) During such relatively brief face-to-face contact, there were probably very few overt cues available to show the judge how his associates differed in their feelings *toward him.* Cues for differences among group members in their general behavior were more likely to have been present, and to have been observed, both by the judge and *by the group members themselves.* Hence the possibility of a better-than-chance performance in second-person sensitivity.

It is, of course, possible that with more items and a longer period of interaction, a reliable measure of first-person sensitivity can be obtained in a situation of this type. We can indeed almost insure this possibility by making one modification: selecting as participants, not comparative strangers, but people who know each other relatively well.[12] The same considerations apply even more forcefully to the measure of second-person sensitivity. Indeed, if we simply increase the number of items, say, from twelve to fifty or sixty, we would expect the reliability to rise to about .90, a level high enough to permit dealing with cases on an individual basis.

So far we have confined ourselves to the question of reliability *across items;* that is, we have asked whether a judge who is able to

[11] An analysis of the psychological significance of these group differences appears below (Section 7).

[12] Tagiuri and his associates (*52, 53*), working with subjects who have known each other for long periods of time and employing a measure of what we would call first-person sensitivity, repeatedly obtain results which are better than chance for the group as a whole.

discriminate others on one set of items will differentiate these same others on a different set of items. But in problems of interpersonal perception there is also the question of another kind of reliability which is at least as important; this is reliability *across persons.* Here we ask whether a judge is likely to obtain a similar score when confronted with a new and different set of people to evaluate. Although our data were not ideally suited to this question because of the small number of persons evaluated by each judge, we made an attempt to explore it.

The five subjects estimated by each judge were subdivided into two sets, Set A consisting of three persons, Set B of two. Assignment of subjects to sets was made at random, except for one restriction. In order to make both sets representative of the total task performed by the judge, we required that each contain persons of both sexes. Specifically, this meant that for each judge Set A consisted in three persons, two of the opposite sex and one of the same sex, while Set B contained two persons of the opposite sex. We cite these details because they turned out to be crucial for the results obtained. For every judge, two separate measures of second-person sensitivity were computed, one based on each set. These measures were then correlated to provide an estimate of across-person reliability.

The results were both sobering and perplexing; the correlation between sets was substantially zero ($r = .12$). On the chance that this value might be exceptionally low because of sampling error, we repeated the procedure employing a new random assignment of subjects to sets. This time the correlation was unequivocal ($r = -.03$). These results seemed to point to the conclusion that our measure of interpersonal sensitivity was wholly unreliable across persons; that is, the score which a judge obtained in estimating one set of persons had no relationship to the score he might obtain with another set of persons. Although discouraged by such a conclusion, we would have been prepared to accept it had it not been for one fact: our analysis had revealed highly significant differences in sensitivity score from one discussion group to another. How could such differences appear, we asked ourselves, if the measure being used were wholly unreliable?

No immediate answer was forthcoming, but in due time there occurred to us a possible explanation which involved several interrelated factors. First, we came belatedly to the realization that, since our groups included both men and women, a judge, in order to obtain a high score, actually had to make three possibly different types of discrimination: he had to recognize how men differed from men, how women differed from women, and also how men and women differed from each other. This last discrimination, moreover, probably included an element of the type we had intended to eliminate from our measuring procedure—a response set, taking the form of a stereotyped conception of how men and women differ in their self-descriptions. Such a stereotype would necessarily enter into any judgment involving a comparison between a man and a woman. Furthermore, if an incorrect stereotype were shared by the majority of our subjects, it would introduce error into all cross-sex comparisons and thus, of course, reduce their reliability. But because of our requirement that each set of two or three persons include members of both sexes, our reliability measures were primarily a function of cross-sex rather than same-sex comparisons. If the latter were reliable, they could contribute to the observed differences among group means, but would not be reflected in the predominantly cross-sex measures of reliability which we had employed.

Also, a judge might be able to discriminate reliably among members of one sex but not the other. A woman brought up in a predominantly female environment, for instance, might be an extremely good judge of her own sex but a poor judge of men. If the correlation between sensitivity toward one sex and sensitivity toward the other were generally zero or negative, it, too, would contribute to the unreliability of our measuring instrument.

Finally, in view of the fact that our subjects had been divided into groups of six, there was the possibility that any correlation between group means would be a function of additional factors not operative in the correlation within the group, with the result that although the relationship *within* groups might be positive, the correlation *among* groups might be zero or even negative. To take a clear-cut example outside the present context: if we consider successive grades in any public school system, there is a high positive correlation between the average chronological age of the pupils in a grade and their mental age; that is, the older the grade, the higher the mental age. But *within* any grade, the correlation between chronological age and mental age tends to be negative—the less intelligent student is often one who has been "left back" and is therefore older than the majority of his classmates.

A similar phenomenon, we surmised, could occur in the measurement of social sensitivity. Specifically, although the relative magnitude of scores of individuals within the group would primarily be a function of their ability in interpersonal perception, the differences in mean score among groups might reflect not only differences in ability but also variation in the difficulty of the task. In other words, some groups might be easy to judge, others more difficult. Any difference in group means might therefore reflect not only variation in sensitivity but also variation in *estimatability*. If the correlation between sensitivity and estimatability is low or negative—if, as Allport suggests (2, p. 515), sensitive people are more difficult to judge than insensitive ones—then any over-all measure of reliability based on a total correlation both within and among groups would tend to approach zero, even though the measure of sensitivity might in actuality be quite reliable.

The preceding considerations imposed two new important requirements for adequate measurement of interpersonal sensitivity. First of all, it was necessary to provide for separate indices of sensitivity toward each sex. Second, in investigating reliability of sensitivity scores or their correlations with other variables, it was essential to obtain separate measures of *within*-group and *among*-group relationships.

The first of these requirements was met by again dividing the five subjects evaluated by each judge into two sets, this time with each set composed of members of the same sex only. As before, separate measures of interpersonal sensitivity were then computed for each set so that for every judge two scores were available, one measuring his skill in discriminating among members of his own sex (same-sex sensitivity), the other his ability in differentiating members of the opposite sex (opposite-sex sensitivity). As measures of relationship *among* and *within* groups, we employed the conventional procedures of analysis of covariance. These procedures yield two correlation coefficients: the first is simply the correlation between group means; the second is a meaure of the average correlation within groups.

The results of this extensive re-analysis of our data on interpersonal sensitivity appear in Tables 1 to 3. The fact that our measures take the form of transformed correlation coefficients makes possible a consideration of the absolute level of proficiency achieved by our subjects. As indicated in the first two colunms of Table 1, the average scores for both types of interpersonal sensitivity are rather low.[13] The question remains whether they are significantly different from zero and from each other. Data relevant to both

[13] Although the means reported in the table are averages of Fisher's z, they can be given the same interpretation as the corresponding correlation coefficients, since, at such low levels of magnitude, the corresponding values are practically identical.

parts of this question appear in the analyses of variance shown in Tables 2 and 3. In these tables, the sum of squares associated with the mean, which is ordinarily of little or no interest and hence not reported, has an important interpretation. The fact that for both variables the corresponding mean square differs significantly from zero indicates that our subjects, when asked to predict how others varied in their self-descriptions, did appreciably better as a group than they could have been expected to do on a purely chance basis. In short, there is evidence for the existence of a genuine ability in interpersonal perception. The analysis reveals no significant difference between the sexes in either type of skill, but marked variation from one discussion group to the next. Possible explanations for this salient finding are considered in some detail below (see Section 7).

We must call attention to an important difference between the data in Tables 2 and 3, to explain why the seemingly comparable

TABLE 1. MEAN VALUES, INTERCORRELATIONS, AND DIFFERENCES IN REGRESSION COEFFICIENTS FOR SCORES IN SENSITIVITY TO THE SAME SEX (x) AND SENSITIVITY TO THE OPPOSITE SEX (y)

	Means		Inter-correlations		Regression Coefficients (x or y)		Differences in Among-group vs. Within-group Regressions	"t" for Difference
	Same Sex	Opposite Sex	Within Groups	Among Groups	Within Groups	Among Groups		
Men	.128	.135	.337	.169	.207	.140	.067	2.82**
Women	.218	.137	−.207	.764	−.129	.661	−.790	7.37**
Both Sexes	.173	.136						
Sex Differences in Regression					3.36	−.521		
"t" for Sex Difference					3.62**	2.69*		

* Significant at the 5% level.
** Significant at the 1% level.

measures of the two types of sensitivity were not treated in a single analysis. The variation in same-sex sensitivity is consistently greater than that for opposite-sex sensitivity; indeed, the error term for the former is almost twice that for the latter. This difference in spread

TABLE 2. ANALYSIS OF VARIANCE FOR SAME-SEX SENSITIVITY SCORES

Source of Variation	Sum of Squares	d.f.	Mean Square	F
Mean Level (.173)	21562.72	1	21562.72†	7.62**
Sex	1458.00	1	1458.00	
Group	31115.28	11	2828.66	2.68**
Sex × Group	17860.00	11	1623.64	1.54 n.s.
Subjects within Sex and Group	50724.00	48	1056.75	
Total (excluding mean)	73157.28	71	1030.38	

†In order to permit generalization to another population of groups, this mean square has been tested against the mean square for groups rather than that for individual subjects which is considerably smaller.
* Significant at the 5% level.
** Significant at the 1% level.

TABLE 3. ANALYSIS OF VARIANCE FOR OPPOSITE-SEX SENSITIVITY SCORES

Source of Variation	Sum of Squares	d.f.	Mean Square	F
Mean Level (.136)	13284.50	1	13824.50†	5.12*
Sex	.50	1	.50	
Group	28527.17	11	2593.38	6.48**
Sex × Group	6835.17	11	621.38	
Subjects within Sex and Group	19202.66	48	400.06	
Total (excluding mean)	54565.50	71	768.53	

† See footnote to Table 2.
* Significant at the 5% level.
** Significant at the 1% level.

is probably accounted for by the fact that the measure of same-sex sensitivity for each judge, being based on a comparison of only two persons, is therefore less reliable than the measure of opposite-sex sensitivity, which involved a comparison of three persons. The hypothesis of lower reliability would explain both the larger error term found in the analysis of variance for the same-sex sensitivity scores and also the more reliable group differences revealed in the corresponding analysis for measures of opposite-sex sensitivity. The small number of subjects remaining in each set precluded the possibility of computing separate coefficients of reliability for the two measures, but presumptive evidence in favor of modest reliability for both appears in the reliable differences between means and between correlation and regression coefficients shown in Tables 1 to 3 and in subsequent analyses to be reported below.

One final question regarding mean differences remains which cannot be answered from the data of Tables 2 and 3—whether people are more skilled in judging their own sex or the opposite sex. Although in Table 1 the over-all mean score for same-sex sensitivity is slightly higher than that for opposite-sex sensitivity, neither this difference nor the even greater one for women taken separately turns out to be statistically significant.[14] From our data, therefore, we cannot conclude that one skill is any more difficult than the other.

We now turn to the question of the correlation between same-sex and opposite-sex sensitivity. The relevant coefficients appear in the center section of Table 1. Our primary interest is in the within-group correlations, for it is these which tell us whether a person with a high score in one skill is likely to excel in the other as well. It turns out that the answer to this question depends on the sex of the person involved. For men the relationship between the two skills is positive; for women, negative. In order to determine whether this sex difference is reliable, we tested the difference between the two regression coefficients. The resulting "*t*" was significant at the 1% level. It appears that men who are sensitive to men are also likely to be sensitive to women, but the more sensitive a woman is to her own sex, the less likely she is to be sensitive to men. We shall be in a better position to consider the implications of this finding after we have examined the behavioral correlates of each type of sensitivity, which turn out to be quite different for the two sexes.

[14] In testing these differences an appropriate procedure was employed taking into account the fact that the variances were not homogeneous.

Before proceeding to this topic, however, we have to complete our examination of the relationship between same-sex and opposite-sex sensitivity by considering the among-group correlations between the two variables. As we had thought possible, these correlations differ appreciably from what might have been expected on the basis of the within-group trends. The difference is particularly marked in the case of women, for whom the negative within-group coefficient of —.21 contrasts sharply with the high positive value of .76 for correlation among groups. As shown at the extreme right of Table 1, the difference between within- and among-group regression coefficients is highly significant for both sexes. In other words, the relationship between the two skills at the level of the group is quite different from the relationship at the level of individuals.

A clue to the possible source of this difference lies in the contrast between the high among-group correlation for women and the much lower one for men (.17). If the three women in a group get a high score in judging one sex, they seem likely to do well in judging the other as well; but the corresponding relationship is by no means so strong for men. This fact suggests that *the marked variation from group to group observed with both variables is, at least in part, a function of some property peculiar to the women in the group.* We shall pursue this lead in a subsequent discussion of possible explanations for the marked variation in group score (Section 7 below).

6. Some Correlates of Individual Differences in Interpersonal Sensitivity [15]

Method of Analysis

The basic information on the correlates of sensitivity in the Statler experiment comes from ratings given each judge by his associates

[15] A preliminary and, unfortunately, highly misleading report on the results of our investigation of the correlates of interpersonal sensitivity appears in a published abstract (7) for a paper read at the 1955 Annual Meeting of the American Psychological Association in San Francisco. Although it was possible to correct the errors in the paper as finally presented, the results cited in the abstract are, ironically enough, in many instances diametrically opposed to the correct findings presented in the succeeding pages. This happened because the earlier conclusions regarding the correlates of interpersonal sensitivity were based on a hasty analysis employing the conventional correlation coefficient, a measure of association which reflects primarily the relationship among group means rather than among individuals within groups. Since, as we have already seen, the among-group and within-group relationships in our data are likely to be quite different and, in the case of women, even opposite in sign, the inferences drawn in the published abstract are largely invalid and, in a number of instances, inversely related to the actual facts.

on each of 24 adjectives sampling a variety of "desirable" and "undesirable" characteristics. By summing the ratings received by each judge from his five associates and correlating this sum against his sensitivity score, we can investigate relationships between the person's sensitivity and the way in which he is perceived by the fellow members of his group.

Since our first interest is in the correlates of individual differences in skill rather than in relationships at the group level, the appropriate measure of association is again the within-group correlation coefficient. Furthermore, inasmuch as we have already shown that same-sex and opposite-sex sensitivities represent different skills, it is obviously important to investigate separately the correlates of each. We should like to know, that is, what kinds of behavior are associated with skill in judging one's own sex, and how such behavior differs (if it does) from that of persons who excel in judging the opposite sex.

A special problem arises in this connection by virtue of the fact that the two variables are not independent, the correlation being positive for men and negative for women. Accordingly, if we wish to identify the characteristics associated with only one of these skills, we must in some way hold constant variation in the other skill. Ideally, this might be accomplished by comparing behavior in persons who varied in one ability but were all equal in the other. Our sample, unfortunately, was too small to permit experimental controls of this kind. Instead, we approximated the ideal situation, by employing a statistical control in the form of a partial correlation coefficient. Thus, in order to obtain an estimate of the relationship between rating by associates (w) and same-sex sensitivity (x)—holding opposite-sex sensitivity (y) constant—we computed a within-group partial correlation $r_{wx \cdot y}$. The corresponding partial coefficient $r_{wy \cdot x}$ provided the analogous measure of association for opposite-sex sensitivity.

One final methodological problem remained. Since our primary concern was with general ability in interpersonal perception rather than with skill in judging one sex only, we wished also to obtain an index of overall sensitivity to both men and women. Such an index could then be correlated against ratings from associates to indicate how a person who is generally sensitive to others is perceived by his fellow group members. An obvious and seemingly altogether appropriate method for obtaining a measure of this kind would be simply to add each person's scores on same- and opposite-sex sensitivity and to employ the sum as an overall measure. Unfortunately, the fact that the variance for same-sex sensitivity scores is considerably larger than that for opposite-sex sensitivity means that a procedure of simple addition would result in giving the former variable a good deal more weight than the latter. Such an outcome becomes particularly undesirable when we recall that the greater spread in same-sex sensitivity scores is probably attributable to errors in measurement (pp. 57-58 *supra*). In order to avoid this unwelcome effect, we converted the two types of scores into standard scores, and then added them together—a procedure frequently employed in psychological measurement when scores from distributions having different variances are to be combined. The resulting sums were correlated with the ratings by associates to provide a measure of the relationship between the person's general sensitivity and the way in which he is perceived by his fellow group members.[16]

Since we had reason to doubt the reliability of our measures of first-person sensitivity across items (see p. 52 *supra*), the correlational analyses described above were carried out only for scores of second-person sensitivity—the judges' skill in recognizing how others differed in their self-descriptions. Table 4 summarizes the relationships between the subject's score in each of three types of sensitivity (same-sex, opposite-sex, and overall) and the sum of ratings given him by his associates on each of 24 adjectives.[17] The adjectives have been grouped into clusters in such a way as to highlight the patterns formed by the correlation coefficients. As a summary for each cluster, an average value has been computed based on the r corresponding to the mean of Fisher's z's for the correlations in the cluster. Although these clusters derive in part from the purely semantic relationships between the adjectives, which could have been specified before the statistical analysis was per-

[16] Actually, since we had no particular interest in the individual score values, the final correlations were computed directly. As before, all calculations, including the standard score transformations, were performed on a within-group basis.

[17] Although 12 of these 24 adjectives are the same ones used in obtaining the ratings and estimates from which sensitivity scores were computed, it is our belief that correlations between these scores and ratings from associates are not susceptible to artificial linkages arising from similarity between the judge and the person being judged. Several considerations make such linkage extremely improbable. In the first place, the indices involved are based on two completely different sets of ratings. The ratings given each judge by his associates do enter as criteria for evaluating accuracy of first-person sensitivity, but the correlations in this instance are all with second-person sensitivity, which is based on the associate's self-rating. Moreover, even if the same ratings had been used, the fact that one index is a mean (average rating received) and the other a correlation based on individual deviations around that mean, removes the possibility of bias insofar as the correlation coefficient is independent of the mean of the distribution.

TABLE 4. CORRELATIONS BETWEEN INTERPERSONAL SENSITIVITY SCORES AND RATINGS BY ASSOCIATES

		Men			Women			Men and Women
		Sensitivity toward			Sensitivity toward			Sensitivity to Both Sexes
Cluster	Item	Men	Women	Both Sexes	Women	Men	Both Sexes	
Withdrawn and Insecure vs. Outgoing and Self-Assured	Submissive	—.29	.37	.08	.49*	.47	.57**	.23
	Not influential	—.46*	.43*	—.04	.38	.26	.40*	.07
	Not persistent	—.17	.42*	.22	.18	.31	.52**	.32**
	Not warm	—.33	—.04	—.32	.26	—.03	.18	—.17
	Shy	—.38	.42*	.04	.34	.36	.43*	.18
	Uneasy	—.41*	.10	—.27	.26	.09	.39	—.06
	Worried	—.22	.33	.11	.38	.20	.36	.15
	Immature	.02	—.20	—.16	.22	—.07	.10	—.14
	Average †	—.29	.24	—.04	.32	.20	.38	.07
Ability to Relate vs. Offensive Behavior	Not domineering	—.37	.52**	.15	.45*	.52**	.58**	.27*
	Not annoying	—.11	.48*	.34	—.02	.16	.20	.29*
	Considerate	—.19	.62**	.41*	.25	.19	.48*	.40**
	Accepting	—.26	.37	.10	.01	.38	.42*	.22
	Reasonable	.00	.29	.25	.03	.41*	.24	.29*
	Average	—.19	.46*	.25	.15	.34	.38	.30*
Uninhibited vs. Controlled Behavior	Impulsive	.36	—.30	.06	—.42*	.12	—.35	—.10
	Not serious	.44*	—.33	.10	—.20	.12	.09	—.08
	Enthusiastic	.28	—.11	.16	—.06	—.16	—.24	.03
	Frank	.14	—.18	—.04	—.23	.18	—.06	—.02
	Not indifferent	.19	—.23	.04	—.13	—.15	—.31	—.11
	Average	.28	—.23	.06	—.21	.02	—.18	—.07
Talented and Resourceful vs. Incompetent and Dull	Imaginative	.44*	—.16	.25	—.21	—.32	—.34	.00
	Interesting	.39	—.10	.26	—.46*	—.31	—.47*	
	Constructive	.49*	—.19	.28	—.12	.10	—.24	—.06
	Helpful	.38	—.19	.17	—.40*	—.21	—.38	.04
	Observant	.34	—.20	.13	—.18	.14	.13	.08
	Practical	.05	—.01	.05	—.26	.11	—.17	.03
	Average	.34	—.14	.20	—.27	—.08	—.26	.02

† The value for the average is the r corresponding to the mean of Fisher's z's for the coefficients in the cluster.
* Significant at the 5% level. ** Significant at the 1% level.

formed, the items were not assigned to clusters until we had become familiar with the general character of the results. Accordingly, the hypotheses below regarding the patterns shown by the correlation coefficients must be regarded as "after the fact."

Behavioral Correlates of Interpersonal Sensitivity

A. *In men.* Looking first at the relationship between men's sensitivity to their own sex, and ratings by their associates, we note that although in general the coefficients are low, about 20% of them are significantly different from zero at the 5% level.[18] More impressive, however, is the consistent pattern exhibited by the correlations. The more sensitive a man is to his own sex, it would seem, the more likely he is to be perceived as resourceful, dominant, and outgoing—although at the same time somewhat egocentric and tactless ("domineering," "not accepting"). In general, this is the stereotype of the "All-American boy"—aggressive, self-sufficient, ebullient, friendly, a bit superficial and boorish. Conversely, the man who is insensitive to his own sex is seen as relatively incompetent, withdrawn, and insecure, but at the same time accepting and considerate rather than annoying or domineering.

We must put this contrast in perspective by keeping in mind that our subjects were for the most part college sophomores and juniors—late adolescents, still going to school. For males at this stage and station in life, identification with one's peer group is still a matter of considerable importance, and the activities shared by the group tend to emphasize the "masculine" qualities of aggressiveness, initiative, and uninhibited expression. It is not surprising, therefore, that the young man who is especially sensitive to his fellows is one who himself acts in ways that are regarded as appropriate and desirable by his age group, while the man who is insensitive to his own sex is seen as deficient in these characteristics so valued by the group. Naturally one wonders whether the man who is sensitive to his own sex is perceived in the same way by both the men and the women in the group. An adequate answer to this question would have necessitated separate analyses for ratings received from each sex, thus doubling the already-extensive computations required for Table 4. So arduous a task was beyond our means, but we were able to sample a few of the relationships in order to get a notion of the general trend. The results were in

[18] Such apparent deviation from chance expectancy cannot be interpreted at its face value, since the several coefficients, and the items on which they are based, are not independent of each other.

the expected direction. Specifically, men sensitive to their own sex were perceived as aggressive primarily by women rather than by men. One suspects on the basis of this finding that had our subjects been rated not by their age-mates but by parents, teachers, or other adults, the resulting picture would have been appreciably different from that reported above, with the negative qualities of the men sensitive to other men becoming even more salient.

It seems reasonable to conclude from our data that the behavioral correlates of same-sex sensitivity in men involve peer- and sex-group identifications. Unfortunately, correlation coefficients, while providing evidence for association, do not resolve the problem of cause and effect—we cannot determine whether interpersonal sensitivity is an antecedent or consequent of the behavior pattern. It is possible, on the one hand, that sensitivity to others' behavior is a necessary first step in the process of identification; before one can identify with something, one must first perceive what it is. On the other hand, it could also be true that sensitivity is learned through interaction with others, that only the person who shares the activities and values of a group can come to recognize individual differences with respect to these activities and values. Under the first hypothesis, sensitivity to his peers becomes a prerequisite for the male's identification with his peer group; under the second hypothesis, the opposite would be true. It is possible, of course, that both explanations may apply, each process simultaneously reinforcing the other. This problem of causal interpretation is a recurring one. Although it cannot be resolved from the data at our disposal, some further light is shed on it by material to be reported below.

When we turn to the data on the correlates of men's sensitivity to opposite sex, shown in Table 1, the findings are in striking contrast to those for sensitivity to the same sex. Men who are especially sensitive to women are characterized by their tact, their tolerance, and their timidity. They are, in addition, likely to be perceived as somewhat controlled in their behavior and as relatively insecure and incompetent. The man who is particularly insensitive to women presents the opposite side of the coin—socially aggressive, self-assured, expressive, and able; but, at the same time, likely to offend.

Once more it is helpful to view these results in the perspective of the social group and the social situation to which they apply. What we have learned is that in a small group composed of college students of both sexes, men who are especially sensitive to women are likely to be described by their associates as polite, retiring, and, perhaps, over-inhibited. The general impression shows us a somewhat over-socialized, precociously serious, and "mature" young man who lacks youthful spontaneity and does not share the less-inhibited interests and activities of the late adolescent. Again one suspects that a different judgment might have resulted if our raters had included mature adults; they might have described the behavior of such a man in somewhat more favorable terms. One cannot dispel completely the impression, however, that the man who is especially sensitive to women may often be regarded as something of a Caspar Milquetoast—a man who has been unable to break the maternal tie and to arrive at a satisfactory identification with his own sex role.

The correlations most relevant for us are, of course, those between ratings from associates and general interpersonal sensitivity to either sex. Unfortunately, from our point of view, the correlations for men's sensitivity to other men and to the opposite sex are almost invariably opposite in sign, which means that the correlations with overall sensitivity to both sexes are low in magnitude. Indeed, only one of the 24 within-group correlation coefficients differs significantly from zero. One can still say something, however, about the pattern of relationships. The highest correlations, all of them positive, appear in the cluster labelled "ability to relate." The adjectives with the highest coefficients are in the following order: considerate, not annoying, warm, constructive, not uneasy, interesting, reasonable, and imaginative. To the extent that the picture is reliable, we may conclude that men sensitive to both sexes seem to lack the extreme characteristics associated with sensitivity to either sex alone. They show neither the dominance and somewhat self-centered aggressiveness of the man sensitive to other men, nor the introverted ineffectuality of the man especially sensitive to women. What remains is a modest degree of thoughtfulness, tact, warmth, self-confidence. This conclusion must be regarded as a tenuous one, however, in view of the low magnitude and questionable reliability of the correlations.

B. In women. In a set of correlations characterized by marked sex differences, the sharpest contrast appears in the comparison between the correlates of sensitivity to the same sex, in men and in women. Three-quarters of the 24 pairs of correlation coefficients are significantly different from each other at the 5% level. In contrast to the man sensitive to his own sex, the woman who is especially perceptive toward her own sex is described by her associates predominantly in unfavorable terms. They see her as submissive, insecure, inhibited, unattractive, and ineffectual; her saving grace is a mild chance of being perceived as inoffensive and considerate of others. All in all, the woman sensitive to other women presents a pattern similar to but even more extreme than that for the man sensitive to women—that is, both are perceived by their associates as submissive, dependent, inhibited, and socially impotent. The pattern calls to mind the clinical picture of the over-protected adolescent (37) who is immobilized by the ties of an unresolved Oedipal relationship. Of interest too is the fact that a sampling of the relevant correlations reveals that women sensitive to their own sex are judged somewhat more harshly by women than by men.

Turning to the correlates of women's sensitivity to men, we find a much more favorable picture. The outstanding general characteristic of the woman who is perceptive toward men is her ability to establish and maintain a smooth, but at the same time subordinate, relationship with others. Thus she is described as submissive, not domineering, reasonable, accepting, shy, and the like. The woman sensitive toward men resembles the woman sensitive to her own sex in meekness of word and action. This fact is reflected in the correlates of overall sensitivity of women toward both sexes shown in the next to the last column of Table 4. Women who are generally perceptive of individual differences in others are described as socially retiring, ill at ease, somewhat lacking in spontaneity, but at the same time as able to effect viable interpersonal relationships (not domineering, considerate, accepting, reasonable, not annoying). Moreover, the relationships in this instance are somewhat more reliable than previously, with one-third of the correlations significantly different from zero at the 5% level.

C. In both sexes. We come now to the question most relevant to our research interests: what behavioral characteristics, if any, are associated with interpersonal sensitivity irrespective of the sex of the person judging or being judged? The answer to this question appears in the last column of Table 4. Although the correlations are low, the pattern is clear and, because it is based on all 72 cases, reliable. Virtually all the significant correlations appear in the cluster labelled "Ability to relate vs. offensive behavior." The general picture suggests a person who is "sensitive" in both senses of the term; that is, perceptive and responsive to others' needs, but, perhaps because of this very quality, hesitant and passive in his behavior toward them. By refraining from any kind of aggressive behavior, he avoids hurting the feelings of others, but at the price of failing to realize his own capacities for creative expression and social leadership.

Lest we be carried away by the challenging social implications of some of the conclusions drawn in the preceding paragraphs, we must emphasize once again the tenuous quality of many of our data. Correlations below .40—particularly non-significant ones—are hardly a firm basis for generalization.[19] In only one respect can our findings be regarded as unequivocal; they do raise doubts about some of the common assumptions regarding the nature and presumed advantages of ability in interpersonal perception. For instance, there can be little question that the notion of empathy or ability to judge others as typically conceived gives considerable emphasis to what we have called interpersonal sensitivity. Empathy has, moreover, been generally regarded as a social asset, almost as a guarantee to effective social behavior. In our own speculation about the correlates of interpersonal sensitivity, we foresaw a different possibility; namely, that acute awareness of individual differences in feeling might be rooted in anxiety regarding the consequences of one's own and others' social behavior.

Accordingly it is a matter of some interest that our data, inadequate as they are, tend to contradict the conventional assumption. But even this inference must be made with caution. While our re-

[19] This caution applies in two directions, for the possibility exists not only of overestimating but also of underestimating the nature and magnitude of the behavioral correlates of interpersonal sensitivity. Such underestimation could occur, for example, as a function of the low reliability of our measures of skill in interpersonal perception. Although we were unable to obtain a numerical estimate of reliability (because of the impossibility of further subdividing the individuals to be judged), there can be little doubt that scores based on a comparison of only two or three persons can have only modest reliability at best. Since measures which are themselves of low reliability are not likely to show high correlations with other variables, it is possible that our obtained correlations are consistently lower than the true correlations between the variables.

A second factor that might lead to underestimation derives from the fact that our measure of association, the Pearson product-moment coefficient, assumes a linear relationship among the variables. If the true relationship is nonlinear, its magnitude could be seriously underestimated by the type of index used. To check on this possibility, we constructed tables which would reveal the actual character of the joint distribution. Since the tables had to be constructed in such a way as to reflect relationships within groups only, the procedure employed was fairly complex and need not be reported here. It made possible the comparison of mean scores for each adjective obtained by sub-groups of persons representing different combinations of skill; e.g., high in sensitivity to same and opposite sex, low in both, high in one but low in the other, medium in both, etc. The results of this analysis indicated that the assumption of linearity had not done serious violence to our data. Substantially the same items emerged as characteristic of the several sub-groups as would have been expected on the basis of the correlations reported in Table 4.

sults suggest that the sensitive person tends to be passive and withdrawn, there is no explicit evidence to show that he anticipates hostility or is easily hurt; and the fact that our high scorers tend to be perceived as "accepting" does not altogether fit the "anxiety" hypothesis. A second and more likely possibility is that these results are a function of our particular experimental situation; they represent a *first impression.* Had the discussions continued later into the evening, the sensitive person might have been perceived differently.

Even if the sensitive person does tend to create an initial, or even an enduring, impression of meekness, this does not mean of course that it is a mistake to think of sensitivity to individual differences as an important factor in social talent. We know that this meekness is associated with positive qualities such as considerateness and acceptance of others; and, perhaps more important, we think of interpersonal sensitivity as a necessary but not sufficient condition for correct judgment of other persons as individuals. Another essential condition is accurate knowledge of the social norms—what we have called sensitivity to the generalized other. Our analysis of this skill, its behavioral correlates, and its relation to ability in interpersonal perception should shed further light on the relationship between skills of social perception and social behavior.

In concluding discussion of our findings regarding the correlates of interpersonal perceptiveness, we would call attention again to the inference suggested by our data that interpersonal sensitivity plays a functional role in the basic need system of the individual. Such a relationship in turn implies that the nature of sensitivity and its behavioral correlates will vary with the developmental stage of the individual and, what is more, will depend on the particular needs that may be activated in a given social context. Probably the most serious limitation of our research findings is that they are based on a sample of college undergraduates, a group highly selected in terms of age and social background. This group was tested, moreover, in only one social situation, an artificially contrived situation at that. Whether the conclusions we have drawn from our data are applicable to other populations or even to the same population in another situation can be discovered only by further research.

7. Situational Correlates of Group Differences in Performance

Among the most reliable differences revealed in our analysis of interpersonal sensitivity are the marked variations in mean scores of the discussion groups, which, as we have already seen, cannot be explained as a function of individual differences in ability but must be a function of properties peculiar to the group as a group. In this section we shall deal with our efforts to determine the nature of these special group properties.

Motivation vs. Difficulty of Task

We began by considering two general types of explanation. The first is the possibility that in some groups, for reasons essentially unrelated to the personal characteristics of the persons involved, the participants were more strongly motivated to use their abilities in interpersonal perception. Such motivation could, for example, be a function of the group's decision to carry on its discussions in an informal or a formal fashion. The second explanation, discussed previously, is the possibility that the judgmental task varied in difficulty from group to group. If, for instance, one group happened to adopt a procedure in which each individual was given an opportunity to express his views, the members would probably have found it easier to make accurate discriminations than would a group in which no such opportunity had been provided. In order to determine which type of explanation was in closer correspondence with the facts,[20] we needed a measure of "estimatability," the degree to which a person was easily and accurately differentiated from the other members of the group. The only measure available to us, our correlational index, would necessarily have reflected any differences in estimatability at the group level, but unfortunately these differences would also have been confounded with variations in sensitivity resulting from differences in actual ability or in motivation to perceive.

One possibility, however, remained open to us. While our resources did not permit us to develop individual measures of esti-

[20] We attempted to explore this question also by studying the reports of nonparticipant observers, one or two of whom had been assigned to each discussion group. These reports turned out to be of little value, however, for identifying intergroup differences—probably because each observer saw only one group and hence had no basis for comparison. The reports were concerned mainly with accounts of gross behavior that tended to be duplicated from one group to the next.

matability for each of our subjects, we could, by a relatively simple manipulation of available data, make separate approximations of the sensitivity and the estimatability of the two sexes in each discussion group. We could then determine whether the observed variation among groups was more strongly associated with the sensitivity or the estimatability level of the sub-groups of any one sex. A higher correlation with sensitivity would be consistent with an explanation of group effects in terms of differential motivation. A higher degree of association with estimatability would point to an explanation in terms of the relative difficulty of the task involved.

The relative contributions of sensitivity and estimatability to differences among groups were determined in the following manner. For each group of six, we computed the mean scores in sensitivity to the same and to the opposite sex, for both men and women. Thus for each group we had four values: MM, or the men's score in judging their own sex; MW, their score in judging the women in the group; WM, the women's score in judging the men; and WW, the women's score in judging themselves. Any one of these means necessarily reflects both sensitivity and estimatability. For instance, the men's score in judging their own sex is a function of their interest and skill in recognizing how they differ from each other, and also it is a function of the difficulty of the task—that is, whether the men in the group had acted in such a way as to be easy to judge.

But let us assume for the moment that the factor which actually operates to produce differences in score from group to group is estimatability rather than sensitivity. If so, then when men are easy to judge for one sex, they should also be easy to judge for the other. At the same time, the fact that the men in the group are readily estimatable does not guarantee that the same will hold true for the women. Under these circumstances the relationship between men's sensitivity to men and their sensitivity to women should not be particularly high. In other words, if estimatability is the principal factor determining differences in performance from group to group, then the correlation, over the twelve groups, between MM and WM should be higher than that between MM and MW. Correspondingly for women, the relationship between WW and MW should exceed that between WW and WM. The data of Table 5 show that this is indeed the case, the respective correlations being .60 vs. .17 for men and .90 vs. .76 for women. In short, the evidence suggests that differences in the difficulty of the task played a more important part in producing the marked variation in group performance than did differences in motivation. Whether the group did well or poorly depended in large measure on whether or not the members of the group were easy to judge.

TABLE 5. INTERCORRELATION AMONG GROUP MEANS OF SAME-SEX AND OPPOSITE-SEX SENSITIVITY SCORES
($N = 12$)

		MM	MW	WM
Men judging men	MM			
Men judging women	MW	.17		
Women judging men	WM	.60*	.71**	
Women judging women	WW	.27	.90**	.76**

* Significant at the 5% level.
** Significant at the 1% level.

We cannot, nevertheless, rule out the influence of motivation as a relevant factor, for one feature of the correlations in Table 5 cannot be explained completely on the basis of differential difficulty. This is the fact, first noted early in our discussion, that group differences seem to be a function of certain properties associated with the women in the group. One of these properties is apparently their estimatability, for the correlation reflecting this variable is appreciably greater for women (.90) than for men (.60). But this is not the only important factor linked with the women. The correlation for women's sensitivity is considerably higher for women than the corresponding correlation for men (.76 vs. .17); indeed, the former coefficient is the second highest in the table. Apparently, that group performs best in which the women are not only easy to judge but are also better judges, perhaps because they have been more highly motivated to observe others. The crucial contribution of the women to group performance, both in estimatability and sensitivity, is further reflected in the fact that the three highest coefficients in Table 5 represent combinations tapping simultaneously the sensitivity of women and their estimatability. In contrast, the three lowest coefficients are those which involve men's judgment of their own sex; the only one of these three coefficients which differs significantly from zero is that reflecting men's estimatability by both sexes. We may infer, then, that while the ease with which men can be judged played some part in determining the performance of the group, the most important factor affecting group differences had to do with the "degree of communicability" associated with the women in the group. A situation of high communicability would be one in which the women both recognized how others felt (i.e., showed high interpersonal sensitivity) and, at the same time, were themselves understood by their associates (i.e., had high interpersonal estimatability). Low communicativeness would be the case when the women both misjudged their follow group members and were themselves misperceived.

Behavioral Correlates of Group Differences in Sensitivity and Estimatability

Although the preceding analysis sheds some light on the problem of group differences, it poses more questions than it resolves. What accounts for the variation in women's communicability from group to group? Why is it that in some situations they were both understanding and understood, whereas in others they were unperceptive and misperceived? And why should this phenomenon be observed primarily for women and not for men?

For possible answers to these provocative questions we began by examining the behavior ratings for men and women in those groups in which the sensitivity or estimatability of either sex was exceptionally high or low. We reasoned that, if our analysis was correct, the behavior of men and women in such groups should exhibit sharp contrasts, which might offer clues for an explanation of the marked variation in women's communicability.

Accordingly, correlation coefficients were computed, over the twelve groups, between the average level of sensitivity or estimatability and the ratings received by the two sexes separately on each of the 24 adjectives. A separate sensitivity and estimatability score was obtained for the men and women in each group by combining in appropriate fashion the sensitivity scores to the same sex and opposite sex for a particular sex sub-group. For example, the estimatability index for the women in a group was based on a combination of the score obtained by the women in judging themselves and that of the men in judging the women. Since, as already noted, the variance among sensitivity scores for the same sex was considerably greater than that for sensitivity to the opposite sex, we avoided bias in the composite index by converting all scores into ranks, and using the average rank as the final measure.

In view of the fact that the complete analysis involved well over 200 correlation coefficients, it is impractical to report the results in full detail. The general findings may be summarized as follows. As we had foreseen, the correlations for women's sensitivity and estimatability tended to be high and very similar in pattern; in other words, there were consistent differences in behavior from group to group associated with variation in what we have called the degree of communicability for the women members of the group. Also as expected, in those groups in which such communicability was exceptionally high or low, there was a marked contrast in the observed behavior of men and women.

What we had not anticipated, however, was the fact that the communicability of the women was related primarily not to their own behavior but to the behavior of the men. Specifically, in those situations in which the women were both sensitive and estimatable, the men's behavior was described as generally ineffectual and inappropriate—not constructive, not helpful, immature, indifferent, not reasonable, not frank, shy, etc.[21] The correlations for women's behavior in these groups were lower, but equally instructive;[22] in contrast to the men, they were perceived in generally positive terms—helpful, not annoying, influential, observant, practical, enthusiastic and warm. At the same time, the women apparently exerted their influence in an unobtrusive and even self-abnegating manner, for they were also described as shy, submissive, not frank, serious, and worried.

It is important also to notice that the preceding descriptions apply in reverse to those groups where the women's communicability was low; that is, in such situations the men were described as behaving in highly appropriate fashion, while the women were perceived as aggressive, disruptive, incompetent, and unfriendly.

Once again the empirical findings take on richer meaning when viewed in the perspective of a broader social context. Thus, in our American middle-class culture, men are expected to take, and ordinarily do take, a dominant role in group discussions such as those of the Statler experiment. At the same time, college women (particularly when, as at Cornell, they represent a minority in a predominantly male world) are under such circumstances likely to challenge the dominant position of the man and compete with him on his own terms. If the men in the given situation are reasonably capable and attractive, the woman's position becomes especially frustrating. She reacts, according to our data, by behaving aggressively and non-constructively in such a way as to arouse the antagonism of her own as well as of the opposite sex. And—most

[21] The magnitude of the corresponding correlation coefficients ranged from .58 for shy to —.80 for not constructive. All of these coefficients were significant at the 5% level for an N of 12. Of the 48 relationships involved, approximately 20% exceeded the 5% level of confidence.

[22] Out of 48 coefficients, only 4, or 12%, were significant at the 5% level. The correlations for the items cited range from the low .30's for warm, not frank, worried, and submissive to the 50's and 60's for helpful, not annoying, shy, and serious.

relevant from our point of view—she tends not only to misjudge others but to be herself misjudged. When, on the other hand, the men in the group fail to function effectively as leaders, the woman comes into her own. Confronted by male inadequacy, she no longer has to compete; instead, she takes a role that is highly approved for women in our culture (*46*), especially in terms of relationship to men: she is the tactful helpmate who aids and encourages, but does so indirectly, in order not to threaten the man's self-esteem.[23] It is precisely under these conditions—when the woman is functioning effectively in a supportive and non-threatening role—that she is shown by our measurement procedures to be both most understanding of others and best understood by them.

The preceding considerations, then, point to the conclusion that the property of a group which we have referred to as women's communicability is primarily a function of the degree of conflict or compatibility between the roles of the two sexes. Communicability is lowest when the women are in competition with the men; it is highest when the men and women have complementary roles. Further support for this general conclusion comes from the analysis of behavioral correlates of sensitivity and estimatability in sub-groups of men. Although, as expected, the correlations are lower in magnitude, they indicate clearly that men also tended to be most perceptive and most clearly perceived in those situations in which the role relationship between the sexes was complementary rather than antagonistic.

This finding, in turn, underscores the importance, for interpersonal perception, of viewing the behavior or psychological state of the person not solely in *individual* terms but also in terms of the *relationships* in behavior and psychological state that exist among the persons judging and those being judged. Thus, in the present instance, men were most sensitive and estimatable when they were being unimaginative, unconstructive, and immature, but the women were at their best when they were helpful, practical, submissive and not annoying. In terms of facilitating accurate interper-

[23] Additional weight is given to this interpretation by the fact that, in the situations under discussion, the ratings of women as submissive, shy, and not domineering came primarily from men, while more flattering terms, such as influential, were applied by the women themselves. Also, the women were not so critical of men's failure to live up to the requirements of the leadership role as were the men themselves, but here the ratings showed much greater convergence. Indeed, the fact that the two sexes tended to differ more in their characterizations of women than of men probably explains why the correlations between performance scores and ratings by associates were higher for men's behavior.

sonal perception, what is probably most significant about these two sets of behavioral characteristics is not their content as such but the fact that they reflect a reciprocal or symbiotic relationship between the men and women in the group.

One additional line of evidence lends support at a more general level to the conclusion that accuracy of interpersonal judgment in the various experimental situations was related to patterns of interaction peculiar to the group as a group rather than simply to the behavior of individuals as such. We made an analysis of regression comparing relationships within groups and among groups between sensitivity scores and ratings from associates. For over half the items for each sex, the among- and within-group regression coefficients were significantly different from each other. In other words, the relationship between behavior and judgmental performance at a group level was quite different from what might have been expected from the relationship between these two sets of variables at the individual level.

In summary, then, we may say this. The striking differences in performance from group to group observed in the Statler experiment seem to be primarily a function of varying degrees of conflict and compatibility in the roles and relationships between the two sexes in each group. Judgments of differences in feeling are least accurate in those situations where women compete unsuccessfully for positions of leadership held securely and capably by men. Under such circumstances women are described as aggressive, disruptive, incompetent, and unfriendly, and it is they in particular who tend to misjudge others and be misperceived by them. In contrast, interpersonal judgments are most accurate in those situations where men fail to function effectively as leaders; thereupon, women assume a role which is at once supportive, solicitous, and subordinate, and again it is they in particular who are most understanding and best understood.

Our findings are consistent with the general hypothesis that interpersonal sensitivity will be highest in those social situations where there is complementarity among the roles and relationships of group members. Conversely, distortions and "blind spots" in social perception are most likely to occur in situations of role conflict and interpersonal tension. Once again, the direction of causality remains ambiguous. In all probability we are dealing with circular relationships which, once established, become progressively vicious or benign.

8. An Analysis of Accuracy in Judging the Generalized Other and Some of Its Correlates

Although not always explicitly recognized as such, two methods are currently used for measuring a judge's ability to predict the social norm. Both of them, having been described in earlier sections, will be summarized only briefly here. The first involves asking the judge to predict directly the typical or modal response of a large group or class; we may, for example, ask a subject to estimate the percentage of persons agreeing with a particular item in a questionnaire. The second method gets at the same variable indirectly by asking the judge to make predictions for a series of specific individuals, and then comparing these estimates (or their mean) with the average response of a group. The latter, in effect, was the method employed by Lindgren and Robinson (*38*) to demonstrate that the conventional accuracy score, when employed on an individual basis, was largely a function of correspondence with the group norm; in this approach, in other words, we tap the judge's implicit assumptions regarding the modal patterns of response.

The two procedures are by no means equivalent. It is possible, in fact, that they measure somewhat different variables, each important in its own right. Thus the first or direct approach may be relevant for tasks requiring explicit predictions of group trends (for example, forecasting prices on the stockmarket), while the second or indirect method may gauge the judge's ability to evaluate the common characteristics of people whom he meets in the flesh.

In the present research, we have selected the direct procedure as the basis for obtaining a measure of sensitivity to the generalized other. Several considerations have prompted this decision. First, in order to assure adequate sampling of the norm, it is necessary in the indirect approach for the judge to make predictions for a relatively large number of specific others. This situation involves cumbersome problems of administration and statistical analysis. Second, if the judge appraises others in a group situation, and if *sensitivity to the face-to-face group* involves other abilities beyond awareness of social norms, the resultant index would represent a composite of several skills rather than the single one we wish to measure. Finally—and this is the most important consideration—our conception of sensitivity to the generalized other has included the element of explicit recognition or prediction of the norm. On this basis we have assumed that persons with sensitivity to the generalized other might be able to function more effectively in tasks requiring accurate appraisal of public opinion and response, as in advertising, finance, etc. The question of the relationship of this skill to implicit discrimination of group norms remains an important area of research, both basic and applied.

Outcome vs. Ability

Whether one employs a direct or indirect method for measuring sensitivity to the generalized other, he is still left with the problem of what type of index to use. As already indicated, the conventional accuracy score, based on the sum of absolute errors, is likely to be affected in substantial degree by the judge's rating pattern and its similarity to the normative pattern for the group. At this point, two divergent lines of logical argument may be pursued.

The first takes the position that it is the result rather than the process that is most important. What counts, from this point of view, is the absolute accuracy of the judge's prediction, irrespective of the factors that make such accuracy possible. This argument in effect legitimizes what we have previously described as the built-in circularity in many correlations between accuracy score and related variables. That all persons tend to assume similarity, so that the conventional individual turns out to be right and the eccentric wrong, is simply a point in favor of the former. The important fact is that his predictions are accurate.

The second line of argument emphasizes the importance of measuring an "ability" in Baldwin's sense of the term [24]—the judge's capacity to recognize properties of the external reality situation at will and independently of his own characteristic patterns of response. From this point of view, we are interested in the accuracy score only to the extent that it reflects awareness of "what is really out there," as against mere correspondence, for whatever reason, between the judge's predictions and the criterion.

Because both of the preceding points of view are of theoretical and practical importance, we have, in the course of our research, investigated each. Following the pattern employed above for interpersonal sensitivity, we shall report first the results of an analysis of what is perhaps referred to most precisely as *accuracy in judging the generalized other*—the person's skill in predicting the typical responses of persons in his own sub-culture—as measured by an adaptation of the conventional difference score. Second, we shall explore the problem of developing a "pure" measure of ability in

[24] See Chapter 5 of this volume.

sensitivity to the generalized other, and the degree to which various types of indices meet the requirements of such a measure. The results of this inquiry will enable us to return to the problem of absolute accuracy, and to advance hypotheses regarding the conditions under which factors other than "real ability" lead to accuracy of prediction.

Procedure for Obtaining Accuracy Scores

Our measure of accuracy (second-person only) was obtained in the following manner. A total of 179 Cornell students (including 72 who later participated in the Statler experiment) was asked first to check from a list of 25 desirable and 25 undesirable adjectives those that applied to them, and then to estimate the percentage of college students who would do the same.[25] The accuracy score is based on the difference between the actual percentage of college students who checked an adjective and the subject's estimate of this percentage. Rather than use the absolute difference score, which does not lend itself to conventional statistical analysis, we have taken as the basis for our index the square of the difference, and employed an appropriate logarithmic transformation to permit statistical manipulation.[26] The split-half reliability coefficient for this index (corrected by the Spearman-Brown formula) was .85. There was no significant difference in mean accuracy score for men and women.

Correlates of Accuracy in Judging the Generalized Other

Table 6, which corresponds to Table 4, shows the relationship between the judge's accuracy score and the sum of the ratings given him on each item by his associates. In order to be sure that we are dealing with relationships at the level of individual differences rather than of group effects, the correlation coefficients have

[25] Unfortunately, at the time that these data were gathered we did not recognize the importance of obtaining criterion responses and estimates for each sex separately. Had we done so, we would have obtained measures of accuracy analogous to our indices of same-sex and opposite-sex sensitivity. The fact that such measures are not available sets important limitations on our subsequent discussion of the relationship between sensitivity to individual differences and accuracy in judging the modal response for the group.

[26] Since small errors are more likely to occur than large ones, a distribution of absolute difference scores is likely to be heavily skewed at one end. Using a logarithmic transformation of the square of the difference eliminates the skewness. (Cf. Bartlett, M. S., "The Use of Transformations," *Biometrics*, 1947, 3, No. 1, pp. 39-52.) The exact mathematical formula for the accuracy measure we have used appears in Table 7.

again been computed on a within-group basis. As before, a positive value indicates a direct relationship between skill in judging and the rating received. Even though less than 10% of the coefficients attain the 5% level of significance,[27] the results are not without interest, particularly when contrasted with the corresponding data for interpersonal sensitivity (see Table 4).

First, there is the fact that the correlations are generally of lower magnitude, despite the unquestionably higher reliability of the accuracy score. From this, one infers that skill in predicting correctly the absolute level of self-ratings for people in general is not as closely related to how a person is perceived by his associates as is his ability in recognizing how individuals differ from each other. Second, turning to the behavioral correlates of accuracy in men, we find that the pattern resembles that observed for interpersonal sensitivity of men for other men. Thus the accurate man tends to be perceived as outgoing, uninhibited, and self-assured, but at the same time somewhat irritating personally. While not as salient, the picture is again reminiscent of the youthful social extrovert, self-assured, friendly, but not always tactful. In line with this impression of similarity is the contrast in the correlation coefficients (shown at the bottom of Table 6) between the man's accuracy score and his sensitivity to his own and the opposite sex. The relationship is positive in the first instance, negative in the second. It seems likely that both of these correlations would have been considerably higher, and the contrast between them even more marked, if our measure of accuracy had tapped knowledge of the modal self-percept, not of college students in general, but of college men.

A similar consideration applies to the relationship between accuracy and sensitivity in women: it is possible that the contrast between the correlations for sensitivity to the same sex and the opposite sex might have been greater had we known the woman's accuracy in predicting the modal response of her own sex. As to the

[27] Since these correlations are susceptible to "built-in circularity" arising from the operation of assumed and real similarity, it may seem surprising that they do not show the commonly-found high positive relationship between accuracy on the one hand and socially desirable characteristics on the other. This seeming contradiction illustrates the importance of distinguishing skills in social perception in terms of referent. Had we employed a measure of first-person accuracy, such relationships would undoubtedly have emerged, for here the criterion for evaluating accuracy varies from judge to judge; some persons make a good impression, others a poor one. In general, however, most people expect to be liked and those who are liked turn out to be accurate. With a second-person index, however, the criterion for evaluating accuracy, i.e., the typical self-rating, is identical for all so that persons who make the same predictions cannot, as in a first person situation, obtain different accuracy scores.

TABLE 6. CORRELATIONS BETWEEN ACCURACY SCORES AND RATINGS BY ASSOCIATES

($N = 72$)

Cluster	Item	Men	Women	Both Sexes
Withdrawn and Insecure vs. Outgoing and Self-Assured	Submissive	—.24	.30	—.10
	Not influential	—.41*	—.21	—.18
	Not persistent	—.11	.10	—.06
	Not warm	—.17	—.10	—.12
	Shy	—.23	.17	—.04
	Uneasy	—.22	—.01	—.16
	Worried	.14	—.05	—.09
	Immature	—.14	—.50**	—.15
	Average†	—.18	—.04	—.11
Ability to Relate vs. Offensive Behavior	Not domineering	—.16	.24	—.02
	Not annoying	—.35	.38	—.04
	Considerate	—.09	.01	—.06
	Accepting	—.05	.15	.02
	Reasonable	.15	.40*	.15
	Average	—.10	.24	.01
Uninhibited vs. Controlled Behavior	Impulsive	.07	—.47*	—.13
	Not serious	.34	—.64**	—.02
	Enthusiastic	—.13	.16	.02
	Frank	.07	—.23	—.09
	Not indifferent	.00	.03	—.05
	Average	.07	.26	—.05
Talented and Resourceful vs. Incompetent and Dull	Imaginative	.23	.15	.08
	Interesting	.18	.23	.12
	Constructive	.13	.32	.12
	Helpful	.10	.36	.07
	Observant	.11	.26	.05
	Practical	—.19	.26	—.07
	Average	.09	.26	.06
Interpersonal Sensitivity	Same-sex	.30	.19	
	Opposite-sex	—.21	—.07	
	Overall (both sexes)	.09	.08	.05

† The value for the average is the r corresponding to the mean Fisher's z for the coefficients in the cluster.

* Significant at the 5% level.

** Significant at the 1% level.

behavioral correlates of accuracy in women, we find what by now we should have come to expect—that these correlates differ from those for men. The better a woman is in predicting the modal self-percept of the group, the more likely she is to be perceived as controlled, well-socialized, and competent. It is perhaps no mere coincidence that the contrasting clusters of traits associated with accuracy in the two sexes resemble the sex role stereotypes for young men and women in American middle-class culture—the man socially aggressive and outgoing; the woman sociable, but more controlled and submissive. The person who knows the modal self-percept for his sub-culture, one suspects, is himself one who has found a place in that sub-culture through identification with its expectations for his particular sex role.

In view of the contradictory character of the correlations for the two sexes, it is not surprising that for both sexes the over-all relationships between accuracy score and ratings from associates are very low. As indicated by the coefficients in the last column of Table 6, there is a slight tendency toward an association between desirable social characteristics and accuracy; but the magnitude of the relationships is so small that, even if the trend is reliable, it cannot be regarded as important. Above all, these data make it clear that skill in judging the modal response of a group is not the same as what we have called interpersonal sensitivity. Persons scoring high in this ability (cf. Table 4) consistently received higher ratings in the cluster labelled "Ability to Relate vs. Offensive Behavior"; specifically, three of the five correlation coefficients in this cluster were significantly different from zero, and average value for all five was .38. In contrast, the corresponding average for accuracy is .01, and none of the coefficients differs significantly from zero.

Thus we come back to a question that is central to our research. In our initial exploration of the problem, we were led to the hypothesis that the ability to judge others, which has ordinarily been regarded as a single generalized capacity, might in fact involve a number of quite different skills. In particular, we foresaw the possibility that a person's accuracy in gauging the typical response of the group might be relatively independent of his ability to recognize differences among individuals with the group. Now we are in a position to test the validity of this assumption. Inasmuch as our data suggest that accuracy tends to be positively correlated with a person's ability to differentiate members of his own sex and negatively with his sensitivity to the opposite sex, it is to be expected that the correlation between accuracy and general sensitivity will tend to approach zero. As indicated in the last line of Table 6, the specific coefficients are .09 for men, .08 for women, and .05 for the sample as a whole. Since the behavioral correlates of these two variables are by no means the same, we may conclude that they do in fact represent different skills rather than related facets of a single generalized ability.

Relationships between Accuracy and Sensitivity at the Group Level

One question regarding the relationship between accuracy and sensitivity scores remains to be considered. Thus far we have confined ourselves to an examination of the correlations between these variables within the groups and not between groups. Being interested primarily in individual differences rather than group trends, we have wanted to know whether a person who excels in one skill is likely to excel in the other as well. But now let us ask a different kind of question. Suppose we have a discussion group composed of subjects all of whom have high accuracy scores; that is, all have correctly predicted the modal self-percept of college students. Are the members of such a group likely to do well or poorly in recognizing how they differ among themselves in their self-ratings?

The empirical answer to this question is unequivocal and, perhaps, surprising in terms of what we know about the relationship between the two skills at an individual level. The correlation, over the twelve groups, between group means for accuracy and general interpersonal sensitivity is high and negative,[28] —.72. In other words, a group composed of accurate judges of the social norm will tend to score low in interpersonal sensitivity.

This finding, however, is not entirely out of line with what we already know about the factors associated with accuracy. We have cited evidence from other studies (and corroborative data from our own research will be reported below) to the effect that the person who is himself similar to the group is likely to do better in predicting the average response than one who is dissimilar. The former needs only to put down his own response to be correct. We also know that, in general, a judge who "assumes similarity" is likely to do better than if he ascribes to others reactions that are markedly different from his own. People, particularly of the same age and social position, tend to have many values in common. In Harry Stack Sullivan's (*50*) picturesque phrase: "People are more simply human than otherwise." To follow one circular statement with another,

[28] Significantly different from zero at the 1% level.

what this means is that a group composed of accurate judges is also a group composed of persons who regard themselves as, and who actually are, similar to the norm. It follows, of course, that they are also likely to be similar to each other, to believe that their fellow group members are like themselves, and to be correct in this belief.

Now, let us consider the implications of these facts. In the first place, when self-descriptions are similar to each other, differential prediction will be extremely difficult. Moreover, since under such circumstances each judge tends to assume that others will make the same responses as he, he is not likely to catch the relatively few idiosyncratic reactions which do actually occur. Hence the probability of a negative correlation between the means of group scores in accuracy and sensitivity.

The preceding argument has been essentially statistical and devoid of psychological content. Fortunately, we are in a position to fill in the void by taking advantage of our findings on the behavioral correlates of group differences in sensitivity score. Our statistical argument tells us, for example, that members of groups composed of accurate judges of the norm are likely to have self-percepts both similar to each other's and typical for students at the university. But the majority of students at Cornell are men. This means that such groups contain men and women who share what is in large measure a masculine self-percept. How do such men and women behave when brought together for a group discussion?

Since a group composed of accurate judges tends also to be a group with low sensitivity scores, our data on the correlates of group differences in sensitivity should suggest an answer. We already know that in insensitive groups the men perform effectively in a leadership role, while the women strive unsuccessfully for recognition. Now we are in a position to offer an explanation. These are all persons who, even before the Statler experiment began, apparently shared a predominantly masculine self-percept. It is not surprising, therefore, that the women tend to compete with the men for leadership status. In addition, interpersonal sensitivity in such groups becomes difficult on two counts. First, there are smaller differences in self-percept to be detected. Second, the role conflict between the sexes leads to misperceptions of the differences that do in fact exist.

The same considerations apply in reverse to groups composed of inaccurate judges. Again our statistical reasoning suggests that in such situations the men and women are likely to have self-percepts which are both different from each other and atypical for the college population as a whole. Thus neither sex has a particularly masculine self-percept. Appropriately enough, our data on the correlates of group sensitivity indicate that when such men and women are brought together in the same discussion, the men perform inadequately, thus failing to live up to the cultural stereotype for male behavior, and the women—since they neither aspire to a male ideal nor need to respond to the challenge of male dominance—are able to function effectively in the traditional feminine role of the outwardly submissive supporter.

The foregoing analysis has implications which permit us to test the validity of our interpretation in terms of consistencies within the data. These implications relate to the presumed nature of the behavioral correlates of group accuracy. Since accuracy and sensitivity are negatively correlated at the group level and hence should have correlates which are mirror images of each other, we would expect that men in groups composed of accurate judges would be seen as capable, outgoing, and dominant, whereas women in these same groups would be described as aggressive, disruptive, and unfriendly. The characteristics thus expected of men in groups of accurate judges are similar to those already identified (cf. Table 6) as correlates of accuracy for men at the individual level; that is, among groups as within groups, accuracy should be associated with competence, extroversion, and group dominance on the part of men. If our interpretation is correct, however, no such parallelism is to be expected for the woman. We already know from Table 6 that, within any group, the more accurate woman tends to be described as serious, not impulsive, mature, reasonable, submissive. But our analysis now leads us to conclude that when a number of accurate women turn up in the same group with men who are also accurate, the women behave quite differently. Frustrated by male superiority in a group which shares a predominantly masculine self-concept, the women apparently throw over their controls and become aggressive, outspoken, and tactless.

The preceding statements have not, as yet, been established as facts; they are expectations derived from a miniature theory intended to explain the high negative relationship between group means for sensitivity and accuracy scores. In order to check the validity of our interpretations, we computed for each sex the intergroup correlations between accuracy scores and ratings by associates on each of the 24 adjectives employed in our experiment. Although the results are too extensive to present in detail, they conform nicely with our expectations. A regression analysis showed that, as anticipated, the intergroup relationships for men were much the same as those revealed by the analysis within groups. The corresponding regression coefficients did not differ appreciably from chance, and, in both instances, accuracy tended to be associated with outgoingness and general competence. For the women, on the other hand, the regression coefficients differed in almost half of the items; and, as we would have expected, women in groups with high mean scores in accuracy were characterized as persistent, annoying, not shy, and inconsiderate.

In summary, our analyses of group trends indicate that the low magnitude of the coefficients in Table 6 may belie the true importance of measures of accuracy (and the related variables of real and assumed similarity) as predictors of behavior. Although it is probably true that the accuracy score of a particular individual will tell us very little about how he will behave in social situations, nevertheless if we are given the scores of several persons who will be placed in the same social situation, we may be able to predict with appreciable success their pattern of interaction. In the present instance, for example, it would have been possible, on the basis of accuracy scores obtained prior to the Statler experiment, to identify in advance those groups in which interpersonal sensitivity would be exceptionally high or low and to predict the roles taken by the men and women in each group.

A word of caution here, however, is not out of place. *It is important to recognize that the preceding assertion is made possible only through hindsight.* Moreover, even though the results of our analysis of group effects in interpersonal perception and behavior exhibit a highly consistent pattern, the fact remains that they are based on only 12 groups. Finally, the degree to which these results can be generalized to other, non-student populations or to other types of social situation remains a problem outside our research. At best, the principal contribution of our analysis lies, not in the realm of established fact, but in the areas of method and hypothesis.

We are now ready to return to the problem of developing a "pure" measure of sensitivity to group norms which will be independent of the judge's similarity to the group being judged.

9. A "Pure" Measure of Sensitivity to the Generalized Order

The development of a "pure" measure of interpersonal sensitivity was made possible through the method of differential comparison, i.e., forcing the judge to make discriminations among different social objects of the same class. This same strategy could be followed to obtain a measure of sensitivity to *intergroup differences* to obtain for example, an index of a judge's ability to predict how various organizations, neighborhoods, or factions, might differ in their responses to a questionnaire. But when we approach the question of measuring sensitivity to the generalized other, we are faced with a somewhat more difficult problem. There are no comparisons to be made; we want to know how familiar the individual is with a single sub-culture, usually his own. The method of differential comparison, which enabled us to partial out factors associated with the person's own response pattern and his similarity to the norm, is therefore no longer applicable, at least in its usual form. We may still attempt, however, to apply the logic inherent in this procedure—that of partialing out extraneous factors—and see how close we can come to the ideal of a "pure" measure of this type of ability.

Eliminating Level and Spread: The Profile Accuracy Score

Two extraneous components can be eliminated rather easily. These relate to what Cronbach (*14, 15, 16, 27*) and others have referred to as "response set"—the tendency of the judge to use a similar mean and similar standard deviation regardless of what he is trying to predict. Each judge, in other words, tends to have a characteristic rating pattern in terms of "level" and "spread." The fact that the mean of his estimates coincides with the mean of the criterion ratings *may* reflect sensitivity on his part—but it may equally well be the result of chance similarity between his characteristic "level" of rating and that of the average individual with whom he is dealing. It also seems likely that the "spread" of estimates used by a particular judge is more dependent on his characteristic rating habits than it is on any ability to "empathize" the standard deviation of the criteria he is predicting.[29]

If one is willing to make the conventional statistical assumptions regarding normality of distribution, the effects of level or spread can be controlled rather simply through the use of a simple correlation coefficient (r_{xy}) between the subject's estimates (x) for a series of modal responses and the modal responses themselves (y). Such a measure is independent of any chance similarity between the judge's characteristic level of rating and the average level for the

[29] If a judge *were* to recognize the standard deviation of the criteria, and conformed to this standard deviation in his estimates, the conventional accuracy score would penalize him for doing so. The optimum standard deviation for a set of estimates in terms of the accuracy score is not the standard deviation of the criterion ratings, but this standard deviation times the correlation between estimates and criteria—ordinarily a much smaller figure.

group of subjects. Similarly, the tendency of the judge to vary his ratings widely from item to item, which could appreciably influence the conventional accuracy score, is also controlled by a correlational index. What the coefficient measures is the correspondence between the shape or relative ordering of the modal responses over a series of items, and the shape or relative ordering of the judge's estimates for these items. For this reason we have referred to this index as a Profile Accuracy score.[30] In terms of our data on predictions of typical self-ratings, a person with a high Profile Accuracy score (i.e., a high correlation) is one who correctly estimates the relative frequency with which each adjective is checked by college students as applicable to themselves.

We computed Profile Accuracy scores for each of the 179 students for whom conventional measures based on difference scores were also available. To permit statistical manipulation, the correlation coefficients were again transformed into Fisher's z's. The basic data for the Profile Accuracy score are shown in Table 7. The measure yielded a corrected split-half reliability of .76 as compared with .85 for the conventional or "Total" accuracy score. Since the basic index is itself a transformed correlation coefficient, we may, by looking at its mean value, gain some notion of the general level of proficiency exhibited by the group as a whole. As shown in the first column of Table 7, the mean Fisher's z corresponded to an r of .85, indicating a substantial relationship on the average between the pattern of the judge's prediction and the modal pattern of response. The relationship between Profile Accuracy and Total Accuracy is .80, a value of the same order as the reliability of the two variables involved.[31] In other words, in the present situation individual differences in level and spread have comparatively little effect on the relative position of the judges in terms of their skill in making accurate predictions. The effect would in all likelihood have been considerably greater, had we not included both favorable and unfavorable items on the same questionnaire, so that individual differences in favorableness on the part of the judges tended to be canceled. Had there been more opportunity for such a "halo" effect (which occurs in many judging situations) the Accuracy score might have been markedly affected by the degree of correspondence

[30] This type of measure has been used, with much the same purposes in mind, by Gage and his associates *(28)*.

[31] In a similar comparison of measures of accuracy based on absolute difference score vs. a correlational coefficient, Gage and Suci (*28*) report substantially the same result ($r = .77$).

between the judge's tendency to make favorable ratings or estimates and the general level of self-esteem in the group.

Partialing Out Similarity

The preceding consideration points up a crucial limitation of the Profile Accuracy score as a "pure" measure of sensitivity. Although virtually free of influences attributable to mean and variance effects, this index is likely to be appreciably affected by the degree of similarity between the pattern of the judges' own self-ratings and the profile of the average responses for the group; a person who is similar to the group has only to put down his own self-ratings as estimates (i.e., to assume similarity) in order to obtain a high score. To show the actual magnitude of the relationship involved, we computed for each judge an Assumed and Real Similarity score. The former was based on the simple correlation (r_{xw}) between the subject's estimates (x) on each of the 50 adjectives and his own self-rating (w). In analogous fashion, the Real Similarity score took the form of a correlation (r_{yw}) between the self-rating (w) on an item and the actual response of the group (y). In each instance the r scores were transformed into Fisher's z's. The reliabilities, mean values, and intercorrelations for these z scores are shown in Table 7. As expected, the correlations between Real Similarity, on the one hand, and Total and Profile accuracy, on the other, are positive and significant (.21 and .35 respectively).[32] The coefficients are sufficiently low, however, to suggest that the accuracy scores are substantially independent of the judge's own self-ratings and hence reflect the operation of genuine sensitivity to group response.

Two other features of the table support this conclusion. The first is the sharp drop in the average level of the r score for Real Similar-

[32] The question may be raised whether these and subsequent intercorrelations should not be based on different sets of items rather than on the same set of 100 adjectives. From a purely practical point of view, this question is largely answered by the split half reliability coefficient appearing in the diagonal of Table 7. These coefficients are sufficiently high to indicate that although the absolute levels of intercorrelations might be expected to drop somewhat when different sets of items are used, their relative magnitudes are likely to remain much the same. From a theoretical point of view, the question becomes simply one of which hypothesis one wishes to investigate. For example, if one wishes to examine whether a person who resembles the group in one set of characteristics is likely to be more accurate even when judging a *different* set of characteristics, then indices based on different sets of items are obviously appropriate. But if one merely wishes to know whether the person who resembles the group in a particular set of qualities is also likely to be more accurate in judging these *same* qualities, then the same set of items must be used. In the present research our interest has generally been in hypotheses of this second type in which the content of the items is held constant.

TABLE 7. AVERAGE LEVELS, RELIABILITIES, AND INTERCORRELATIONS AMONG DIFFERENT MEASURES OF ACCURACY AND SIMILARITY *

		INTERCORRELATIONS †				
Variables **	*Average Level* ***	*Total Accuracy*	*Profile Accuracy*	*Differential Accuracy*	*Assumed Similarity*	*Real Similarity*
Accuracy						
Total Accuracy ($\log_e [1 + \Sigma(x - y)^2]$)		.85‡	.80	.62	.33	.21
Profile Accuracy (r_{xy})	.80		.76‡	.69	.49	.35
Differential Profile Accuracy ($r_{xy \cdot w}$)	.65			.67‡	−.23	−.35
Similarity						
Assumed Similarity (y_{xw})	.60				.86‡	.87
Real Similarity (r_{yw})	.66					.91‡
$N = 179$						

* Since all sex differences in mean or correlation were negligible, we report in each instance the single overall value for both sexes.

** In the algebraic expressions below y denotes the actual percentage of college students who checked an adjective as applying to them, x denotes a judge's estimate of this actual percentage, and w refers to the judge's self-rating (on a six-point scale) of the degree to which the item applied to him. Wherever a variable was measured by a correlation, the coefficient was transformed into a Fisher's z, which was then employed as the person's score.

*** The value cited is the r corresponding to the average Fisher's z.

† All coefficients are significant at the 1% level.

‡ Reliability coefficient corrected by the Spearman-Brown formula.

ity (.66) as compared to that for Profile Accuracy (.80). Apparently our judges were able to predict with more accuracy than would have been the case had they simply assumed complete similarity between themselves and the group. Second, there is the strikingly high correlation of .87 between Assumed and Real similarity. Although most students assumed a substantial degree of similarity with the group (average r score $= .60$), they evidently did not do so uncritically. To a remarkable degree the typical person knew that he was typical; and, what is more, the eccentric person knew that he was eccentric.

There is a third line of evidence corroborating the existence of genuine social awareness on the part of our subjects. In a final, and futile, attempt to develop a "pure" measure of sensitivity to the generalized other, we explored the possibility of partialing out the judge's similarity by conventional statistical procedures; that is, we computed a partial correlation coefficient ($r_{yx \cdot w}$) between estimates and criteria, holding constant the judge's own self-ratings. Such a measure, we reasoned, would reflect the degree to which a judge could differentiate those aspects of other people's behavior that were unrelated to his own responses. In devising this index, we recognized that in all probability judges could also accurately perceive similarities to themselves: but we wished to limit our *measurement* of their sensitivity to the recognition of behavior unrelated to their own—in the hope that our index would contain *only* sensitivity and not a mixture of sensitivity plus actual similarity to the group.

Since the partial correlation coefficient taps the judge's ability to recognize in what respects the typical pattern of responses differs from his own, we have referred to this index as a measure of Differential Profile Accuracy. The basic data for this variable also appear in Table 7. The measure is moderately reliable (corrected $r = .67$), and the r score corresponding to the mean z value is .65. In other words, even with the self-rating partialed out, our judges were able to make accurate discriminations of a fairly high order. In more concrete terms, this figure indicates that the average student in our experiment had a fairly good idea of the proportion of other students who would say that a particular adjective applied to them, whether or not he thought it applied to himself.[33] Finally, the substantial

[33] The relatively high degree of discrimination exhibited by our subjects is not so surprising when one recalls that the adjectives employed represented extremes on a continuum of "favorable" to "unfavorable." In other words, to obtain a high score in Differential Profile Accuracy one simply had to know which qualities most college students are likely to regard as desirable and which undesirable. This is not a very

correlation between this index of Differential Profile Accuracy and the measures of Profile and Total Accuracy ($r = .69$ and $.62$ respectively) adds further weight to the conclusion that virtually any type of accuracy score—including the conventional score—is likely to reflect in substantial degree the operation of a genuine ability in social perception.

But what of our hopes for a "pure" measure of this ability? Unfortunately they were ill-founded, as evidenced by the correlation between Differential Profile Accuracy and Real Similarity ($r = -.35$). The coefficient is equal in magnitude to that between straight Profile Accuracy and Real Similarity, but it is negative in sign. In other words, just as the Total Accuracy and Profile Accuracy scores penalized the dissimilar person, so the partial correlation measure handicaps the judge who is similar, and favors the eccentric, who has an easier discrimination to make. Because the eccentric differs markedly from the group norm, he has no difficulty in recognizing the difference. In contrast, the conformist must make much finer discriminations in order to obtain the same score. The partial correlation coefficient, in short, is inadequate as a pure measure of sensitivity to the generalized other for essentially the same reason as its predecessors—it is not independent of the judge's own similarity to the group.[34]

It would, of course, be possible deliberately to "adjust" the accuracy score for each judge so that for all judges the correlation between such an adjusted score and the measure of real similarity would be zero. This can be accomplished by utilizing the appropriate regression coefficient to "correct" each accuracy score for the corresponding level of real similarity. The procedure is analogous to that occasionally used in adjusting achievement test scores for differences in I.Q. Although it avoids the principal difficulty described above, this method too is questionable as a "pure" measure of sensitivity to the generalized other. First, since the adjusted values are all based on a single regression coefficient derived from the data themselves, the scores of the different judges are no longer

difficult type of information to acquire, and by and large, the students in our sample seem to have acquired it. At the same time, as indicated by our data, there are appreciable individual differences among them with some persons being comparatively unaware or even misinformed.

[34] The same basic criticism applies to Bender and Hastorf's (*5, 6*) "refined empathy score" which represents an attempt to correct for similarity by subtracting from the conventional accuracy score a component associated with assumed similarity. The effect of this procedure, as with our partial correlation measure, is to penalize the person who is similar. Hastorf and Bender (*31*) have recently acknowledged that their measure suffers from difficulties of this type.

statistically independent of each other. Second, like the Differential Profile Accuracy measure, the adjusted score rests on the assumption that the person's skill in predicting responses similar to his own is purely a function of assumed similarity; genuine ability or knowledge are presumed to play no part in his success. As our analysis has repeatedly indicated, such an assumption does not seem warranted. Finally, from a purely practical point of view, the resulting measure, like all the others we have examined, is likely to show a high correlation with an accuracy score of the conventional type, but with reliability appreciably reduced.

In summary, we have a certain measure of success to weigh against a certain measure of failure. For, unsuccessful in our attempt to develop a satisfactory "pure" measure of ability in sensitivity to the generalized other, we have been able to demonstrate that in our experiment the conventional accuracy score was predominantly a function of genuine skill in social perception. Although factors associated with the judge's characteristic pattern of response (level and spread) and with his similarity to the group affected the accuracy score, these influences were always overshadowed by the component attributable to recognition of objective properties of the external social world. In the light of these facts and in the absence of a satisfactory "pure" measure, the accuracy score must remain our best choice for assessing ability in recognizing the generalized other. Clearly it is preferable to such other indices as the simple or partial correlation coefficient or the "adjusted score," on grounds both of reliability and of ease in computation. Some caution must still be exercised in its use as an ability measure, of course, in view of its susceptibility to extraneous influences.

Factors Other than Ability Affecting Accuracy of Judgment

The preceding discussion adds weight to the importance of identifying those psychological conditions, other than ability, which tend to increase accuracy of prediction. From two points of view their recognition is essential. First, in the absence of a pure measure of sensitivity to the generalized other, awareness of the manner in which extraneous influences operate makes possible a more judicious evaluation of the degree to which the accuracy score is spotting genuine ability in social perception. Second, and perhaps more important, insofar as accuracy of prediction is of practical value in its own right, knowledge of the psychological factors facilitating such accuracy provides a basis for manipulating the social situation so as to minimize the likelihood of errors in prediction.

The general nature of the more important factors, other than ability, influencing accuracy of prediction has already been indicated. What remains is to specify insofar as possible the precise way in which these factors operate, the combinations which are most likely to make for error or for accuracy. We shall attempt to make these specifications systematically, beginning with some general propositions which are more or less self-evident but basic, and ending with formulations of concrete relationships susceptible to empirical test.

Hypotheses

I. Accuracy of prediction is a function of at least four factors:
   (1) Direct observation by the judge of the objective properties of the person or group being judged (the social object);
   (2) Previous knowledge not based on personal observation (for example, from reading, hearsay, etc.);
   (3) The feelings of the judge toward the social object;
   (4) The judge's own attitudes or perceptions with respect to the *content and referent* being evaluated.

II. When information is available either from personal observation or personal knowledge, accuracy of prediction will be influenced in large measure by the accuracy of this information.

III. To the extent that previous knowledge is lacking and cues are minimal, accuracy becomes a function of the judge's own attitudes toward the *social object* and *content*, specifically:
   (1) The more favorable the judge's orientation toward the person or group being judged, the more likely he is to predict that the attitudes or perceptions of this person or group toward a particular content will be similar to his own; that is, the more the judge likes the other, the more likely he is to assume similarity.
   (2) Given (1) above, it necessarily follows that:
      (a) If the judge and the judged have similar views about the same content and if the former is favorably disposed toward the latter, the judge is likely to assume similarity and be correct.
      (b) If the views are similar but the judge is unfavorably disposed, he is likely to assume dissimilarity and be incorrect.
      (c) If the views are dissimilar and the judge is favorably disposed, he is likely to assume similarity and be incorrect.
      (d) If the views are dissimilar and the judge is unfavorably disposed toward the person or group being estimated, the outcome is determinate only if predictions are made in terms of a polar scale, i.e., one which varies along a single continuum. Under such circumstances, the predictor will assume dissimilarity and turn out to be correct.[35]

[35] For example, let us assume that A is estimating how B will vote in the Presidential elections and that he has no objective information or cues regarding B's political leanings. Let us suppose further that A dislikes B and that A himself plans to vote Republican. B is actually a Democrat. If our hypothesis is valid, A will assume

Some Tests of Hypotheses

In order to test the relationships stipulated under III above, we have employed an index *of Favorability toward Others* based on the algebraic sum of each person's ratings of "college students in general" on 25 favorable and 25 unfavorable adjectives. This measure showed a split-half reliability of .90. To investigate the basic hypothesis represented by III (1), we computed The correlation between Favorability toward Others and Assumed Similiarity. The resulting coefficient (based on 179 cases) was .49, which gives solid support for the general conclusion that the more favorable the judge's orientation toward the person or group being judged, the more likely he is to assume similarity.[36] Once this relationship is established, then the four specific effects stipulated under III (2) follow as logical necessities.

Some data illustrating these effects are shown in Table 8. Working for convenience with only the 72 subjects included in the Statler experiment proper, we divided the group at the median on the basis of their scores in Favorability toward Others, and then divided them once again at the median for Real Similarity. This double division made it possible to distribute the subjects into the four groups shown in the table, and to compare them in terms of their mean scores in Total Accuracy. The basic hypothesis requires that errors in accuracy be a function not of a simple direct relationship but of an interaction between Favorability and Similarity, with fewer errors by the two groups exhibiting "symmetrical" properties (Favorable-Similar and Unfavorable-Dissimilar) than by the two with "asymmetrical" features (Favorable-Dissimilar and Unfavorable-Similar). In Table 8 these expectations are borne out in full. The only significant mean square revealed by the analysis of variance is that for interaction, and the two symmetrical groups (A and B) show smaller errors in prediction than the two asymmetrical ones (C and D).

---

that B is different from himself; namely, that he is a Democrat and hence will predict correctly.

It is of some interest that the preceding hypotheses, which grew out of an empirical study, are highly compatible with the theoretical models for analysis of interpersonal relationships recently developed by Heider (*32, 33*), Newcomb (*44*), and Osgood and Tannenbaum (*45*).

[36] Findings in clear support of this same hypothesis are reported in a series of studies by Fiedler and his associates (*21, 22*).

TABLE 8. TOTAL ACCURACY SCORES OF SUBJECTS CLASSIFIED BY FAVORABILITY TOWARD OTHERS AND REAL SIMILARITY

Group	*N*	*Mean Accuracy Score*
A. Similar and Favorable	21	100.52
B. Dissimilar and Unfavorable	21	101.90
C. Dissimilar and Favorable	15	103.07
D. Similar and Unfavorable	15	104.67
	72	

Analysis of Variance of Accuracy Scores

Source of Variation	*d.f.*	*Mean Square*	*F*
Favorability toward Others	1	39.98	2.02
Real Similarity	1	.34	
Interaction	1	123.70	6.41*
Within groups	68	19.31	
	71		

* Significant at the 5% level.

To examine in detail the performance of each of the four groups is rewarding. Thus we find that the person who made the most accurate predictions of others' self-ratings is one who was favorably disposed toward others and who resembled them in his own self-evaluation. Since, in fact, the average college student tended to rate himself high on favorable adjectives and low on unfavorable, the best predictor was a person with high self-esteem who thought well of others and assumed that they thought likewise of him.[37] In contrast, the group which scored second best in accuracy of prediction was composed of persons who had a low opinion of others and who differed from the typical pattern of self-appraisal in having a low opinion of themselves as well. It is as if they were thinking, "Most college students including myself are pretty sorry specimens, but *they* don't even know it; they probably think quite a lot of themselves." Since most of them do, our cynical judges turn out to be right. The relatively poor predictors, on the other hand, are of two types: those favorably disposed toward others but differ-

[37] To confirm the presence of the hypothetical relationship between self-evaluation and real similarity implied by this statement, we employed a measure of Self-Esteem analogous to the index of Favorability toward Others; the correlation between this score for Self-Esteem and that for Real Similarity was as high as the reliabilities of the measures involved: namely, .90. That the indices of Self-Esteem and Favorability toward Others are not merely alternative measures of a single generalized positive orientation is indicated by the fact that the correlation between these two variables is .39.

ing in their own self-evaluation; and, especially, those resembling others but critical of them.

Finally, even though there are significant differences among the mean accuracy scores for the four groups, it is noteworthy that these differences do not appear to be very great in absolute terms. Thus while factors other than ability have some effect, as we have already concluded, on the accuracy score, this influence is not the predominant one; the principal determinant of the judge's score in our experiment was his awareness of the objective social reality.

10. Recommendations for Future Research

The need for further clarification and testing of the concepts, methods, and hypotheses that have emerged from this exploratory research is self-evident. Particularly is this true with respect to many problems which arose in the course of our analysis but could not be investigated with our data. Chief among these are the following:

1. *An analysis of "third-person" sensitivity,* both at the level of sensitivity to individual differences (e.g., the ability of an executive to recognize interpersonal tensions among members of his staff), and at the level of sensitivity to the generalized other (e.g., gauging public opinion toward prominent persons or segments of the population).
2. *An investigation of sensitivity to group differences:* Does this skill represent an ability in its own right or is it merely a combination of *interpersonal* sensitivity and sensitivity to the generalized other?
3. *A study of the reliability of measures of sensitivity from situation to situation:* How stable is a person's sensitivity score from one rating situation to the next? In particular, to what extent does the judge's sensitivity vary as a function of the person or group being judged and his relationship to that person or group?
4. *An examination of the relationship of various types of sensitivity to successful performance:* Do certain occupations require a minimum of one or another type of sensitivity? Will our indices predict differential achievement in various walks of life?

The last question is, of course, the crucial one for talent research; but before it can be pursued directly, considerably more attention must be given to the clarification of variables underlying skills in social perception and the further development of appropriate methods for their measurement.

In addition to the problems arising directly out of our analysis, several other considerations have some relevance for future research, both pure and applied, on abilities in social perception. Most of these relate to the inherent limitations of the method most widely used in this area (and the procedure which we ourselves followed)—that of utilizing a subject's questionnaire responses as criteria for evaluating accuracy in perception and judgment. To clarify the limitations of this approach and to evaluate the applicability of such conventional paper-and-pencil procedures along with the need for new research techniques, we shall outline certain areas of skill in social perception.

Areas of Skill in Social Perception

In general, we may distinguish three types of skill:

1. *Social sensitivity:* the ability to recognize through direct observation the behavior, or psychological states of another person or group.
2. *Predictive skill:* the ability to forecast actions or psychological states that are not being directly observed; that is, that occur at some time other than the one about which the observer has information.
3. *Role-taking:* the ability to act or feel in the manner of another person (imitation) or to act or feel in accordance with the expectations of the other person (responsiveness). The former skill is exemplified by the professional actor or by the undercover agent who must impersonate someone quite different from himself. The second ability, *responsiveness,* includes such skills as "saying the right thing," avoiding *faux pas,* acting as another person thinks appropriate, etc.

These three types of skill are regarded as interdependent. Thus a person's sensitivity may be increased by the fact that he is able to foresee what may happen (predictive skill) through his ability to experience for himself the feelings of another person (role-taking). Also it should be clear that these skills involve more than perception in the strict psychological sense of that term. To the extent that sensitivity utilizes previous experience and integrates it with immediate observation, we are dealing with cognition rather than perception. Similarly, where role-taking involves actual behavior as well as mere awareness, it represents a complex skill that incorporates perceptive, cognitive, and behavioral features.

Areas of skill in social perception may be viewed from still another perspective—the *content* or kind of material to which a person responds. Such content must be considered with reference to two different contexts or situations. First, there is the *objective stimulus situation,* that which is regarded as being "really out there" in terms of some dependable external criterion. To the extent that a person is sensitive, the cues to which he initially responds are presumed to lie in the objective stimulus field. Second, there is the subjective view of the observer, his *phenomenal field,* which may or may not correspond in its content to the objective stimulus situation. Moreover, whatever correspondence does exist, may be direct or indirect. Where the content of the phenomenal field is a representation of properties of the objective reality, correspondence is direct. A person's lip quivers, his fingers stiffen, his face blanches; and these are what the observer reports as his perception. This type of point-for-point correspondence is analogous to that posited by Köhler (*36*) in his theory of isomorphism. On the other hand, the quivering lips, stiffened fingers, and blanching face may not be recognized as such by the observer; he may not even be able to describe these features when asked about them. Instead, if asked to report his observations, he states that the other person seems frightened, without being able to identify any of the specific cues that gave rise to his impression.

Rather than take a rigid position with respect to the way in which social perceptions occur, we have regarded the matter as an open question and have therefore attempted to develop categories of analysis which would be applicable both to the objective and to the phenomenal field, leaving the relationship between the two to be investigated as an empirical problem. Thus in our own thinking we have distinguished four major aspects of the social situation as it may exist either in the perceptions of the subject or in objective reality as determined by some adequate criterion.

1. *Physical:* overt physical characteristics of the other person, such as dress, complexion, facial features, body proportions, etc.
2. *Actional:* overt behavior of the other person—his posture, his movements, what he does, or says.
3. *Characterological:* properties of the other person which, while they may be rooted in physical characteristics or behavior, in addition reflect the person's impact as a social stimulus; e.g., he is seen as amusing, overbearing, irritating, awe-inspiring, etc.
4. *Experiential:* properties that represent internal psychological states of the other person, his thoughts, feelings, desires, etc.

Although the lines between these four aspects cannot always be clearly drawn, there is a distinct gradient from the first, which is concerned with external properties of the person, to the last, which deals wholly with internal states. It is our general hypothesis that people are likely to exhibit consistent individual differences with respect to the saliency in their phenomenal field of these four types of content. Some people tend to see others primarily in terms of physical characteristics; for others, overt behavior predominates; for others still, the most salient feature about another person is his emotional state.[38] Such variations deal solely with the content of the phenomenal field and leave aside the question of correspondence to external reality. There is, therefore, the further possibility of consistent individual differences in the accuracy with which a person observes each of the four areas of content. At one extreme, one thinks of the familiar master-detective of popular fiction, the Sherlock Holmes who notices the shiny cuffs, the mud-spotted shoes, the tell-tale stain; at the opposite pole, perhaps, is the astute clinician, who may not miss such cues but who is primarily attuned to the experiential area and correctly senses the psychological state of the patient.

Limitations of Questionnaire Responses

In the light of the preceding analysis, the limitations of questionnaire responses as criteria become increasingly apparent. It is evident that conventional procedures can tap *social sensitivity* only in so far as such sensitivity is reflected in predictive skill. Moreover, by their very nature such procedures emphasize sensitivity to attitudes and psychological states rather than to overt characteristics or behavior. Except in so far as the questionnaire responses of the person being judged represent accurate descriptions of his own overt acts, the conventional paper-pencil technique does not enable us to appraise the judge's ability in recognizing whether other people actually behave in an influential or submissive manner, etc.; what we appraise is the judge's sensitivity to whether or not another person *regards himself* as having behaved in a particular fashion. In terms of the distinctions we have introduced, the questionnaire method focuses on recognition of *experiential* aspects as against the *physical, actional* or *characterological.* Yet we have every reason to believe

[38] Support for this general hypothesis is reported in a recent doctoral dissertation by Wolin (54), described below. Using a sample of fifty subjects, Wolin found consistent individual differences in the person's tendency to focus on a particular area of content in his free descriptions of six fellow group members.

that sensitivity to these other aspects is at least equally important from a theoretical and practical point of view.

Even if we confine our interest to the recognition of experiential properties, we find that the conventional procedures have serious limitations. For example, they by-pass the question of the other person's *actual* psychological state as distinguished from what he is *willing to say* about his thoughts and feelings. The same is true of the psychological state of the judge. By presenting him with specific questions, we in part determine what he will report; there remains unanswered the question of what the subject spontaneously notices about other people but is not asked to report.

Similar considerations apply to the suitability of conventional procedures as measures of predictive skill. So long as the criteria for evaluating skill are confined to questionnaire responses, they constitute the only behavior that can be predicted—strictly speaking, rating behavior. Such behavior, though as "real" as any other, and probably highly relevant to the action which it may symbolize, is still not equivalent to the action itself. The student of human behavior will want to know also what the person will actually do in important human situations—in the family, on the job, under stress.

Paradoxically, the conventional method is probably least adequate in the very area in which it has been most enthusiastically applied in recent years—the measurement of ability in role-taking. Perhaps by stretching the imagination we may regard the standard technique as measuring the ability of a person "to act like another" in responding to a questionnaire or to anticipate what kinds of responses are expected of him. (Indeed, the last effect probably enters into our indices to a far greater extent than we have realized.) But, even so, here again we are dealing with behavior which may be rather academic compared with situations from life.

These considerations should not, of course, invalidate the use of questionnaires for the measurement of social skill, but they do set limitations on their fruitfulness, both theoretically and practically. What we need are methods which tap more directly the specific variables involved in different types of skill. A number of such methods are indeed already available, and we have only to recognize their potentialities in order to put them to use. We now turn to some of these.

A Broader Approach to Research on Social Perception

First, with regard to the measurement of social sensitivity, our critique of conventional methods leads us to emphasize the use of *direct observation* in situations where wide differences in the social stimulus situation (i.e., cues) have been insured, preferably through experimental control. Second, there is the necessity for *analyzing the content of social perception;* and, third, the importance of *securing data on the spontaneous as well as the guided observations of the subject.*

The way in which such principles can be applied is illustrated by a doctoral research recently completed at Cornell by Wolin (*54*). This investigator took advantage of an experiment of the Asch-type (*4*), already under way for another purpose, in which there were six "stooges" who had been previously trained to play differing roles in relation to each other and to a naive subject. One of the stooges consistently agreed with the naive subject in his judgments and defended him in subsequent discussion; another was hostile, a third inquisitive, a fourth digressive, etc. The persons playing each role had received training and extensive practice under the guidance of a dramatic coach prior to the beginning of the experiment proper. Although the roles were constant from one situation to the next, they were played by different people. For each stooge there was available—from observers' reports, questionnaires, and tape recordings—a fairly complete set of "criterion data" regarding physical appearance, body posture and movement, speed, etc. Fifty different naive subjects, taken one at a time, were used in the experiment, and it is on these that Wolin focused his attention.

Following the experiment proper, the naive subject was asked to write a brief description, first of the group as a whole, and then of each of the participants. Given relatively little guidance, he was told simply to "give as lifelike a picture as you can." This free description or open-ended questionnaire provided data on his spontaneous observations. It was followed by a check-list in which specific perceptions were collected in each of the four areas—physical, actional, characterological, and experiential. Data of this type made possible both qualitative and quantitative evaluation of the subject's sensitivity to individual differences among the group members. The material also permitted an investigation of the degree of interdependence between sensitivities to different types of content. For example, does the person who perceives the feelings of others also notice surface details, or does such perceptiveness involve a Gestalt-like quality in which specific cues cannot be identified?

Any procedure as elaborate as that followed by Wolin would of course be impractical for measuring social sensitivity in large groups. With this in mind, Wolin explored a hypothesis—developed early in the course of our pilot studies—that there may be a correlation between a person's ability to perceive accurately a particular type of content (as measured by his social sensitivity score) and his "approach," or the degree to which references to this type of content appear in his spontaneous description of a social situation. For example, the judge who scores high in identifying external physical characteristics might be one whose spontaneous account would deal primarily with the same type of material—concrete surface characteristics. In contrast, the person who correctly senses attitudes and feelings would, in his free descriptions, go beyond or perhaps even omit reference to external characteristics or overt behavior, and depict others mainly in terms of their emotional states. (One thinks of the contrast in the character delineations of an author like Dostoyevski with those of, say, James Fenimore Cooper.)

Wolin's findings with respect to our general hypothesis are summarized thus (*54*, p. 83):

> Since the Ss differed in both approach and sensitivity, the relationship between these two variables was studied. A distinct but not statistically significant relationship was noted between preference for a given category and sensitivity to that category. More striking was the relationship between approach and general sensitivity to others. Persons who described others primarily in terms of psychological characteristics were more sensitive to all categories than those persons who described others primarily in terms of physical characteristics. This relationship was statistically significant for the characterological approach. It would appear that persons who are set to perceive physical characteristics of others are sensitive only to these characteristics. In contrast, persons who seek meaning—who look for the essentially human, psychological characteristics of others—tend to be sensitive to all aspects of other people, including their physical characteristics.

Another technique which holds promise for the study of interpersonal perception is the use of motion pictures. One can show large groups a constant social stimulus in the form of a movie, and then immediately afterwards ask them to describe what they have seen—first spontaneously and then with reference to specific areas of content.[39]

[39] A motion picture, however, could not readily be used for obtaining measures of first-person sensitivity (particularly to individual differences), since it would be difficult to convince the viewer that the attitudes or actions expressed on the screen were directed at him *personally*. A further problem in the use of motion pictures underscores an undeniable advantage of the questionnaire approach. Who is to judge what is the "real behavior" being displayed in the motion picture? Even if the picture is documentary, the problem of deciding on the intent of depicted action remains to plague the investigator concerned with questions of validity. Whatever faults the questionnaire method may have, it does offer a specific target for estimation.

Whatever procedures are employed for gathering the data, in analyzing the material it would be necessary to apply methods analogous to those developed in the present research in order to provide measures of the different types of sensitivity (e.g., interpersonal vs. generalized other).

Turning from social sensitivity to other areas of social skill, we find that, by and large, the same general principles apply. Thus in future research on the measurement of predictive skill, it is important to shift the emphasis from an estimation of questionnaire responses to the forecasting of directly significant behavior—an individual's interpersonal relationships in the family and on the job, his choice of a career, his performance under stress, and so on. Also it may be important to distinguish between success in predicting what a person will *do* as against how he will *feel*. The latter may very likely require a special sensitivity in the experiential sphere, of the type presumably possessed by some writers, actors, and workers in the field of human relations.

Of relevance also is the problem of anticipating how another person is likely to perceive a particular situation—its probable meaning for him. This leads us directly to what, from a research point of view, is perhaps the most neglected of the three major areas of social skill we have distinguished—namely, role-taking. Certainly, in terms of social talent, the ability *to act* in accordance with the expectations of others is at least as important as the capacity to recognize or predict their attitudes and acts. Indeed, the chief relevance of sensitivity and predictive skill to problems of social effectiveness rests on the assumption that the person who possesses these abilities will also be able and willing to act more appropriately toward his fellows. It would be useful to test this double assumption by investigating the degree to which various types of social sensitivity are associated with the ability to act in accordance with another's expectations. The investigator would, of course, need to bear in mind the general concepts, methods, and hypotheses described in the preceding pages. One can, for example, conceive of a person able to "take the role of the generalized other" in that he behaves in a maner considered normal by the society in which he lives. But beyond this minimal level there is perhaps another kind of ability, analogous to and depending on interpersonal sensitivity, which enables the person to adapt his behavior to the differing expectations of different groups in individuals. Our fictional school superintendent must not only sense and anticipate the reactions of his principal, his board, his teachers, his wife, and the entire community; he must also be able and willing to respond appropriately to the different demands of each.

Moreover, in attempting to measure ability in role-taking, we are again faced with the now familiar problem of similarity: to what extent is a person's capacity to imitate someone else or act in accordance with his expectations a function of the degree to which that other person resembles him? Although it is probably impossible to partial out this factor of similarity, our hypotheses regarding the determinants of accuracy may be applicable, *mutatis mutandis*, to the problem of factors other than ability affecting appropriateness of response. We may speculate, for instance, that the more favorable A's orientation toward B, the more likely A is to treat B in the way he hopes B will treat him. To the extent that A and B have similar needs and goals, A's behavior under such circumstances will be appropriate (i.e., in line with B's hopes and expectations); to the extent that A and B are dissimilar, A will end up "doing the wrong thing" from B's point of view. Mary, who wants to please John, buys him a box of expensive candy on his birthday, something which would make her happy were he to do the same for her. If John likes expensive candy as Mary does, all is well; but if he regards candy as an extravagance and really expects a new pipe. . . . In fact, of course, Mary, being high on sensitivity, predictive skill, and responsiveness as well, has indeed bought John a new pipe along with his favorite tobacco—and perhaps has talked the attractive new secretary into giving him the candy.

We are, of course, not at the point where we can attempt a general theory of social skill. Our main purpose in this discussion is to suggest the direction of possible progress in this difficult area and to indicate that the concepts, methods, and hypotheses developed from a study using conventional questionnaire procedures are applicable beyond this restricted context, and are basic to the investigation of a variety of skills in social perception irrespective of the particular technique employed for their measurement.

11. Summary

Taking as our point of departure current research procedures in the general area of skill in social perception and their underlying assumptions, we have called into question the notion of a single generalized ability in "empathy," "social insight," or the "understanding of others." We have indeed contended that methods now in use becloud and confound a variety of variables which should be distinguished for reasons of both theory and practical application. In pursuit of this view, we carried out a theoretical and empirical inquiry with the following major results:

A. We have proposed a conceptual framework which permits the analysis of skills of social perception in theoretically relevant terms and distinguishes a number of variables which may represent independent abilities in this area. Two of these variables were selected for empirical investigation: *interpersonal sensitivity,* defined as the ability to recognize the ways in which other people differ in their behavior, perceptions, or feelings; and *sensitivity to the generalized other,* defined as the ability to recognize the typical response of persons in one's own sub-culture.

B. Measures of interpersonal sensitivity were secured for 72 Cornell students after they had participated in a group discussion. Each group was composed of three men and three women, all of whom were complete strangers to each other.

   1. The measures of first-person sensitivity—the ability to recognize how others differ in their feelings toward one's self—proved wholly unreliable. It was concluded that this unreliability was the result, primarily, of the experimental conditions which made recognition of such differences extremely difficult.

   2. The measure of second-person sensitivity—the ability to recognize how others differ in their self-percepts—showed a corrected reliability of .67 for two alternate forms of the test based on different items. An attempt to determine the reliability of the test for two different sets of persons judged revealed the necessity of distinguishing between sensitivity to one's own sex and sensitivity to the opposite sex. Specifically, women who were perceptive toward their own sex showed a tendency to be insensitive toward men ($r = -.21$); men sensitive to their own sex, however, were likely to be sensitive to women as well ($r = .34$). In all instances, there was evidence for the existence of genuine abilities in interpersonal perception. There were no significant differences in terms of the sex of the person judging or being judged, but marked variation in sensitivity score from group to group.

   3. An analysis of the behavioral correlates of individual differences in sensitivity score revealed striking contrasts in terms of the sex of the person judging and being judged.

      a. *Men sensitive to their own sex* were described by both men and women as resourceful, dominant, outgoing, but at the same time as somewhat dogmatic and annoying. *Men sensitive to women,* however, were distinguished for their tact, tolerance, and timidity. *Men sensitive to persons of either sex* represented a compromise between the two preceding types and showed relatively few outstanding characteristics. They were most frequently referred to as tactful, inoffensive, warm, and resourceful.

      b. *Women sensitive to their own sex* were perceived as submissive, insecure, inhibited, and ineffectual. In partial contrast, *women sensitive to men,* while still somewhat retiring, were seen as maintaining smooth interpersonal relationships. *Women perceptive toward either sex* were described as withdrawn but, at the same time, as considerate and accepting.

c. Qualities associated with *general interpersonal perceptiveness in both sexes* suggested a person who is sensitive in both senses of the term. It is possible that the person who is highly perceptive of other's feelings may pay a price in terms of realizing his own capacities for creative expression and forthright social behavior. This possibility calls into question the prevailing view that the "empathic" person is one who is effective in virtually all types of interpersonal situations, including a leadership role.

d. The preceding findings are interpreted as reflecting differing stages and types of sex-role identification. These considerations, in turn, point to the conclusion that the nature of interpersonal sensitivity and its behavioral correlates is likely to vary with the developmental level of the person and to depend on the particular needs that may be activated in a given social context.

4. An analysis of group differences in sensitivity score and their behavioral correlates indicated that the marked variation in performance from group to group was primarily a function of the relationship between the sexes in each of the twelve groups. These findings are consistent with the general hypothesis that interpersonal judgments are likely to be most accurate in situations where there is complementarity among the roles and relationships of group members. Conversely, distortions and "blind spots" are to be expected under conditions of role conflict and interpersonal tension.

C. Measures of accuracy in judging the norm were computed for our subjects prior to their assignment to discussion groups. These measures were based on the difference between the actual percentage of college students checking a series of adjectives and the subject's estimate of this percentage for each item.

1. The accuracy score showed a corrected reliability of .85. The difference between mean scores for the two sexes was negligible.
2. Despite its higher reliability, the accuracy score turned out to be a poorer predictor of the person's behavior than his score in interpersonal sensitivity. Again there were differences in behavioral correlates for men and women. In contrast to the situation for interpersonal sensitivity, there were no characteristics significantly associated with accuracy irrespective of the sex of the judge.
3. While there was some tendency for a judge's accuracy to be positively correlated with his sensitivity to members of his own sex, the relationship between accuracy and general sensitivity to persons of either sex was substantially zero. This fact, taken together with the differing behavioral correlates of the two variables, supports our original hypothesis that sensitivity and accuracy represent different skills rather than related facets of a single generalized ability.
4. Although sensitivity and accuracy showed low interrelationships at the level of individual differences, the correlation between group means for these two variables was high and negative, indicating that groups composed of accurate judges were very likely to exhibit a low level of interpersonal perceptiveness. The explanation offered for this inverse

relationship implies that knowledge of the pattern of accuracy scores for men and women in a particular group would have made possible forecasting the degree of role-conflict between the sexes and its accompanying problems of interpersonal sensitivity. Accordingly, it is suggested that although a single accuracy score, viewed in isolation, may be a poor predictor of the behavior of a particular judge, the relationship among scores in accuracy (or the related variables of real similarity, assumed similarity, and self-esteem) for several persons may permit forecasting with impressive success the patterns of interaction that would characterize the behavior of such persons as a group.

D. An attempt to develop a "pure" measure of sensitivity to the generalized other which would be independent of the judge's similarity to the social norm proved unsuccessful. At the same time, however, the analysis demonstrated that the conventional accuracy score was predominantly a function of genuine skill in social perception rather than extraneous factors associated with the judge's similarity to the norm. Accordingly, provided it is used with caution, the customary difference-score index is recommended as an acceptable approximation to a "pure" measure of ability in sensitivity to the generalized other.

E. The general hypothesis was offered that, beyond ability in social perception, accuracy in prediction is aided or impaired as a function of two variables: the favorableness of the judge's attitude toward the person or group being judged, and the degree of similarity in the perceptions of judge and judged concerning the material to be predicted. Several specific relationships which follow from this general proposition were tested and confirmed in terms of available data.

F. Because of the limitations of questionnaire methods for the study of skill in social perception, the following series of recommendations was made for a more comprehensive research approach.
   1. Distinguishing between and giving direct attention to three interrelated areas of skill: *social sensitivity, predictive skill,* and *role-taking ability.* The last area, which involves translating one's perceptions and predictions into appropriate action, deserves special emphasis, since it has received comparatively little attention in research to date.
   2. Differentiating the aspects both of the social stimulus to which the judge is asked to respond (physical characteristics, behavior, subjective states, etc.) and of the corresponding content of his social perceptions.
   3. Utilizing actual social situations (as against questionnaires) as the context for research operations.
   4. Securing data on the spontaneous observations and behavior of subjects.
   5. Recognizing the general applicability, in all areas of research on social skills, of the concepts, methods, and hypotheses developed in the restricted context of the present study.

In a word, to the extent that the present research has made a contribution to research in social talent, it is primarily in the area, not of substantive results, but of the definition of problems, concepts, methods, and hypotheses. Although one is naturally tempted to attack the problem of social talent directly—for example, by comparing and analyzing the characteristics of successful and unsuccessful persons—it is our belief that such direct efforts are still premature. We must continue for yet a while the slow and sometimes painful exploration of basic theoretical and methodological problems.

References

1. Allport, G. W. *Personality: A Psychological Interpretation.* New York: Holt, 1937.
2. Allport, G. W., and Vernon, P. E. *Studies in Expressive Movement.* New York: Macmillan, 1933.
3. Angell, R. R. *Psychology; an Introductory Study of the Structure and Function of Human Consciousness.* (4th ed. rev.) New York: Holt, 1908.
4. Asch, S. E. Effects of group pressure upon the modification and distortion of judgments. In G. E. Swanson, T. M. Newcomb, and E. L. Hartley (Eds.), *Readings in Social Psychology.* (2nd ed.) New York: Holt, 1952, pp. 2-11.
5. Bender, I. E., and Hastorf, A. H. The perception of persons: Forecasting another person's responses on three personality scales. *J. abnorm. soc. Psychol.,* 1950, *45,* 556-561.
6. Bender, I. E., and Hastorf, A. H. On measuring generalized empathic ability (social sensitivity). *J. abnorm. soc. Psychol.,* 1953, *48,* 503-506.
7. Bronfenbrenner, U., Harding, J., and Gallwey, M. Two types of skill in social perception and their perceived behavioral correlates. *Amer. Psychologist,* 1955, *10,* 347 (Abstract).
8. Bruner, J. S., and Tagiuri, R. The perception of people. In G. Lindzey (Ed.), *Handbook of Social Psychology.* Vol. 2. Cambridge, Mass. Addison-Wesley, 1954, 634-654.
9. Cooley, C. H. *Social Organization.* New York: Scribner, 1912.
10. Cooley, C. H. Roots of social knowledge. *Amer. J. Sociol.,* 1926, *32,* 59-79.
11. Cottrell, L. S., The analysis of situational fields in social psychology. *Amer. sociol. Rev.,* 1942, *7,* 370-382.
12. Cottrell, L. S., Some neglected problems in social psychology. *Amer. sociol. Rev.,* 1950, *15,* 705-713.
13. Cottrell, L. S., Jr., and Dymond, Rosalind F. The empathic responses: a neglected field for research. *Psychiatry,* 1949, *12,* 355-359.

14. Cronbach, L. J. Processes affecting scores on "understanding of others" and "assumed similarity." *Psychol. Bull.*, 1955, 52, 177-193.
15. Cronbach, L. J., and Gleser, G. C. Assessing similarity between profiles. *Psychol. Bull.*, 1953, *50*, 456-473.
16. Cronbach, L. J., Hartmann, W., and Ehart, M. An investigation of the character and properties of assumed similarity measures. *Technical Report No. 7.* ONR Project N6ori-07135, University of Illinois and the Office of Naval Research, 1953.
17. Dymond, R. F. A preliminary investigation of the relationship of insight and empathy. *J. consult. Psychol.*, 1948, *12*, 228-233.
18. Dymond, R. F. *Empathic ability: an exploratory study,* Unpublished doctor's dissertation, Cornell University, 1949.
19. Dymond, R. F. A scale for the measurement of empathic ability. *J. consult, Psychol.*, 1949, *13*, 127-133.
20. Dymond, R. F. Personality and empathy. *J. consult. Psychol.*, 1950, *14*, 343-350.
21. Fiedler, F. E. Assumed Similarity measures as predictors of team effectiveness. *J. abnorm. soc. Psychol.*, 1954, *49*, 381-388.
22. Fiedler, F. E., Warrington, W. G., and Blaisdell, F. J. Unconscious attitudes as correlates of sociometric choice in a social group. *J. abnorm. soc. Psychol.*, 1952, *47*, 790-796.
23. Freud, S. *A General Introduction to Psychoanalysis.* New York: Boni and Liveright, 1920.
24. Freud, S. *New Introductory Lectures on Psychoanalysis,* New York: Norton, 1933.
25. Freud, S. *The Basic Writings of Sigmund Freud.* New York: Modern Library, 1938.
26. Gage, N. L. Judging interests from expressive behavior. *Psychol. Monogr.* 1952, *66*, No. 18 (Whole No. 350).
27. Gage, N. L., and Cronbach, L. J. Conceptual and methodological problems in interpersonal perception. *Psychol. Rev.*, 1955, *62*, 411-422.
28. Gage, N. L., and Suci, G. Social perception and teacher-pupil relationships, *J. educ. Psychol.*, 1951, *42*, 144-152.
29. Gross, N., and Mason, W. S. Some methodological problems of eight-hour interviews. *Amer. J. Sociol.*, 1953, 59, 197-204.
30. Hastorf, A. H., and Bender, I. E. A caution respecting the measurement of empathic ability. *J. abnorm. soc. Psychol.*, 1952, *47*, No. 2. Suppl., 574-576.
31. Hastorf, A. H., Bender, I. E., and Weintraub, D. J. The Influence of Response Patterns on the "Refined Empathy Score." *J. abnorm. soc. Psychol.*, 1955, *51*, 341-343.
32. Heider, F. Social perception and phenomenal causality. *Psychol. Rev.*, 1944, *57*, 358-374.

33. Jordan, N. Behavioral forces that are a function of attitudes of cognitive organization. *Hum. Relat.*, 1953, *6*, 273-287.
34. Klages, L. *Der Geist als Widersacher der Seele,* 3 vols. Leipzig: Barth, 1929-1932.
35. Klages, L. *The Science of Character.* London: Allen & Unwin, 1929.
36. Köhler, W. *Gestalt Psychology.* New York, Liveright Publishing Corp., 1947.
37. Levy, D. M. *Maternal Overprotection.* New York: Columbia Univ. Press, 1943.
38. Lindgren, H. C., and Robinson, J. The evaluation of Dymond's test of insight and empathy. *J. consult. Psychol.*, 1953, *17*, 172-176.
39. Lipps, T. *Leitfaden der Psychologie.* Leipzig: W. Engelmann, 1909.
40. McDougall, W. *Introduction to Social Psychology,* London: Methuen, 1908.
41. Mead, G. H. *Mind, Self, and Society.* Chicago: University of Chicago Press, 1934.
42. Merton, R. K., and Kitt, A. Contributions to the theory of reference group behavior. In Merton, R. K. and Lazarsfeld, P. F. (eds.) *Studies in the Scope and Methods of the American Soldier,* Glencoe, Ill.: Free Press, 1950, 42-53.
43. Murray, H. A., et al. *Explorations in Personality.* New York: Oxford Univ. Press, 1938.
44. Newcomb, T. M. An approach to the study of communicative acts. *Psychol. Rev.*, 1953, *60*, 393-404.
45. Osgood, E., and Tannenbaum, P. H. The principle of congruity in the prediction of attitude change, *Psychol. Rev.*, 1955, *62*, 42-53.
46. Parsons, T., and Bales, R. F. *Family Socialization and Interaction Process,* Glencoe, Ill.: Free Press, 1955.
47. Scheler, M. *Phänomenologie der Sympathiegefühle.* Bonn: F. Cohen, 1926.
48. Speroff, B. J. Empathic ability and accident rate among steel workers. *Personnel Psychol.*, 1953, *6*, 297-300.
49. Strodtbeck, F. L. et al. Special issue on small group research, *Amer. sociol. Rev.*, 1954, *19*, 651-781.
50. Sullivan, H. S. *Conceptions of Modern Psychiatry.* Washington, D. C.: The William Alanson White Psychiatric Foundation, 1947.
51. Taft, R. The ability to judge people. *Psychol. Bull.*, 1955, *52*, 1-21.
52. Tagiuri, R. Relational analysis: An extension of sociometric method with emphasis on social perception. *Sociometry,* 1952, *15*, 91-104.
53. Tagiuri, R., and Blake, R. R. Some determinants of the perception of positive and negative feelings in others. *J. abnorm. soc. Psychol.*, 1953, *48*, 585-592.
54. Wolin, L. R. *An Analysis of the Content of Interpersonal Perception.* Unpublished doctor's dissertation, Cornell Univ., 1955.

III

Achievement and Social Status in Three Small Communities[1]

JOHN E. KALTENBACH and DAVID C. MCCLELLAND

WHAT do ordinary men and women consider success to be? Do they admire the rich, or the powerful, or the well-educated? Do they judge a man who is none of these a failure? By defining one aspect of what is meant by talented behavior, answers to such questions as these help the behavioral scientist in his analysis of the problem. Theoretically, it is a peculiarly important aspect in that it may dictate the goals which people set up for themselves, perhaps even unconsciously. Because so often these goals turn out to be quite different from what outside observers assumed them to be from an objective point of view, predictions of objective criteria from test behavior may be consistently thrown off; from the subjective point of view, these were the "wrong" criteria.

Take a concrete example. Suppose we decide that one of the easily measured, objective signs of success is earned income. So we try to predict who will make the most money on the basis of, let us say, a test of the strength of motivation for achievement (9). But suppose that in our culture making money is not, from the subjective point of view, the main criterion of success. Then our correlations from achievement motivation score to the income criterion will

[1] The authors gratefully acknowledge help received in planning the project from Fred L. Strodtbeck and Orville G. Brim, Jr., and in carrying through its many technical details from Dorothy Brown and Edward Taras. The study was completed at Wesleyan University in 1952-54.

necessarily be imperfect; it is not the criterion for which our subjects are striving. It may continue to be true that we will want to identify these "deviant" people who will strive primarily for money; but even this practical problem could be better solved if we knew *which activities or "life outcomes" were perceived by potential achievers as relevant to success or achievement.* What we need to know is what "life outcomes" are desirable from the subjective point of view as well as from some objective, perhaps arbitrary, point of view.

The research reported in this chapter is a start in this direction—in the direction of exploring the *perceived dimensions of success.* It is analogous to studies of the class system from the subjective as contrasted with the objective point of view (see Centers, *3*; A. W. Jones, in Bendix and Lipset, *1*, pp. 343-44). It attempts first to discover whether there is any consensus in a small community as to who the successful people in town are. Second, it searches, in the lives of the more and the less successful, for factors which might have led their fellow citizens to categorize them in this way. Finally, it explores the relationship between perceived achievement status and social status as traditionally defined and measured by sociologists like Warner, *et al.* (*12*), Hollingshead (*6*), and Kaufman (*8*).

Procedure

The data were collected by interview with informants in three small towns, called here Shoretown, Milltown, and Rivertown. The towns themselves and the reasons for choosing them will be described below. Because the interviewer (J. E. K.) had lived in the first two towns for some time, he knew them both well; yet, never having been employed in either one, he could still be considered by residents of the town an "outsider." Rivertown he knew considerably less well and visited only in connection with his interviews by commuting from a nearby town.

In each community his first step was to interview a cross section of persons in the town, to get from them nominations of successful members of their community. These persons, called nominators, were queried about their own education, employment, family, and membership in community organizations. They were then asked questions about who was the most successful man in town, who had the best job, who the easiest job, who worked hardest, who had the most money, who had done the most for the town, who were generally regarded in the community as being successful, and finally what they themselves would consider the main end in life to be.

The interviews were conducted in an informal manner, but the questions were introduced in the order listed; generally they led to a discussion of considerable interest to most of the informants. The purpose of the interview and the topic of conversation were to lead people to review in their minds various prominent personages in the town and to make thoughtful nominations for our list of successful people. After seven or eight interviews, the number of new names for the list began to fall off rather sharply; the nominating phase was concluded with 76 names from Shoretown, 77 names from Milltown, and 39 names from Rivertown (which was half the size of the first two towns). The number of nominators in the three towns was 16, 8, and 7 respectively. Their representativeness as a cross section of each community is attested by the fact that six from Shoretown and two each from Milltown and Rivertown were not themselves on the list of nominated "successes"; and by the fact that of those nominated the final achievement rank orders assigned them by our judges ranged from 7–85, 10–77, and 1–29, respectively, in the three towns. Every effort was made to get all possible points of view in the community represented in the nominating phase—from mill hand, to Tax Collector, to editor of the local paper, or leading socialite.

The next step was to have the nominees judged according to their successfulness. First, the interviewer added enough names in each town to bring the totals to 90, 90, and 45, respectively. This he did for several reasons: (a) to provide the judges with "anchoring points" at the low end of the scale (i.e., unsuccessful people) to make the judging easier; (b) to prevent correlations with the final achievement rank from being spuriously low, as would be the case if the range represented were limited to the upper ranks in achievement; and (c) to permit the interviewer to add some names which he felt from his general knowledge of the town should be included. Such a procedure may be criticized for making correlations spuriously high, in that the extremes of the achievement distribution are over-represented. This objection may not hold, however, because most of the people on the list were nominated only once and thus should probably not be considered as representing the upper extreme in success. In any case, it seemed to us that the errors possibly introduced by adding names would be less serious than those of not adding any at all.

TABLE 1. OCCUPATION, ACHIEVEMENT RANK (AR), AND SOCIAL STATUS RANK (SS) OF ACHIEVEMENT AND SOCIAL STATUS JUDGES IN THE THREE TOWNS COMPARED

Shoretown	AR	SS	Milltown	AR	SS	Rivertown	AR†	SS†
Achievement Rank Judges								
Editor, local weekly	12	35	Editor, local weekly	37.5	44	Editor and publisher local weekly	14	8
Bank president	2	10	Publisher, local weekly	12	6	Bank president	8	22
President, Savings & Loan	45	52	Insurance agent, Savings & Loan official	29	31	Egg wholesaler	8	36
Club woman	8	1	Club woman	16	27	Congregational minister	2	14
Lawyer, state gov. official	4	2	Bank president	26	14			
			Supt. schools	2	15.5			
Extra Achievement Rank Judges								
Newcomer woman doctor	6	15				Italian gas station owner	58	44
Factory worker who commutes to nearby city	—	—				Baptist minister	—	—
Social Status Judges								
Bank president**	2	10	Publisher's wife*	12	6	Printer and publisher's wife	12	4
Bank president's wife*	2	10	Real estate man's wife*	19	3	Congregational minister's wife*	2	14
Editor of weekly	12	35	Insurance agent	29	31			

* The AR and SS values given are for the husbands of the women concerned.

** Cases where the same judge or his wife ranked both for AR and SS can be determined by comparing SS and AR ranks for the judges.

† Ranks in Rivertown have been doubled to facilitate direct comparison with the other towns.

In each town about half-a-dozen judges were chosen, primarily on the basis of how many people they would be likely to know. Their occupation, achievement rank, and social status are listed in Table 1. It can be seen immediately that most of them turned out to be themselves fairly high-ranking individuals in their communities, although, of course, the interviewer had no way of knowing this before the judging. The fact raises the objection repeatedly made (see Kornhauser in Bendix and Lipset, *1*, p. 249), to the effect that status studies on American communities reveal a strong bias in the direction of seeing the social structure from the viewpoint of the upper-middle and upper classes. In defense we can say only that it would have been meaningless to have the judging done by someone who knew but a fraction of the persons to be ranked. We had to choose the persons with a knowledge of who most of the people on our list were. These judges turned out to be, by and large, themselves in key positions in the community—which is why they knew so many of the people. To attempt to correct for this bias, we succeeded in getting at least one judge each in Shoretown and in Rivertown who could be relied on to give at any rate a lower-middle class point of view.

The judging process itself was fairly simple, though long; it took from two to three hours for each judge. The names on the final lists having been transferred to individual cards, each judge was handed a pile of cards and asked to sort it first into halves, then into quarters, and so on until he had managed to rank-order all individuals from 1 to 90 (or as in the case of Rivertown, 1 to 45). To get as much information as we could from our judges, ties were not permitted. One judge refused to go beyond the first division saying, "There are only sheep and goats in the world. You either have what it takes for success or you haven't, and this is it."

Most of the judges asked what we meant by "success." This question the interviewer steadfastly refused to answer, stating that the person was to judge by his own standards, whatever they might be. The same procedure was followed in ranking the cards for social standing in the town. If the judges asked what was meant by social standing, the only further explanation that was given was to the effect that it dealt with "who would invite whom to dinner." It should be pointed out here that the ratings for social standing are not so adequate as those for achievement rank, because the nominating procedure centered exclusively around getting the names of successful, not socially prominent, people. Thus there are undoubtedly socially prominent individuals who were not on our lists at all. What we were after was a rating of the social standing of our "achievers" to check on its possible relationship to achievement.

Some time after the ranking had been done, each judge was interviewed to find out what criteria he thought he had used in sorting the cards. These interviews gave us clues about the objective characteristics we should measure in attempting to find out what contributed to perceived success. The wide variety of explanations given by the judges (as also by the nominators) as to what led them to pick people as successful or unsuccessful, we found, could be classified under four main headings: (1) the traditional variables found by sociologists to be associated with prestige, i.e., income, educational level, and occupational level; (2) "service to others"; (3) "overcoming initial handicaps"; and (4) "personality and character."

We were able, as Table 2 shows, to get data on the first three of these four factors. Income, education, and occupation we judged in the traditional way. For "service to others" we found a measure in the number of community activities participated in. An indirect measure of "overcoming initial handicaps" lay in the number of rungs on the occupational ladder the person had moved up over his father. This latter measure was, of course, only partially satisfactory. For one thing, it did not include the other handicaps that our informants had in mind, such as physical disabilities, "no account" parents, a drunken wife, or what not; and for another, it did not measure advance *within* an occupational category. That is, a man's father might have been a poorly paid missionary of a revivalistic church, while he himself has gone on to be a respected minister in an upper-middle class church—an advance which, although taken into account by our judges, would not be apparent in our index of mobility, where both parent and son would be classified as ministers.

Although they undoubtedly played a large part in the achievement rank assigned certain individuals, we were unable to get any objective measure of personality and character factors. We were unable, that is, to think of a way of translating into an index, applicable to everyone, such comments as "He pays his bills," "Honest in all his dealings," "Fulfills his obligations," etc. To some extent these personality factors were measured indirectly in our community service index, since they are undoubtedly taken into account in determining who shall lead in community affairs.

It should also be noted that the community service data for Shoretown are incomplete. When we decided it would be necessary to use this index, we had already completed our interviewing in that town, and we were able to get the information easily on only half of the persons on the final list. But this sample seemed to be sufficiently representative of the whole to provide us with accurate enough information on its importance.

A final limitation of our data lay in the fact, as Table 2 shows, that occupational and income classifications were not applied to the women nominated, on the ground that neither of these classification systems really fits women. Thus we simply did not know how to classify a woman, either as to occupation or income, who had

TABLE 2. DEFINITION OF VARIABLES USED TO DESCRIBE SMALL TOWN LEADERS

AR–Achievement rank

Final rank order assigned an individual by combining judgments of him by several community leaders when asked to rank a group of 90 (or 45) persons from the town on their "success in life."

SS–Social status

Final rank order assigned an individual by combining judgments of him by several "socially aware" individuals when asked to rank a group of 90 (or 45) persons from the town on their "social standing."

OL–Occupational level (modified from Edwards' census classification, used for men only)

6–Major professional and business executives
5–Minor professional (HS teacher), managerial, medium business (drug, hardware stores, etc.), large farms
4–Clerical, ordinary sales, small business (grocery stores, filling station), self-employed skilled workers, small farms
3–Skilled mechanical and public service workers (machinists, postmen)
2–Semi-skilled (millhands)
1–Unskilled (unemployed, janitors, etc.)

IR–Income rank (estimated by bankers in town)

5–$20,000 or more annually
4–$10,000 annually
3–$5-10,000 annually
2–$3-5,000 annually
1–Less than $3,000 annually

EL–Educational level

3–College graduate or more
2–High school graduate or more (up to 3)
1–Less than high school graduate

OD–Occupational differential

Difference between occupational level of person and his father.

CS–Community Service

Number of community activities in which person participated actively (mere membership not counted, if inactive). Community Chest, Parent-Teachers' Association, School Board, Finance Board, Zoning Board, Rotary Club, March of Dimes, Garden Club, Boy's Club, Community Concerts, Planned Parenthood, etc.

been a successful executive in business but who now was one only in respect to the way she managed community affairs and whose separate income was by itself small, although large if her husband's was added to it.

TABLE 3. GENERAL CHARACTERISTICS OF THE THREE SMALL TOWNS COMPARED

Characteristic	*Shoretown*	*Milltown*	*Rivertown*
Population (1950)	c. 5,000	c. 5,000	c. 2,500
Population (1930)	c. 3,100	c. 3,700	c. 2,300
Location	Shore of Long Island Sound, semi-suburban to nearby city	Inland 25-35 mi. from Philadelphia, not suburban	On New England river, not suburban
"Culture complex"	Dominantly old Yankee, Congregationalist, plus small immigrant minorities	Overwhelmingly German Lutheran	About one-half old Yankee and one-half Catholic immigrant (Polish, Italian)
Economic life	Small business, farming, service occupations for tourists in the summer and commuters to nearby city	Heavy industry (iron, glass, textiles)	Agriculture and manufacturing
Religion (est. %)			
Protestant	70%	80%	50%
Catholic	30%	20%	50%
% Republican votes in 1948 Presidential election	78%	63%	53%

The geographical and cultural characteristics of the three towns are summarized in Table 3. Shoretown was studied first. There we found such a clear-cut and surprising difference between achievement rank and social standing and their determinants that we decided to check our results in a town of a different character. For this we chose Milltown, in a different region and much more industrialized. Although the results here were quite different from what we had found in Shoretown, we were not certain whether the divergence was due to the regional difference or to a difference in industrialization. So finally we came back to New England to look for a third town, which would be comparable to Shoretown but heavily industrialized. Unfortunately most of the New England industrial towns that would have been suitable were much larger than the other two; finally we had to be satisfied with a town which was much smaller. This fact in turn forced the difficult decision of whether to ask for the same number of nominees or to be satisfied with about half the number, on the ground that this would provide us with a list roughly comparable to the sample we had obtained in the other two towns. We chose the latter course—the lesser of two evils. On the whole, our work in Rivertown is much less thorough than in the other two towns, and the data from it are presented only as a general check on findings obtained in other types of situations.

Results

Table 4 summarizes the objective characteristics of the persons nominated in the three towns excluding women from the occupational and income classifications, and both women and men whose parents' occupations were unknown from the classification by occupational mobility. Data on community service are not presented, because comparisons across communities are not really warranted where data are available on less than half of the persons nominated in Shoretown and where some improvement is probable in the interviewer's ability to collect this information as he went from one community to the next. Such improvement in the interviewer should not affect seriously, of course, the rank order *within* a given community.

From Table 4 several conclusions are possible. In the first place, there are no significant differences in educational level among the successful people of the three towns. There is, however, a significantly larger number of persons with high occupational level in Milltown as compared with Shoretown ($\chi^2=8.35$, $p<.01$). These men are largely the owners and executives of the several large factories located in Milltown, a fact which is also reflected in a significantly larger number of nominees with incomes over $20,000 a year in Milltown. In all three towns there were only 18 persons whose yearly incomes were judged to be this high. Of these, 13 were in Milltown ($\chi^2=7.82$, df.$=2$, $p<.02$).

But probably the most interesting difference shown in Table 4 lies in the pattern of occupational mobility in the three communities. Shoretown is predominantly a stable community, with nearly

TABLE 4. STATUS CHARACTERISTICS OF PERSONS NOMINATED AS SUCCESSFUL IN THREE SMALL TOWNS

Characteristic	Town	*N*	Percentages in Various Status Categories			Mean*	SD*
			High	Middle	Low		
Occupational level	Shoretown	68	18[1]	51	31	4.87	.68
	Milltown	70	41	33	26	5.11	.89
	Rivertown	31	29	58	13	4.90	1.25
Income	Shoretown	68	28[2]	43	29	2.98	.92
	Milltown	70	40	40	20	3.36	1.05
	Rivertown	31	32	39	29	3.03	1.00
Educational level	Shoretown	76	38[3]	46	16	2.23	.70
	Milltown	77	31	42	27	2.04	.76
	Rivertown	39	46	38	15	2.31	.72
Occupational mobility	Shoretown	52	13[4]	29	58	.71	1.52
	Milltown	57	14	56	30	1.23	1.34
	Rivertown	27	37	19	44	1.26	1.65

* All means and SD's are computed from full data, not data as grouped for percentages in this table.

[1] For occupational level (men only)
High = 6 = Professional and large business
Middle = 5 = Managerial, medium business, minor professional
Low = 4 or less = clerical, small business, etc.

[2] For income (men only)
High = 4 or 5 = $10,000 a year or more
Middle = 3 = $5-10,000 a year
Low = 2 or 1 = less than $5,000 a year

[3] For educational level
High = 3 = College graduate
Middle = 2 = High school graduate or more (up to 3)
Low = 1 = less than H.S. graduate

[4] For mobility (men only)
High = 3 or more step gain over father in occupational level
Middle = 1-2 step gain over father in occupational level
Low = 0 gain or less over father in occupational level

60 per cent of the nominees at the same occupational level as their parents. Milltown, on the other hand, has shown a steady growth in occupational status; an equally large proportion of its nominees have moved up one step on the occupational ladder. Finally, Rivertown shows a distinct split. Although in one respect it is like the traditional New England community, Shoretown, in having a large number of persons who have shown no change in occupational level, it includes in addition a large proportion of persons who have

jumped three steps or more in occupational level. Thus our three communities present three distinct patterns of occupational mobility. How such organization influences the way persons in a town are judged for achievement and social standing will be important to see.

So far we have concentrated largely on the differences among the communities; there are also some similarities. In the first place, it is clear that in any of the towns a person is morely likely to be nominated if he comes from the upper occupational, income, or community service levels. Although we have no information on the distribution of jobs or income for the population as a whole in these particular towns, we know from other studies that the bulk of the population would be classified in our "low" categories. Thus it seems safe to conclude that our nominees come significantly more often from upper economic and occupational levels. The same is certainly true of community service, although no data are presented here bearing on the participation of the whole town in such activities. Because it seems safe to assume that *most* of the people in the community do not participate at all in community enterprises, the fact that a large percentage of our nominees do, sets them off as no mere random sample of the larger population. On the average, the upward mobility of the successful is also high in all three towns; it is not only significantly greater than zero, but considerably higher than the average (+.35) for a general sample in a United States urban setting (Centers, *3*, p. 202) or than the average (.00) for a general sample in Britain (Glass, *4*, p. 185). As to educational level, we can be less sure because we are less certain about the distribution of education in the population at large for these towns; but again it seems highly likely that the upper educational levels are over-represented among our nominees.

A second region of similarity shown by data for all three towns is hinted by the fact that success is a term not applied very often to women. Only eight women were nominated in Shoretown, seven in Milltown, and eight in Rivertown, making the odds that women are as likely to be nominated as men almost infinitesimally small. There is, however, a tendency in the two New England towns for women, if included, to be ranked high (biserial *tau* for Shoretown for sex and achievement rank equals .17, $p \sim .08$). The same is not true in Milltown.

Other similarities in types of persons judged successful are revealed in Table 5, where the top six persons in each community in achievement rank are briefly described. A minister appears in all

TABLE 5. BRIEF DESCRIPTIONS OF TOP SIX PERSONS IN ACHIEVEMENT RANK ORDER IN THREE TOWNS INCLUDING SOCIAL STATUS (SS) RANK

Shoretown	Milltown	Rivertown *
1. A beloved HS art teacher, farmer's son, confidential adviser to many, SS–47	1. President, Teacher's College, farmer's son, SS–17	1. Congregational minister, son of bookkeeper, SS–14
2. President of bank patronized by well-to-do, son of groceryman, SS–10	2. Sup't Schools, minister's son, SS–15.5	2. Nurse, daughter of hotelkeeper, mother, community leader, SS–4
3. Minister, orphaned early, makes many parish calls on foot, SS–40	3. Minister, official in state denominational organization, SS–23.5	3. Egg wholesaler, farmer's son, SS–36
4. Lawyer, important state official, son of unsuccessful factory worker, SS–2	4. President, boiler mfg. co., machinist's son, SS –1	4. Head of a bank, insurance man's son, SS–22
5. Judge of Probate, Town Clerk, farmer's son, SS–24.5	5. Owner, large truck transportation company, drayman's son, SS–23.5	5. Clubwoman, mother, community leader, SS–18
6. Woman doctor, who goes out on night calls, SS–15	6. Undertaker, farmer's son, SS–5	6. Owner publishing and printing plant, owner's son, SS–4

* SS ranks for Rivertown have been doubled to facilitate direct comparisons with the other towns.

three lists, a woman in two, an educator in two, and a banker in two. Perhaps it is significant that a person associated with matters of life and death (a doctor, an undertaker, a nurse) appears in all three lists. Just as obviously, however, it is not the job as such which gives a person his high rank; in each case there are other ministers, others doctors, other teachers, not ranked very high. How a person fills the role rather than the role itself determines his achievement status. Certain positions, however, do expose the person more to the view of the community as a whole, so that if he does his job unusually well, he is likely to be ranked high.

In Table 6 we have data which show the extent to which judges agree among themselves on achievement and social status rank, and the extent to which they differentiate between the two types of ranking. It is clear that the judges in all towns agree significantly and to about the same extent, on the average, about the achievement status of the various people they were asked to judge. The reliability of a combined rank order based on the work of all judges, estimated in each case by the Spearman-Brown prophecy formula, reaches in each town a quite satisfactory level. Agreement on social standing is even higher, particularly in Shoretown.

Such agreement, however, is essentially among community leaders. What about the deviant or lower-class judges? For Shoretown the results are fairly clear-cut. The factory worker's achievement rank order correlated .55 with the combined AR for the other five judges, a correlation which demonstrates that he agreed with them at about the same level as they agreed with each other. The other extra judge, the woman doctor who had moved to town within the last year, showed an even higher correlation (.68)—a fact which apparently reflects her own higher status in the community. Since both of these judges were relative newcomers, it is possible to conclude that the standing of individuals in Shoretown is sufficiently stable and obvious for even newcomers to perceive it and judge it in the same way regardless of their own standing in the community.

For Rivertown the situation is quite different. The two extra judges turned out to be marked deviants. The averages of their agreement coefficients with the other judges were .23 and .25 respectively (calculated as always in this study by the use of z-transformations), and their own achievement rank orders intercorrelated .09. This we interpret to mean that Rivertown is a much less stable and integrated community than Shoretown—or Milltown, for that matter—where no deviant judges were found. In Rivertown one of the deviants was a Baptist preacher who had recently moved to the community from the South and whose standards of judgment were obviously different from those of the community leaders. The latter was true of the other deviant judge, who was an Italian Catholic.[2] Since this was the last town we visited, and since we had not, up to this time, been able to find a judge whose rank order disagreed with the rank order of others, we went out of our way here to prove that in any community deviant judges could be found. It is our conviction—and our agreement coefficients seem to back

[2] It is perhaps worth noting that it was apparently not his Catholicism *per se* which dictated deviance, since one other judge in this community was also a Catholic and his average agreement coefficient with the other three Protestant judges was .59 (perhaps because he was judged to be of high status himself).

TABLE 6. CORRELATION COEFFICIENTS AMONG AND BETWEEN ACHIEVEMENT RANKS AND SOCIAL STATUS RANKS GIVEN BY DIFFERENT JUDGES

Town	Among Achievement Ranks				Among Social Status Ranks				Between Achievement Ranks and Social Status Ranks		
	Number of		Mean Intercor-relation *	r_{xx} †	Number of		Mean Intercor-relation *	r_{yy} †	Number of Intercor-relations	Mean Intercor-relation *	r_{xy} ‡
	Judges	Intercor-relations			Judges	Intercor-relations					
Shoretown	5	10	.56	.86	3	3	.87	.95	15	.45	.56
Milltown	6	15	.55	.88	3	3	.67	.86	18	.58	.83
Rivertown	4	6	.57	.84	2	1	.62	.77	8	.61	.78

* Computed by use of Fisher's z-transformations.

† Estimated reliability of total rank order based on combining the given number of individual rank orders (Spearman-Brown prophecy formula).

‡ Correlation between combined AR and combined SS rank orders.

us up—that in any small community, there is a considerable consensus among the leaders of the community as to who the successful people in town are. In a stable community like Shoretown, this consensus extends rather widely throughout the whole community, and one has to look long and hard to find deviant judges. In a highly mobile community like Rivertown, on the other hand, where the community seems split between an older New England pattern and the newer highly mobile industrial pattern, the consensus is considerably less widespread, and deviant judges are easier to find.

This same occupational mobility may be tied up with another finding shown in Table 6. Only in Shoretown, the least mobile, is there evidence that achievement and social status are separate and distinct. To see whether the average intercorrelation *between* these two types of rank ordering would be less than the average intercorrelation *among* them, we intercorrelated every SS and AR. Clearly this is not the case in Milltown or Rivertown, where the average intercorrelation among AR's and SS's is about what it is between the two. The judges, we suspect, could not make a distinction between the two types of status systems. In Shoretown, although the difference between the average correlations of .45 and .56 is not significant, more of the higher correlations appear among AR's than between AR's and SS's (biserial *tau* = .34, $p < .05$).

Further evidence that these two types of judgments differed in Shoretown is to be found in the fact that two of the judges of social status had also served as AR judges. For one, the intercorrelation between SS and AR was .56; for the other, it was .26. The first judge also re-ranked the cases for AR on a second occasion with a reliability coefficient of .95. Thus in both cases it is quite clear that, for these judges, AR and SS were two different variables. In Milltown, on the other hand, the one judge who ranked both SS and AR apparently had a much harder time distinguishing between the two; the correlation between his two rank orders was .70. And, in Rivertown, the wife of one of the achievement judges produced a social-status rank order which correlated .85 with her husband's for achievement.

The hypothesis that there are two status systems in Shoretown but not in the other two towns is confirmed even more strikingly in Table 7, which summarizes the major results of our study. For Shoretown, occupational level, income and education correlate significantly higher with social standing than they do with achievement rank (especially if the correlations between the correlations are taken into account; see *11*, p. 421). On the other hand, com-

TABLE 7. CORRELATIONS BETWEEN BACKGROUND CHARACTERISTICS, ACHIEVEMENT RANK (AR), AND SOCIAL STATUS (SS) FOR GROUPS OF LEADERS IN THE THREE SMALL TOWNS COMPARED

	Shoretown				Milltown				Rivertown		
Characteristic	*N*	AR		SS	*N*	AR		SS	*N*	AR	SS
Occupational level[x]	82[y]	.48[z]	*	.77	83	.44	*	.57	36	.21	.12
Income	82	.45	*	.65	83	.52		.50	36	.54	.43
Education[x]	90	.47	*	.78	90	.50		.55	45	.20	.08
Community service	45	.86	*	.57	90	.63		.60	44	.68	.62
Occupational mobility	63	.41	**	.18	70	.26	*	.10	29	.01	.04
Achievement rank	90			.56	90			.83	45		.78

Correlations above .40 are significant at the .01 level or beyond, when *N* is 40 or more.

* Difference between correlation with AR and SS is significant at less than .02 level; ** at less than .05 level. For example, $p < .02$ for difference between $r = .48$ and $r = .77$.

[x] Triserial correlations.

[y] The number of cases is sometimes less than 90 or 45 because women were not included in some correlations or because information was not readily available on some individuals.

[z] All correlations have negative signs because high SS and AR rank were assigned low numbers, but since the relationships are positive, the negative signs have been omitted.

munity service and mobility are significantly more highly correlated with achievement rank than with social status. In Milltown the differences in correlational size hold for occupational level as a more significant determinant of social status and for occupational mobility as a more significant determinant of achievement rank, but the differences for the other factors disappear. In Rivertown only income and community service are significantly correlated with either AR and SS, and in each case the difference between them is not significant.

It is interesting that the importance of mobility as a correlate of achievement status decreases the greater the mobility in the community—from Shoretown, to Milltown, to Rivertown (cf. Table 4). This paradoxical decrease is actually somewhat misleading. In the case of Rivertown, for example, there are a number of people who, having raised themselves three or four levels on the occupational ladder, would seem sufficiently successful to get nominated. But, because they have to be compared with other persons at the same level who have not risen but who started there, they tend to lose out. They end by being ranked rather low among the successful, perhaps because in their rapid rise from the lower classes they have not yet had the opportunity to acquire those values and characteristics esteemed by leaders in the community. In a community like Shoretown, where the gains in occupational level are much less extreme and fewer in number, this is not the case. Here a rise in level can be considered an unmixed asset; it is not large enough to be associated with any "lower-class" characteristics, such as lack of interest in community affairs.

If we ignore differences among the towns for a moment, it is obvious that in all towns community service is by far the most important single factor associated with high achievement rank. It is more highly correlated with AR (though not significantly so) in all three towns than is the next important factor, size of income.[3] After income come education and occupation. The importance of overcoming handicaps is probably somewhat underestimated here because we have had to measure it with a mobility index which is apparently less valid, the more mobile the population of the town.

Discussion

The problem which we set out to investigate was this: in a small community what are the objective correlates of perceived success?

First, we come out with the fact that achievement rank is indeed a perceived dimension along which people may be placed with fair agreement by the leaders in a community—even though it is not always distinguished from social standing. The confusion between achievement rank and social standing in the two more mobile towns is not easy to interpret: one could argue either that in these towns achievement rank determines social standing, or just the opposite. Our data cannot, by themselves, settle the issue. It is perhaps worth noting that at the highest levels there is no correlation between the two (see Table 5).

Second, we have found that community service is the single most

[3] There is some slight additional evidence that income may be even more important to lower ranking individuals. In Shoretown there was a slight negative correlation ($p \sim .05$) between income rank of the nominators and income rank of their nominees—e.g., the lower the nominator's income, the higher the average income of his nominees.

important factor correlated with achievement. Since active participation in community enterprises has frequently been found by sociologists to be associated at least with prestige (see Kaufman in Bendix and Lipset, *1*, p. 199) or social standing (see Hollingshead, *6*), this is not surprising. We have given a slightly different flavor to this variable by defining it in terms of "community service," which is the way it was described by our informants, rather than in terms of "memberships in organizations of high social standing," which is the usual way it is described by sociologists. In Warner's studies (*12*) the emphasis is on the fact that memberships in important community organizations often seem to be "reserved" for members of the upper classes; lower-class persons could not participate even if they would. While this may be true of certain social clubs in certain other towns, it does not accurately describe the picture as we were given it in our communities. Here the emphasis, at least so far as achievement rank is concerned, is placed on the time and energy a person is willing to devote to community affairs. A person certainly has to have a certain minimal level of acceptability, of income, of education, and the like to be asked to serve as director of a Community Chest Fund Drive; but of all the eligibles for such a position, those who pitch in and work, or who have volunteered for other jobs around the community, are the ones who receive the highest rating for success.

Such a result may seem a little surprising, since one might have expected judges to rate success in terms of more individualistic criteria, such as amount of money earned, regardless of contribution to the community. Evidence that we are not dealing with a hitherto unnoticed phenomenon is to be found, however, in Henderson's report on the "mass-produced suburbs": "Since no one can acquire prestige through an imposing house, or inherited position, activity—the participation in community or group affairs—becomes the basis of prestige" (*5*, p. 26). What we are adding to his observation is that the same thing seems to be true not only of uniform housing developments, but of small American communities of all types.

Our empirical finding on the importance of community service, furthermore, has ample backing in recent theoretical analyses of what makes for leadership in small groups. Thus Homans writes: "In the small group the person of the highest social rank is the person who comes closest to realizing in his behavior the norms of the group. . . . The leader must live up to the norms of the group—all the norms—better than any follower," (*7*, pp. 426-427). For a small town to function, some of its inhabitants must devote themselves to community activities. Voluntary participation in such activities has become in the United States a group goal or norm, and to those who pursue it most actively we accord the highest achievement status.

After community service in importance comes either occupational mobility or income, depending on whether one chooses the factor which differentiates between achievement rank and social status or the factor which correlates next highest with achievement rank regardless of its connection with social status. Both are important. There is clear support here for the widely held view that a man's success is judged partly in terms of the money he makes. Actually mobility would probably loom even larger if we had a measure of it which was not so easily influenced by the mobility pattern in the town, and which could be broadened to cover the more general category, discovered in our interviews, of "overcoming handicaps."

Last come education and occupational level, both significantly associated with perceived success in two out of our three communities and nearly so in the third. It is interesting to note that, of all the variables studied, occupational level, which is considered by Warner and his associates (*12*) to be the best single measure of social status, is probably the least associated with achievement rank in all our three towns. Why is this so? Possibly because it may be more often inherited than other variables; that is, when the ownership of a business is passed on from father to son, a certain occupational level goes with it. Where the other characteristics are concerned—with the possible exception of income—a person must attain his ultimate level on his own. In the towns we are dealing with here, as a matter of fact, there is not much inherited wealth, so that the actual income is largely earned. Thus we might conclude —not too surprisingly—that achievement rank is likely to be associated with achieved status factors, and social standing with ascribed status factors.

Since we initially raised the question of what goals a person with high achievement motivation would pursue because he perceives them as achievement-related, we were interested to know whether individuals in our communities with high achievement rank or with a high score on the factors which correlate with achievement rank would in fact make higher scores on a test of achievement motivation (*n* Achievement). Fortunately we were able to assemble fifteen individuals in Shoretown for a testing session under standard conditions (see McClelland *et al.*, *9*). Their achievement rank ranged from 2 to 64 and yielded a correlation of .77 with their community service scores, a fact which suggests that the sample is representative of the parent population (see Table 7). For this sample the correlation of *n* Achievement score with achievement rank was .60 ($p<.05$) and with community service .63 ($p<.05$). Thus we derived some support for our hypothesis that those with high achievement motivation tend to engage in activities that lead their fellows to judge them as successful. The corresponding correlation with social status is less as expected (.42) and reduces to .32 if achievement rank is partialled out; whereas partialling out social status in the relationship between *n* Achievement and AR reduces the correlation only from .60 to .55. Although the number of cases is too small to establish significance, it seems likely that achievement motivation is, as predicted, more highly related to achievement rank than it is to social status.

Suppose we ask if there is any way to establish a man's perceived achievement in a small town without going through the elaborate interviewing and ranking procedure we had to adopt. Answering this question might seem to involve a multiple correlation analysis in which all the objective factors should be correlated with each other and with achievement rank. But a glance at the data warns us that such an elaborate procedure would in fact add very little to what is apparent in Table 7: community service correlates so highly with achievement rank that the other variables would add little to the multiple correlation. *Our conclusion must be that community activity by itself, irrespective of all other factors (income, occupational level, etc.), is the best index of perceived achievement that can be objectively obtained.* Since participation in many community enterprises presupposes such things as a minimal level of education, occupational status, money, honesty, etc., this conclusion is perhaps to be expected.

Although the major objective of our study was to discover the perceived dimensions of success in small towns, it did shed light also on problems of current interest to students of social structure. For one thing, it strongly suggests that the Warner Index of Status Characteristics (*12*) provides a good measure of social standing only in a fairly stable community like Shoretown, which seems in many ways comparable to Yankee Town on which Warner did his original work. Occupation, education, and size of income all seem to be highly correlated with social status in Shoretown, but the correlations tend to drop off as mobility increases from Milltown to Rivertown, where the situation is most anomalous. In Rivertown even occupational level, which is Warner's best single indicator of status, does not correlate significantly with social standing. It is true, of course, that the correlation might be considerably higher if a larger segment of the population were studied and cruder step-intervals used. But the fact that the correlation is so low in Rivertown and so high in Shoretown raises doubts as to whether occupational level can be considered a *universally* good index to social standing.

In addition, the fact that in the two mobile towns achievement rank and social standing are highly correlated indicates to us, at least, the possibility that even social standing may be determined in such towns more by what a person does than by who he is. In this connection it is perhaps worth noting that two out of the top three persons in social standing even in Shoretown were individuals who had moved to the community from elsewhere and about whose antecedents no one in the town apparently knew anything. They could scarcely be called "old family" in Warner's sense. Our towns may, of course, have been so small that they included no real upper class; though even this is doubtful, for in Milltown there was such a considerable number of factory owners earning over $20,000 a year, many of whom had inherited their positions from their fathers. Although one of these factory owners ranked highest in social standing, a number of others were well down the list; and the next two highest were insurance men of moderate means. All of these considerations strongly suggest that social standing in our towns is largely determined by achievement, the exception being the most static, non-mobile one, where other factors traditionally emphasized by Warner and his associates enter in *along with* actual achievement.

On still another issue of real interest to students of social structure our data shed some light. This is the question of whether there are within a community one or several status systems. Warner has been criticized (see Kornhauser in Bendix and Lipset, *1*) for lumping all possible status distinctions under one general heading. Most of his critics have argued for the importance of distinguishing between status systems based on prestige, on economic factors, or on power. Merton, for example, has pointed out that "populations may be socially stratified in different hierarchies . . . the sociological problem here is manifestly to explore the interrelations between the several hierarchies, and not to blur the problem by *assuming* that they can be merged into a composite system of ranking" (*10,* p. 217).

Empirical examples of such different hierarchies in the literature are—at least on the subjective side—few and far between. Thus Warner might well retort that, while the social analyst can make a number of such distinctions, members of a community subjectively do not. In our study, however, we have concrete evidence that at least in one community—one with low occupational mobility—judges do make a distinction between achievement standing and social standing. These are correlated but distinguishable variables. To this extent, at least, our data lend support to the hypothesis that there may be subjectively, as well as objectively, hierarchies in a community based on different factors.

References

1. Bendix, R. and Lipset, S. M. (Eds.). *Class, Status and Power.* Glencoe, Ill.: Free Press, 1953.
2. Centers, R. Occupational mobility of urban occupational strata. *Amer. sociol. Rev., 13,* 197-203, 1948.
3. Centers, R. *The Psychology of Social Classes.* Princeton: Princeton Univ. Press, 1949.
4. Glass, D. V. (Ed.), *Social Mobility in Britain.* Glencoe, Ill.: Free Press, 1954.
5. Henderson, H. The mass-produced suburbs. *Harper's Magazine,* 1953, *207,* 25-31, (November).
6. Hollingshead, A. B. *Elmtown's Youth.* New York: Wiley, 1949.
7. Homans, G. C. The *Human Group.* New York: Harcourt, Brace, 1950.
8. Kaufman, H. Prestige classes in a New York rural community. In Bendix, R. and Lipset, S. M. (Eds.) *Class, Status and Power.* Glencoe, Ill.: Free Press, 1953.
9. McClelland, D. C., Atkinson, J. W., Clark, R. A., and Lowell, E. L. *The Achievement Motive.* New York: Appleton-Century-Crofts, 1953.
10. Merton, R. K. Patterns of influence. In Lazarsfeld, P. F., and Stanton, R. N. (Eds.), *Communications Research, 1948-49.* New York: Harper, 1949.
11. Peatman, J. G. *Descriptive and Sampling Statistics.* New York: Harper, 1947.
12. Warner, W. L., Meeker, M., and Eells, K. *Social Class in America.* Chicago: Science Research Assoc., 1949.

IV

Family Interaction, Values, and Achievement*

FRED L. STRODTBECK

AT THE time when the Committee on Identification of Talent was formed and was deciding to use its resources in a search for new perspectives, the writer was engaged at Yale University in studies of family relationships and cultural values. The implications of such research for the identification of talent seemed to open a frontier area worthy of exploration. If it was to be explored, however, it could not in this instance be in terms of long-term designs. Terman had earlier, and inspiringly, demonstrated that to follow a set of young persons through a life career takes a life career. Although, like Terman, we faced the problem of relating whatever *analytic* variables we chose to work with to *outcome* variables, the requirements of the committee's program precluded the use of a longitudinal design. Indeed, in retrospect, our decision on an outcome, or criterion, variable appears to have dictated the design of much of our ensuing research.

* This chapter is based upon the "Cultural Factors in Talent Development," a project conducted under the direction of the author largely at Yale University. The contributions of Bernard C. Rosen, Florence Sultan, and Leslie L. Clark as staff members during the development of the questionnaires and procedure and the collection and analysis of data, are gratefully acknowledged. George Psathas, Robert A. Ellis, and William Vosburg conducted a number of the interviews. Margaret R. McDonald did the bulk of the computing, Marian R. Winterbottom performed the *n* Achievement scoring, and Hava Bonné Gewirtz assisted in the preparation of the manuscript. The writer wishes to express his debt to Orvill G. Brim, Jr., who, during the year before collection of the data, performed a notable job of evaluating prior work in the field, and to Florence Kluckhohn for her guidance in the area of cultural values.

The problem of a criterion necessitated the search for a way of evaluating performance in the larger community—a criterion of performance in the community as broadly understood and universally accepted as are grades in the academic community. The stubborn difficulty and appropriateness of the question "What is talent?" was for the time being only uneasily resolved. The Committee came to use the term to refer to the *exercise* of an ability in a social setting, i.e., a talented performance. Mere possession of ability was not enough; activity of social consequence was required.

In the literature on small groups it has become commonplace to speak of social *rank* in the group as being a product of activities which have been carried out in conformity with group norms (*10*, p. 140). With regard to the larger society—although it is somewhat more difficult to demonstrate in particular cases—rewards, prestige, and control of important resources also tend to be allocated in terms of the importance of the job and the length of training required to perform it. The more responsible positions in society come to be coveted, in part, because of the consensus which exists concerning their worth to the group.

Unusual attainment in community service, the professions, or business generally results in high social status. More modest advances of the order of the shift from immigrant laborer to small business operator have similar, though not identical, consequences for status. There is, of course, always some difficulty in distinguishing between status which is gained by personal effort and status which accrues from family membership. When the mobility of *groups* is under consideration, this difficulty is somewhat less serious. For example, if one of two groups who arrived in this country at about the same time has been markedly more upwardly mobile than the other, our inability to attribute the mobility exactly to the responsible generation does not prohibit comparison between the groups.

The essential strategy in such a group approach is that it enables us to utilize an indicant of performance which arises within society itself: status. The assumption is that the abilities of the more upwardly mobile groups have been used in activities of greater social consequences. To be sure, many difficulties arise, such as when one attempts to compare the work of a chemist with that of a devoted nurse; and these are not always squarely met. But so long as the values of different men, or the same men at different times, are to be reconciled, it is doubtful that any fully satisfactory criterion can be found. "Relative rise in the status structure" appears to have the advantage of being an ubiquitous measure which applies to many activities and which implies the operation of a community-wide system of evaluation. By this reasoning, at any rate, we have concluded that *status mobility* deserves serious consideration as a criterion of talented performance by groups.

This decision, made early in the research, at first seemed to create more problems than it solved. If social mobility were to be the criterion of differential talent development, how were we to get data helpful in understanding and identifying talented adolescents? Were we to be dependent in our research on the recall by adults of the attitudinal dispositions—and interpersonal relations—they believed themselves to have had as early adolescents? Time forbade our following groups of adolescents in their status climb; was there, then, an alternative to longitudinal research?

There was a chance that we could seek groups with differential mobility rates, just as Durkheim had sought groups with differential suicide rates. Although social group rates have the disadvantage of ordinarily having low predictive value for particular individuals, based as they are on the average of acts by many persons, it is nonetheless possible that theoretical understanding may be advanced by the study of factors associated with difference in group rates. For even if group predictions fall far short of the desired predictive efficiency, the mechanisms believed to differentiate between groups may later be found to differentiate between families within particular groups. Thus we should have a more crucial test of our understanding.

To illustrate, there is a popular impression that Presbyterians, Quakers, and Mormons are outstandingly industrious and successful, and they are believed to have produced a disproportionately high number of public leaders and men of science. Presbyterians historically represent the prototype of ascetic Protestantism which Weber suggests is particularly consistent with the requirements of modern capitalism. Quakers and Mormons represent, in differing degrees, slight departures from the typical ascetic Protestantism, but there are still common emphases in the teaching of all three.

From the standpoint of research design, it would be desirable to have a classification of cultural groupings such that extreme cases could be selected with markedly different achievement rates. One would hope that differences might be found among such groups—differences which would clarify understanding of the requirements for achievement in particular situations. While such a design leaves much uncontrolled, it may well be considered as a source of new hypotheses. Whatever findings result may then be verified by other means.

In New Haven, where our research was to be conducted, there were only two large ethnic groups with similar periods of residence in this country: Southern Italians and Jews. The Irish were also numerous, but they had been in New Haven for a longer period. When it became apparent that for Italians and Jews it would be possible to locate second-generation families with early-adolescent (third generation) sons in the public and parochial schools, a detailed review was made of the demographic data relating to the time of arrival, respective economic situation upon arrival, and their subsequent socio-economic attainment. The results of this inquiry (presented in Appendix A: Jewish and Italian Immigration and Subsequent Status Mobility) indicated that while Jews upon arrival had a slight advantage in terms of occupational status and urban skills, this original advantage widened appreciably during the period 1910-1940. In the United States as a whole, Jews consistently have higher occupational status than the population at large, while, in contrast, that of Italians is lower. Later in this chapter we shall see that the status differentials in New Haven in 1952 correspond to the national differentials for these two ethnic groups.

The next step was to discover what differences there might be between Italians and Jews in values, beliefs, child-training practices, family structure, etc. In deciding on research instruments and the like, three sources were of particular importance: (a) studies of religion and social activity; (b) studies of child rearing and adult character; and (c) studies of face-to-face behavior in small groups. Let us consider now in more detail what each of these can contribute to our empirical study of Italian and Jewish differences.

Belief Systems and Social Activity

The classic study of the influence of a religious ethic upon social activity is Max Weber's *The Protestant Ethic and the Spirit of Capitalism* (*44*). For the present study, Weber's argument has two implications. First, his propositions concerning Protestantism, taken together, constitute a logically closed ethical system, justifying the transformation of this world, in contrast with emphases on another. In this sense Weber's concept of the Protestant ethic may be regarded as the paradigm of an achievement ethic. Perhaps specific components of the ethic, which are differentially present in the attitudes of particular persons, might prove helpful in identifying high achievers. Secondly, since our work was to be in America, Protestantism might have an historical relevance; it was, after all, the predominant religion among those who founded this country and from whose beliefs the current American ethic should largely derive. Weber's thesis, as summarized by Parsons (*26*), consists of four main propositions:

(1) The Calvinist belief in God as absolutely transcendant and inscrutable excluded the possibility of a mystical union with the divine spirit.

(2) The Calvinist belief that the world was God's work, set in motion by decisions which last for eternity, encouraged faith in the order of nature and the development of rational science.

(3) The Calvinist belief that man was by nature sinful and that it was man's duty to labor to suppress this sinfulness led to an ascetic dedication to duty.

(4) The Calvinist belief that man was predestined to be saved or damned created an anxiety to know one's status, an anxiety which was transformed into social activity in the belief that worldly success would identify the chosen.

Taken together, these religious premises shaped both a conception of the external world and a way of relating ourself to it. It was a system in which there were no priestly intercessors; it involved a relationship between God and man so intense and exclusive as to result in both a devaluation and mistrust of human relationship.[1] Most important, there was, along with this "inner isolation of the individual," a dedication to duty from dawn to dusk which served the development of both science and early capitalism.

Before inquiring into the ways in which Southern Italians and Jews are similar to Protestants, our first question must be: are such Protestant attitudes still of superior value for success today? Do the achievers in our country—the successful scientists, the executives, the professional people—tend to believe that ours is an orderly universe whose problems can be solved? What have they substituted for the belief in a transcendental God? What is the equivalent now for the former anxiety over being saved? Let us look at some of the relevant research.

M. Stein, in a study of research chemists, reports (*38*) that the successful industrial research man is expected to be congenial, not

[1] "The net result was," as Weber puts it, "an unheard-of 'inner isolation of the individual' which placed him squarely on his own responsibility in all things, and involved a radical devaluation, not to say mistrust, of even the closest human ties. God always came first." (*26*, p. 525; see also *44*, p. 108.)

sociable, on the job; and sociable but not intimate off the job. With neither superiors, colleagues, nor subordinates must he become too involved, so long as he accords them the proper courtesy. Within the organization, he may be a lone wolf on the job only if he is very creative. Otherwise he must not be too inaccessible to others, nor too uncommunicative with his superiors; it is taken for granted that he will know his place without being either obsequious or sullenly submissive. He is expected to be sincere and purposeful in his attempt to gain a point, to get more funds, to obtain personnel; sharp, cunning deals are frowned upon as highly inappropriate. In the intellectual area he must do good work but avoid being overcritical, pedantic, or superficial in his relations to others with regard to their work. In short, what is required are disciplined, reserved, functionally specific modes of relationship.

Outside of business and engineering research, the professions afford another example of a field where great individual responsibility must be assumed after a prolonged training in a subordinate status. Not only is the individual's career worked out to assume progressively more responsibility, but the rewards which go with status are contingent upon satisfactory fulfillment of lesser assignments. It is the more experienced men who evaluate the accomplishments, as well as provide the training and assistance required. This interdependence within the professional community, as a factor controlling level of achievement, lessens as a career advances, but it never wholly stops. The successful lawyer may wish to become a judge; the physician may be promoted to the staff of the training institution operated by his hospital; and professional men everywhere continue to encounter tough problems on which they need help.

According to Warner and Abegglen (*43*), and Henry (*8*), successful executives conceive of themselves as being happy only when they are working hard. They are doers, not dreamers. They want to be sure they are not losing ground, and they gain pleasure from the prestige they have attained; but even more real for them "is the continual stimulation that derives from the pleasure of immediate accomplishment." They are active and alert—not so much physically as mentally and emotionally; they find it hard to take vacations. Far from cutting short their advancement by thinking of authority as distinctive and prohibiting, they generally view it as part of a wider and more final authority system. Thus they are free to turn to their superiors in areas where the superiors' advanced training and experience are helpful. Henry believes that the successful executive's ability to look at his superior as a symbol of his own potential achievement facilitates the interim identification essential to good work. And along with their strong self-structure and decisiveness, Henry reports that the business executives have a perpetual sense of the unattained. As he expresses it, "There is always some place to go, but no defined point at which to stop."

Concerning relations to parents, there is a slight disagreement between Henry and Warner. Henry (*8*, p. 288) feels that for executives the relation to the father is positive but non-restraining, whereas Warner (*43*, p. 103) speaks of the break of close and intimate ties with parents. In both of their accounts, the successful executive emerges, in terms of interview and projective data, as a person who has become psychologically freed of parental influence and is acting on his own. Henry draws the fine distinction that a *few* successful executives who prefer complete independence manifest a higher element of narcissism; their loyalties are only to themselves rather than to the company (in Henry's terms, an impersonal counterpart of a father-image). By implication Henry suggests that earlier identification with father images has in the typical instance generalized to more impersonal value systems. Henry's analysis makes one curious to know more about the relations between parent and child and the interpersonal relations in the family, in connection with the child's performance in non-family situations. Some steps in this direction are taken in the Italian-Jewish study.

It should be noted that the criteria for success among business men and industrial research workers alike stress some sense of isolation and self-determination, but, more important, a dedication to impersonal goals within the framework of a functioning rational bureaucracy. For the professions, the framework of control does not have the simple locus that it has in business; community roles and the evaluations of fellow-professionals are involved. Although the grid on which status at a particular time is reflected is less clearly defined, it is in no sense absent. If one were to speculate about the typical career lines of men in business, industrial research, and the professions, one would guess that they have successfully identified with parents, teachers, superiors, and finally, organizational objectives. At each transition, more diffuse relationships have been sloughed off in favor of those that are functionally specific to the job. With this progressive depersonalization of motivational goals there is possible, later in life, that sense of isolation which a Puritan might well have felt earlier and for different reasons.

While it is put forward as no more than an hypothesis based on impressions, one could say that attempts to connect interpersonal relations and achievement may be thought of as providing, in Weber's sense, *a self-contained achievement ethic* in our society. Consider first the many careers which, if pursued with the concentration necessary for achievement of the highest order, must result in interpersonal relations of lessened intimacy. Executives, for example, must maintain greater social distance if they are to retain the prerogative of shifting personnel in terms of organizational demands. Time for business, moreover, must frequently be found at the expense of time with the family. Scholarship requires a disciplined alternation of contact with colleagues and isolation. In so far as our culture teaches that depersonalization of relationships is bad, then the depersonalization involved in achievement may create anxiety. Some men will ease up to relieve the anxiety; others will find that their own interests and the expectations of others make the reversal of the depersonalizing trend difficult or impossible. The fact that status, power, and related rewards exist as positive inducements to achievement makes possible a resolution to the dilemma: the chronic achiever expiates depersonalization with more achievement. Perhaps non-achievers reduce anxiety over low achievement by the cultivation of more gratifying interpersonal relations. The average man may split the difference between the two emphases, and the neurotic will vacillate from one to the other.

In the nineteenth century there was a slightly different image of the achieving man, summarized by a reviewer of Wyllie's recent study of the "self-made man" (9):

> The "self-made man" is one who ambitiously improves his inborn aptitudes, talents, and interests by cultivating qualities of Christian piety—honesty, diligence, patience, perseverance, industry, frugality, sobriety, and will power—who is punctual, reliable, obedient, and thorough, and who, by abstaining from vices and excesses of all kinds, keeps himself physically fit, energetic, vigorous, and capable of engaging in manual labor. . . . Once he has achieved success, he will be a responsible "steward of wealth," reinvesting his fortunes in legitimate businesses and providing future generations with opportunities for attaining success.

The essential Calvinist prototype is prominent, but perhaps as a reflection of the earlier business organization of our country, individual entrepreneurial enterprise rather than large-organization achievement is implied.[2] A twentieth-century picture would accord

[2] R. Richard Wohl's analysis of Horatio Alger's heroes in his study of success ideologies (in manuscript only) provides an interesting commentary on this point. He reports that there seemed to be a recognition of the need for sponsorship, but within

skill in interpersonal relations a prominence formerly reserved for the skills in shaping materials or abstract ideas. In the Italian-Jewish comparisons, differential skill in the newer *interpersonal* requirements of modern capitalism might be found to be as much a determinant of achievement as the long diligent hours of the Puritan.

Although the Calvinist conception of a system directed by an impersonal, transcendental God has no direct survival, is there not a functional equivalent? As a man works out his career, his successive jobs become a cumulative record available for impersonal review. His particular history is distinct from the success or failure of the organizations in which he has worked. Ideally, if his career goes well, his record should show progressive increases in responsibility and salary, with shifts to higher status. Whenever a shift to a better opportunity is considered, the record is reviewed. The achiever must face the question, "Can I do the job; can I get along with this new set of superiors and subordinates?" If he fails, status in the system is sacrificed. At each "point of no return" the rising executive stands alone before this system. His punishment for failure is no delayed affair; an unwise job move or an extreme stand within the organization can produce immediate consequences. The successful executive, who has faced perhaps a dozen of these moments of decision, learns to anticipate them. His decisions, which he must face alone, are effective to the degree that they are private and well-timed.

If we take as an hypothesis that achievers in America today have an ethical orientation derived from the Protestant ethic, we make three assumptions: (1) they tend to believe that ours is an orderly universe, and that, no matter how complicated the problem, there is a combination of research and organization which will solve it; (2) they believe that one must reckon with a supra-individual system which is impersonal (though in no sense directed by a transcendental God); (3) they have hit upon ascetic dedication to work as a solution to the tension between diffuse interpersonal gratifications and the requirements for achievement. This hypothesis, which has in no sense been confirmed, gives us a working assumption. *If* these prove to be the kinds of individuals who make superior use of their abilities, *then* how does it appear they are produced?

Our concern differs from Weber's in that the orientation in question is not presumed to affect all categories of Americans equally.

---

the framework of the stories there were no regularized ways in which it might be obtained. As a result, a rescue of the boss' son from the river or some similar fortuitous incident was typically employed.

Some elements are believed to be widely held, but the particular dynamic (or neurotic?) element of substituting achievement for interpersonal gratification is believed to develop only in adult years, and only in people who have been in some sense specially prepared. Not only is it necessary that they hold certain beliefs about the nature of the external system, but the implication of performance in it for interpersonal relations may also be involved. It is in search for leads in this connection that we turn to the second set of background materials, those relating to early training as a motivational preparation for achievement.

Childhood Training and Achievement

The general importance of socialization for personality development has by now been so well documented and treated so extensively elsewhere that there is no reason to review the material here (*12, 14, 15, 18*). Specifically relevant to our research are the studies which show a positive relation between emphasis upon early mastery by children and later attitudes toward achievement. In one of these studies, folk tales were scored for evidence of success in competition with a standard of excellence. With such folk tales, G. A. Friedman has demonstrated that in a sample of eight cultures McClelland's measure of *n* Achievement imagery is directly related to early and severe child training (*24*, pp. 288-297).

In another study, Winterbottom has matched mothers' stated expectations for age of mastery with their eight- to ten-year-old children's *n* Achievement scores (*24*, pp. 297-311). In keeping with the hypothesis, children with high *n* Achievement scores were associated with mothers who had reported that they expected mastery at early ages. The relationship was particularly marked where mothers required such extra-familial skills as:

(1) That the child know his way around the city so that he can play where he wants without getting lost;
(2) That he be willing to try new things on his own without depending on his mother for help;
(3) That he do well in competition with other children; try hard to come out on top in games and sports;
(4) That he make his own friends among children his own age.

It is notable that Winterbottom's discriminating items all relate to behavior which make the child more *independent* of the family (*24*, p. 304).

Do parents who insist on such independence produce in their children the psychological feeling of "inner isolation" we have ascribed to Puritans and to achievers? On this question the evidence is mixed. Consider the following:

(a) One investigator found that for thirty college boys a conception of parents as friendly or helpful was *negatively* correlated with *n* Achievement scores. This finding was *not* confirmed on high-school boys, who were both younger and of lower socio-economic status (*24*, pp. 280-284). In so far as age and socio-economic status are confounded here, the interpretation of the two results is not clear.

(b) Clarke, Dinitz, and Dynes [3] have demonstrated that for ninety male Protestant college students, a reported lower satisfaction with family relationships is positively and significantly related to "willingness to sacrifice to attain a higher-level occupation." The questions were based upon reports of not feeling wanted, favoritism to other siblings, attachment to parents, and happiness of childhood. For sixty male non-Protestant (Catholic and Jewish) college students the relationship did not hold.

(c) Stein and Shannon (*36*) have found that more creative research chemists tend to report greater isolation from their parents in early adolescence.

(d) Robinowitz (*32*), using Q-sorts on a group of college students, concluded: "It may be inferred that students who are doubtful of their own acceptance by family and peers seem to be seeking a more secure status by means of academic (over-) achievement. . . ."

The studies mentioned above were not available at the time the present research was undertaken and therefore our results touch on the unresolved points only obliquely. The general impression to be drawn from these studies, however, is that striving for achievement is more frequently noticeable among boys who perceive their parents as reserved and their relationship with their parents as unsatisfying. Because these studies utilize the boy's own perception of his parent's behavior, it is uncertain whether the report is biased by the particular needs of the subject or whether it is, on the whole, accurately descriptive of parental behavior.

Let us go back for a moment to Winterbottom's four items of expected mastery, mentioned above (*25*). In a door-to-door survey of parents representing different educational levels and different religious or ethnic groups, McClelland and his collaborators asked for the ages at which children were expected to have mastered these items. The average ages for the various groups were as follows:

[3] An unpublished study by A. C. Clarke, S. Dinitz, and R. R. Dynes, "Levels of Aspiration, Affection and Family Types," supported by special tables prepared at the writer's request; see also 5, p. 30.

Group	*Average Expected Age for Mastery*
Jewish	6.1
Protestant	6.2
Irish Catholic	7.1
Italian Catholic	8.2

While there were only approximately forty respondents in each group, a significant difference was found between the Jewish and (Southern) Italian Catholic mothers; no significant difference between Jewish and Protestant mothers. Since the greater stress among Jewish parents on early mastery corresponds to our earlier finding that Jews have achieved more in the status hierarchy, this finding may count as a partial confirmation of our belief that early training is relevant to status mobility and, perhaps, to other forms of achievement.

As yet unpublished results of work by Child, based upon cross-cultural comparisons, suggest that achievement imagery and achievement training in a culture are related to greater needs for masculine strength and skill in the means of subsistence adopted by the culture—for example, in hunting big game.[4] In such "achievement-oriented" cultures there tends to be greater role differentiation—greater stress in childhood on achievement skills for boys and on other skills, such as obedience and nurturance, for girls. Such findings make us curious to know more about other family relationships—as between father and son, or mother and son—and their implications for the transmission of values and motives related to achievement.

These, then, are some of the empirical reasons which convince us that family behavior is related to achievement; let us pause for a moment to consider *why* this may be so. If the family is conceived as a small and relatively independent social subsystem with a culture, norms of behavior, mechanisms for reward and punishment, and a capacity for growth and change, then the roles of its members within the subsystem can be seen to have implications for attitudes toward the system outside the family group. Take school as an example of part of the external system. Although Italian and Jewish families have somewhat different attitudes about the value of education, this is a minor difference in attitude compared with their essential unanimity; all families in our culture tend to see the school

[4] Personal communication from Irvin Child to the writer, concerning results of a current cross-cultural study of role differentiation, socialization, modes of livelihood, and characteristics of folk tales.

system as a means of improving their position in the status structure, and the emphases of the schools are consistent with this ambition. Failure to achieve in school has a simultaneous negative significance both within the family and outside it. And by and large, the ability of a family to keep its son achieving in school is a reflection of the ability of the family to adjust to this aspect of the external system. Failures in external adjustments may be expected to have implications for family functioning just as failures in family functioning may be expected to have implications for external adjustments. Thus we come to the third set of background materials, the way in which role differentiation in the family and other small groups is related to adjustments inside and outside the group.

Power in the Family and Achievement

Previous research on small groups has demonstrated that experimental modifications of the power of its members affects their performance in various ways—in the extent to which they feel hostile toward a frustrating agent, in the effectiveness of their communication with one another, and in the efficient performance of various tasks (*11*). Since we have already spoken of the family as a small group, it takes no great stretch of the imagination to suppose that the way power is handled in the family will have an effect on the son's attitudes toward achievement within the family and outside it.

From previous research by Strodtbeck on the Navaho, Mormons and Texans (*39*), we know that cultures differ characteristically in the way power is apportioned among fathers, mothers, and children. It is thus possible that certain cultures may structure the power situation within the family in such a way as to make the adjustment of its sons to power situations "in life" easier and more successful. One might even predict that, if adjustment to power is a factor in achievement, then differences between Italian and Jewish families in this respect would help explain the higher achievement of the Jews. The general question is: what is the arrangement of power and support among the three roles of father, mother, and son which is maximally related to attitudes for achievement and to subsequent adjustment to success outside the family? Specifically, are there differences between Italians and Jews in the matter of allocation of power and supportiveness which are consistent with their differential achievement?

Two possible ways in which power relationships may affect a boy's subsequent achievement immediately suggest themselves.

The first involves the ease with which the son identifies with his father. Proper father-identification, which is probably related to adequate performance in the male role, could very well be facilitated or inhibited by different power relationships among father, mother, and son. The second concerns the fact that the power distribution in the family will condition the way a boy expects power to be distributed in the outside world, and that his adjustment to family power will, therefore, generalize to external systems.

Certainly there is ample evidence that variations in power structure within the family have marked effects on personality, whatever the precise mechanism finally turns out to be which mediates them. Kohn and Clausen (*17*), for example, reported a concentration among schizophrenic patients, both male and female, of family backgrounds presided over by a "mother with strong authority role—father with the weak authority role." Their comparison was based upon a set of carefully matched controls, and the patients' reports about the authority structure were corroborated by interviews with others who knew the family. The authors go on, indeed, to review a broader literature, which they find to be essentially consistent with their findings.

Or again, King and Henry (*16*) found that male subjects who described their fathers as strict disciplinarians, and as the principal disciplinarians in their families, had a cardiovascular reaction under stress similar to that of an organism mobilized and outwardly aggressive. Subjects who described their fathers as mild disciplinarians, and not the principal disciplinarians in their families, experienced a cardiovascular reaction under stress like that of a depressed organism; perhaps, as psychoanalytic theory suggests, the biological equivalent of turning aggression toward the self. Such studies as these indicate that the way power is distributed among father, mother, and son has such important effects as to make its study imperative.

This stress on the family influence, however, has tended toward a neglect of the effect of other groups. Eisenstadt (*6*, pp. 269-323) has argued ably that, in a society like our own composed of individualistic families, it is a particular function of youth groups to give adolescents an appreciation for the importance of the group as a whole. Such an appreciation may make it easier for teachers or members of a profession to relate the young people to large impersonal bureaucratic power structures in a way which goes beyond anything that experience in the family alone normally provides. If we here neglect the role of such other groups in preparing individuals for achievement, it does not mean that they are unimportant;[5] it happens that they are touched on less directly in our empirical work than the family.

Italian-Jewish Cultural Values

It is to be assumed that successive generations of Italians and Jews in this country have progressively become more acculturated and thus more like one another. For guidance in the formulation of hypotheses about the way in which value differences between these cultures may have influenced their differential achievement, one needs to turn first to the original cultures from which they emigrated. For the Southern Italian background we found some nine substantive sources (*4, 7, 21, 22, 23, 28, 29, 34, 35*), all fairly consistent. For the Jews, the relevant literature was much larger. The present account was based primarily on Zborowski and Herzog's *Life is with People* (*46*). Their treatment of *shtetl* culture—perhaps idealized—is sympathetic but sharply focused on attitudes of great relevance to contrasts between Italians and Jews.

To begin with one of the most striking differences, Jews have traditionally placed a very high value upon *education and intellectual attainment.* The Jewish parent was expected to provide as much education as the sons showed themselves capable of absorbing, but not in a ritualistic manner. Learning in the *shtetl* society gave the individual prestige, respect, authority—and the chance for a better marriage. The Jews have a folk saying that "parents will bend the sky to educate their sons." Every first-generation Jewish parent can tell heroic stories of the sacrifices made by fellow parents, both in Eastern Europe and in this country, to educate their children.

The essential nature of education is further attested by the prestige associated with "brainwork," and the corresponding lack of prestige associated with physical accomplishments. This pattern of evaluation starts early in the child's career. Traditionally, a 3- or 4-year-old starting *kheyder* (elementary religious school) was regarded as a serious student; brilliant students, though youngsters, were treated with a deference ordinarily reserved for important adults. The weight of the opinion of the young scholar is reflected

[5] See Inkeles and Levinson (*12*, pp. 998-1003) for approximately 30 references to the role of sociocultural systems in the formation of modal personality in this so-called "latency" period. These authors urge that greater attention be given to this area of inquiry.

by the fact that a bearded man would not be ashamed to bring a difficult Talmudic question to a boy of thirteen.

Religious learning and the satisfactions of family life were not in this culture separated, as they were in monastic systems. It was the custom, indeed, to arrange the young scholar's marriage while he was still in his middle teens. In order that such scholars might give more attention to their studies, many of the economic responsibilities of the family were assumed by the wife.

In Southern Italian culture, on the other hand, the traditional attitude toward education was (and is) very different. School and book-learning were alien pursuits, remote from everyday experience. Priests were taken from their families and even their villages in order to be educated. To the typical Southern Italian peasant, school was an upper-class institution and potentially a threat to his desire to retain his family about him. Although education might well serve for some as a means of social advancement, the peasant was disposed to believe that this avenue was not open to his children—in their case, education was not functional. Family life, local political power, and other objectives were stressed as alternative goals to learning.

Even in this country, the attitude of the first-generation Southern Italian was, in part, negative to education. As an Italian educator reports, "Mother believed you would go mad if you read too many books, and Father was of the opinion that too much school makes children lazy and opens the mind for unhealthy dreams." Intellectualism, in itself, was not valued in Southern Italian communities. Learned men were of another class, or, alternatively, they were men of the church. Status in the community changed slowly; property was in all cases more important than learning. Property could be accumulated faster by a trickster-trader than by a scholar (3). Scholars were like monks: good men, but not of the real world.

La famiglia in the Southern Italian culture was an inclusive social world. The basic mores of this society were primarily family mores; everyone outside the family was viewed with suspicion. Where the basic code was family solidarity, there was a strong feeling that the family should stay together—physically close together. The essence of the ethos has been most forcefully captured by Edward C. Banfield, who states the one premise from which the political orientation would seem to flow: "Choose so as to maximize the shortrun advantage of the family and assume others will do likewise." [6]

[6] An address to the Society for Social Research, June 1956.

Though the Jewish family was also traditionally a close-knit one, it was the entire Jewish *shtetl* community rather than the family which was considered the inclusive social unit and world. Relatives might be more important than friends, but all Jews were considered to be bound to each other. The primary unit, to be sure, was the family of procreation, but physical proximity was not so heavily stressed. Mandelbaum (*20*, pp. 28, 31) and Joffe (*13*) have both pointed out that the dynamics of benefice for the Jews was not in the nature of reciprocal exchange. Parents' gifts to their children were to be paralleled in the next generation. In the home, as in the community, giving must move in a descending spiral. Giving served not only to enrich the donor and succor the recipient, but also to maintain the constituency of fundamentally equal persons, and in this way, to enrich the community. The charitable contributions of American Jewish communities today owe much to this tradition.

For the Jewish parents, whose theme was so definitely "*Alles für die Kinder*", there was an emphasis upon a bettered condition in the *future* which made them willing to let children leave the community for opportunities elsewhere. For the Italians, there was less of this emphasis upon the future. The external world for the Jews was hostile, to be sure, but it was by nature solvable. For all goods there is a proper price, they say; for all labor there is a best way of doing something. For the Italian the equivalent phrasing is perhaps, "There is work which must be done." Perhaps he might go so far as to say that there are ways of doing the work which are more expeditious than others—but no matter how it is done, there is always the chance that fate will intervene. The unpredictable intervention of fate may be for good or evil, but *Destino* is omnipresent. If a man works all his life for something which *Destino* may deny him, well then, why should men look so far ahead? There is always the present, and the chance of a lucky break.

Zborowski, in his study in this country of the reactions of hospitalized Jews and Italians to pain, employs Florence Kluckhohn's well-known *time* orientation to differentiate the cultural responses (*45*). He finds that both Jews and Italians complain more about pain than do "old Americans." But, more important, sedation alone is enough to relieve the Italian; for the Jew, sedation is not enough. He continues pessimistic, concerned about the implication of the sedation for his eventual recovery. For the Italian there is a *present-oriented* apprehension of the sensation of pain; for the Jew there is a *future-oriented* anxiety concerning the symptomatic meaning of the pain. Neither group wishes to suffer alone; neither group believes it necessarily masculine to deny the existence of pain; neither group believes in suffering as an end in itself.

In the use of folk medicines and in such things as a dread of the "evil eye," Jewish and Italian cultures shared many common elements of irrationality. Religious ritual was strong in both cultures. The behavior involved in an individual's participation in his own salvation, however, deserves separate attention.

In Italian folk theology, Catholic doctrine was popularly understood as requiring sheer obedience to arbitrary prescriptions for the sake of an arbitrary reward. Where the formula did not apply, the matter was of no real significance. Faith in the mystery of the Trinity and the timely interventions of the priest were all that was required. For the Jews, religious improvement was always possible and perfection always denied. The scholar proceeded at his own rate after becoming a Rabbi. There were none to grant a learned and respected man a more advanced degree; his job was ever undone. During the middle years he might have to give more attention to business, but as he grew older he could spend his full time in discussion, study, and prayers.

In the East European *shtetl,* no man could occupy a position so humble that it could not in part be redeemed by his religious scholarship. Without that religious scholarship, a man of means alone could be *prost*—simple, common, vulgar. A diploma of any type which signified learning—even in non-religious fields—came to be accorded respect like that accorded religious scholarship. It is important to stress that if Talmudic scholarship taught precision, juridic care, and dedication, it taught also attitudes toward learning which might, with a growth of heterodoxy, be transferred to other learning. As long as the ghetto confined the Jew's area of attainment, goals of religious scholarship were highly coveted. Upon release from the ghetto, the status and financial rewards available in such disciplines as law and medicine were also attainable by work of an intellectual character similar to Talmudic scholarship. Jewish mobility has in all probability been facilitated by the transformation of a complex of behavior which had not existed for the Italians.

A peasant's mistrust of books in contrast with veneration of learning does not exist in isolation from other attitudes. Zborowski and Herzog tell us that in the *shtetl* the hair line of babies would in some instances be shaved back so that the child would have a high forehead—hence, appear intelligent. Short, thick hands were thought to be inapproriate and ugly—*prost.* The Jewish attitude toward the body was not ascetic; the body was neither ugly nor inherently evil. Rather, it was looked upon as a vessel for containing the spirit. Rest, food, and procreation on the sabbath were sanctioned, and keeping one's body at full efficiency was fully approved; but a specialized interest in physical development *per se* was improper. For the Jews the mind was the great tool—but ever under discipline and purposeful direction. In the early morning prayers, the mind is turned to sacred matters; on the Sabbath to non-business matters, etc. There is never a question of whether the mind can win over impulse.[7]

It is perhaps true that the Italian emphasis on good food and proper relaxation is superficially similar to Jewish practice—and, for that matter, to the practice in many cultures. The essential difference as we perceive it is that the Italian manual worker was never ashamed of his strength; to keep his body fit was a desirable end in itself, for it was never perceived to be in competition with other necessarily more important activities.

The contrast in child training in the old Italian and Jewish cultures may be further illustrated by data from one comparative American study which has come to our attention. Field workers from the Harvard University Laboratory of Human Development interviewed an area sample of families in greater Boston concerning methods of child-rearing. For second-generation Italians and Jews, the division of the families by social class was as follows:

	Italian	*Jewish*
Middle	7	64
Lower	36	15

As is consistent with the predicted differential status mobility, Jews are concentrated in the middle classes, Italians in the lower. Unfortunately, for purposes of comparison, this distribution does not provide many middle-class Italian or lower-class Jewish families, although the class distribution appears to be roughly "modal" for second-generation members of these two groups (see p. 159 *infra*). In an unpublished report of this work, the following points are made:[8]

(a) In the amount of time spent in taking care of the child and in affectionate interaction with it, in the warmth of the mother-child relationship, and in the amount of enjoyment derived from child-care, there is no difference be-

[7] See Charles R. Snyder's exhaustive analysis of factors that account for the low rates of inebriety among Jews *(37)*.

[8] Summarized from B. Tregoe, "An Analysis of Ethnic and Social Class Differences," unpublished manuscript.

tween the two groups. Both are relatively high in infant nurturance, save only for the greater severity of the Italian mothers in toilet training. With regard to sexual play with other children, masturbation, or nudity in the home, Italians are markedly less permissive than Jews.

(b) Italians are less permissive also of aggression toward parents, and impose more restrictions on such things as table manners, conversations with adults, being a "nice" boy or girl, being careful of the furniture, and freedom to leave home. Jewish children admit deviant behavior more frequently than Italian children and, in addition, tend to require more attention from adults.

(c) At the five-year level, both groups of children are about equally dependent, but the Jewish mother is significantly more accepting of dependent behavior. In general, the emotional atmosphere of parent-child relations is somewhat warmer in Jewish than in Italian families, although at the same time Jewish families think more highly of the benefits to be gained by spanking.

(d) Jews expect much longer school attendance, but there is less insistence on the child's doing well in school. Perhaps there is implied a disposition to permit the child to set his own level of performance.

There were some marked differences between the 64 middle-class Jewish families and the 15 lower-class Jewish families. While this latter number is small, the lower-class families were significantly more severe in weaning and toilet training, took less pleasure in caring for their babies, and were less warm and nurturant when the child was an infant. Differences between Italians and Jews are greatly attenuated when class level is constant. Since class level was not controlled in the comparisons quoted above, the exact contribution of "class" in contrast with "culture" cannot be ascertained. So, too, the marked difference in "mastery expectations," reported previously from McClelland's work, is not confirmed by the Harvard study, but this may arise simply from differences in the categories of behavior considered.

From all this material, only briefly summarized here, we had now to choose those values which appeared most likely to have accounted for the differences in occupational achievement after these two groups came to the United States. This task entailed likewise a comparison of Italian-Jewish values, with the values we used earlier to describe the Protestant ethic of achievement. Finally the problem narrowed to a comparison at five points, as follows:

(1) *Man's sense of personal responsibility in relation to the external world.* The Calvinist's world was the work of God, its mysteries profound and not to be understood by the slacker. To work to understand and transform this world was the true Christian's personal responsibility. In such a scheme, misfortunes had a definite place; they were the tests which God sets before men. Although

hard work was thus understood to be a prerequisite for all worldly accomplishment, there was still no guarantee that even a lifetime of hard work would necessarily be rewarded.

For the present-day achiever in the United States, rational mastery of the situation has taken the place of the "hard work" of the Calvinists, and the threat of almost continuous review of his record has been equated with anxiety over eventual salvation. There is no necessary personal deprivation which must be endured; indeed, one's accomplishment can be facilitated by "breaks." But the breaks are now of the individual's own making; it is a matter of being available with what is needed at the right place and at the right time. Just as the breaks are not doled out by a beneficent power, neither are failures. Whatever failure an individual has suffered could always have been foreseen and circumvented if the individual had been sufficiently alert. For the modern achiever there is no legitimate excuse for failure. His sense of personal responsibility for controlling his destiny is enormous.

Old-culture Jewish beliefs appear to be congruent in many, if not all, respects with such a belief in a rational mastery of the world. For the Jew, there was always the expectation that everything could be understood, if perhaps not controlled. Emphasis on learning as a means of control was strong. Neither religious nor secular learning, once attained (unlike the Protestant's salvation and the achiever's status), was in continual jeopardy. For men who were learned in trades but not religious scholars, the expectations of charity to others of the community who were less fortunate was a continuing goad to keep working; but if misfortune befell a former benefactor, the community understood. The sense of personal responsibility existed along with a responsibility of the community for the individual which eased somewhat the precariousness associated with "all or none" expectations of the individual.

For the Italian, there was no real logic in striving; the best-laid plans of man might twist awry. Misfortune originated "out there," out beyond the individual. *Destino* decreed whether a particular event would or would not come to pass. A sort of passive alertness was thus inculcated. Although no one knew when he might be slated for a lucky break, at the same time there was no motivation for any rational undertaking of heroic proportions; such an undertaking might be *destined* to fail.

(2) *Familism versus loyalty to a larger collectivity.* The essence of familism is an emphasis on filial obedience and parental authority. Familistic social organization tends to involve a particular locus

of activity and a hierarchy of responsibility based upon age and kinship rather than upon impersonal technical requirements. Calvinism was almost anti-familistic in its emphasis upon a first obedience to one's own soul and to God. The achiever in the United States tends, like the Calvinist, to be anti-familistic. Otherwise, the desire to keep two or more generations together would compete with the job and with educational opportunities which require residential moves. On the basis of his technical qualifications alone, the present-day achiever is ready to move with his wife and children to whatever spot offers him maximum opportunities. At the early stages of his career he may even avoid a line of work in which his father could help him, so as to win for himself the privilege of being judged for his own competence.

The old Jewish pattern sanctioned separation from the family for purposes of business and education, and there was a distinct consciousness that a man's first responsibility was toward his children. That is, obligations were primarily from those who have more to those who have less—from which, practically speaking, it followed that children need not always stay to nurture parents who might be better off than they were. Although the Jews did not go so far as the present American achiever in weakening the ties to parents, the pattern contrasts sharply with that of the Southern Italians who put loyalty upward to the extended family first.

(3) *Perfectability of man.* An aspect of Calvinism perhaps best captured for popular consumption in *Poor Richard's Almanac* by Benjamin Franklin is the insistence that at every moment of every day a man must work to improve himself. The old Jewish culture also, with its emphasis on religious scholarship and study, represented a similar belief in the responsibility for self-improvement. For the achiever in the United States, this perfectability has, in one sense, been relaxed; but insofar as it remains, it has become even more stringent. Now, we are told, the improvement should be acquired in a relaxed manner, with no apparent effort; self-improvement is something to be "enjoyed" not "endured" as earlier. But in any case, an interest in education should be (and has been) high because it is so obviously one of the ways in which man perfects himself.

For the Southern Italian there has always been considerable doubt as to whether man could perfect himself or, indeed, whether he need try. According to his interpretation of Catholicism, he must conscientiously fulfill his duties, but his "good works" do not form a rationalized system of life. Good works may be used to atone for particular sins, or, as Weber points out, stored up as a sort of insurance toward the end of one's life; but there is no need to live in every detail the ideal life, for there is always the sacrament of absolution. Furthermore, the Southern Italian sees man as living in an uneasy peace with his passions, which from time to time must be expected to break through. Man is really not perfectable—he is all too human. So he would do well not to drive himself or his mind too relentlessly in trying to reach that impossible goal, perfection.

(4) *Consciousness of the larger community.* The Calvinist's dictum that "each man is his brother's keeper" has given way in the United States to a less moralistic rationale based upon a recognition of the interdependencies in modern society. Just as the whole Jewish community could vicariously participate in the charities of its wealthiest members, there is a sense in which the strengthening of various aspects of American society is recognized as contributing to the common good.

The Jew from the older culture, enabled by his success to assume a responsibility for the community, had little choice in the matter. The social pressures were great, and they were ordinarily responded to with pride and rewarded by prominence in the community forum. The identification went beyond the extended family. The giver was not to be rewarded in kind; his reward came from community recognition. Such community identification—as contrasted with family identification—has not been highly developed among Southern Italians. Reduced sensitivity to community goals is believed to inhibit the near altruistic orientations which in adolescence and early maturity lead individuals to make prolonged personal sacrifices to enter such professions as medicine or the law.

(5) *Power relations.* Insofar as differences in status are perceived to be legitimate—because indeed the person involved *is* technically more competent—then the person in the subordinate position can still give his full commitment to organizational goals without feeling or acting as if he were being dominated by his superior. Early Calvinism laid the groundwork for such limited and specific relationships by insisting that each man had a post assigned him by God and that no one should feel inferior or superior. Today's bureaucracies create for modern achievers a greatly increased number of positions in our society where a person has a specific role to perform in a large impersonal system.

The old-culture Jew, on the other hand, did not see power in the context of some external system of pre-established impersonal relationships. He tended, like the Calvinist, to translate power questions into other terms—to the equity of a particular bargain, for example; but unlike the Calvinist, he saw these relationships always as specific, both as to persons and content, and not part of a larger system. His primary concern was to make his relationships good with others with whom he was in close contact over a particular issue. The specificity of his relations with others, including his separation of business and family matters, is also like the functional specificity of modern bureaucratic society, but again unlike it in overlooking the *system* of such functional relationships.

The old-culture Italian tended to see power entirely in immediate interpersonal terms. Power was the direct expression of who can *control* the behavior of another rather than who knows more for a job in an impersonal system. "Who's boss?" was his constant inquiry. Every relationship he turned into a "for me-against me" or "over me-under me" polarity.

The New Haven Sample

In the process of developing the sampling frame in New Haven, further data were obtained which bear upon Italian-Jewish cultural differences. A questionnaire was administered to 1151 boys between the ages of 14 and 17 (and a somewhat larger number of girls) in the New Haven public and parochial schools. Data obtained on this questionnaire were utilized primarily to identify a set of third-generation Italian and Jewish boys, who were in turn stratified by their school performance and socio-economic status. The questionnaire touched generally upon values and more particularly upon materials relating to occupational choice, parental expectations, parental control, educational aspirations, and balance of power within the family.[9]

Boys from Catholic families who reported one or more paternal and one or more maternal grandparent born in Italy were considered Italian. Boys who reported the religion of both their parents as Jewish were considered Jewish. Socio-economic status was determined from information provided by the son relating to his parents' education and his father's occupation. Classification was

[9] A more detailed form of this questionnaire has been deposited as Document number 5501 with the ADI Auxiliary Publications Project, Photoduplication Service, Library of Congress, Washington 25, D. C. A copy may be secured by citing the Document number and by remitting $2.50 for photoprints, or $1.75 for 35 mm. microfilm. Advance payment is required. Make checks or money orders payable to: Chief, Photoduplication Service, Library of Congress.

largely in terms of the seven occupational groupings listed in Chapter 3, Table 1, with education an additional criterion for some categories. In terms of these two criteria the following frequencies were obtained:

Socio-economic Status	*Italian*	*Jewish*	*Other*
High (classes 1 and 2; owners of large businesses; major and minor professionals)	8	24	52
Medium (classes 3 and 4; owners of small businesses; white-collar workers; supervisors)	80	66	213
Low (classes 5, 6, and 7; skilled workers; laborers)	182	17	455
Unclassified	15	2	59
	285	109	779

To demonstrate even more clearly the differential status distribution of the two groups, one may construct an index number using the distribution of "Others" as a base. For example, 52 out of the total 720 in column 3 (excluding the unclassified "Others") are of high socio-economic status. On a pro rata basis, 19.5 Italians of high status would be expected. Significantly fewer than this—only 8, or 41 per cent of the expected—turn up. For the Jews of high status, 310 per cent of the expected are observed. The full set of indices is as follows:

PERCENTAGE OF EXPECTATION

Socio-economic Status	*Italian*	*Jewish*
High	41	310
Middle	100	209
Low	107	25

We used the boy's achievement in school as a criterion of his own performance, just as the status of the family might be used as a criterion of the father's performance. Toward this end, each boy's performance on intelligence and achievement tests was inspected, and his grade performance in terms of the norms of the particular school predicted. When the boy's school grades exceeded the expected performance, he was considered an over-achiever; when his grades fell short, he was classified as an under-achiever. The different standards and testing systems of the various schools made it necessary to adjust slightly the degree to which the boy had to depart from expectation before he was considered an over- or under-achiever.

Being an over-achiever proved to be positively related to higher socio-economic status. This may be illustrated with the 674 "other" students for whom full information was available.

Socio-economic Status	*Percentage of Over-achievers*	
High	47%	(47)
Medium	35%	(201)
Low	27%	(426)

It thus becomes apparent that since socio-economic status is not an analytic element of central interest, provision must be made for controlling or removing its effect if other variables are to be understood. The standard procedure for making this correction is a factorial design. Forty-eight boys, according to our estimate, could be studied intensively, and they were selected from the larger frame of cases to be allocated as follows.[10]

	Italian Boys		Jewish Boys	
Socio-economic	*School Achievement*		*School Achievement*	
Status	"Over"	"Under"	"Over"	"Under"
High	4	4	4	4
Medium	4	4	4	4
Low	4	4	4	4
		Total 48		

This decision to work with a stratified sample both simplified and complicated our ensuing analysis. From the standpoint of the statistical analysis, it was possible to isolate with great precision the effects associated with each of the classificatory variables. From the standpoint of generalizing the findings to other Italians and Jews, or to other over- and under-achievers, major difficulties arose. Our sample had a disproportionately large number of higher-status Italians, and more lower-status achievers than would be expected in a probability sample, etc. In addition, the size of the sample was small—too small to enable us to weight and correct it. In short, the stratification served our theoretical curiosity about effects of

[10] In making the final selection, it was necessary in scattered instances to use families with parents who were born elsewhere, but who had come to this country as very young children. The socio-economic status classification is in all cases based upon the interviewer's notes obtained in the interviews with the parents. One Italian family was obtained from a residential community adjacent to New Haven.

combinations of classificatory factors rather than the straightforward descriptive objective of efficiently estimating parameters of incidence for particular populations. While in the present instance this decision is irrevocable, the reader should bear in mind that other investigators with different objectives might choose to select their samples in different ways. Certainly further study of some of the relationships revealed in this research would have to be examined with different types of samples.

To initiate our relations with the families, each of the 48 boys was first contacted in the school during his study period and told that he had been selected by a random process to assist with the development of a new kind of test. The "test" consisted of a set of six 8 x 10 pictures, similar in appearance to the TAT cards, designed to elicit *n* Achievement scores.[11] These pictures were presented to the boy one at a time, with instructions to make up a good story around the picture "about real people and real problems." The administration procedure adopted was comparable to what McClelland and his co-workers have described as "neutral" (*24*, pp. 100 ff.), and it was not assumed that the boy's achievement motivation was any more mobilized than it would ordinarily be in a school situation. The girl psychologist who administered the pictures was young and attractive; the atmosphere was casual and businesslike.

After the session, the boy's cooperation was sought in arranging a visit to his home at a time when it would be possible to talk with him and his parents. On that same day, a letter was sent from the principal explaining the investigation and stating a hope that the parents would cooperate.[12] The experimenter then phoned the parents and completed arrangements to visit the home. The objective of the investigation was explained to the parents as an effort to illuminate ways in which parents and sons go about making occupational decisions.

The parents were almost unanimously cooperative (as soon as they were assured that we did not have anything to sell). Our only

[11] Briefly described, the pictures are as follows: (1) boy in classroom; (2) operation in background, boy in foreground; (3) man and boy in foreground, horses in background; (4) young man in foreground, crossroads in background; (5) two male figures in workshop; and (6) boy with broom in foreground and several teen-agers in background.

[12] We wish to express our appreciation to Mr. Forrest Le Vine and Miss Florence Donohue, Hillhouse High School; Miss Mildred Feldman and Miss Marguerite Healy, Wilbur Cross High School; Mr. Thomas Flaharty, West Haven High; and the instructional staff of Notre Dame High School and North Haven Junior High School, all in greater New Haven, for facilitating our research.

refusals came from two families—one where there was illness and one in which the father would not participate.

THE EXPERIMENTAL PROCEDURE

In addition to the questionnaire administered to the boy at school, questionnaires were given to the father, mother, and son in the home. Some questions were asked of the son both in school and at home so that instances of shift in response might be checked against other family information.

The team visiting each home consisted of an experimenter and an assistant, who carried portable sound equipment. As soon as the answer sheets had been completed, the assistant compiled a set of items for discussion. These he selected, if the distribution of original responses made it possible, with an eye to making three coalitions of the following type:

(a) Mother and son agree, father disagrees;
(b) Father and mother agree, son disagrees;
(c) Father and son agree, mother disagrees.

While this collation of responses was being carried out by the assistant, the experimenter gave the family other forms to fill out and subsequently moved them into position around the recorder. He then presented the first item to the family with the following instructions:

> We've looked over your responses to the first set of items and, in many cases, all three of you answered the items in the very same way. In some cases, two of you agreed, but the third person picked a different alternative. What we would like to do is ask the three of you as a group to consider again some of these items on which the agreement was not complete. We would like you to talk over the item until you understand clearly why each person marked the item as he did. We want you to try to agree on one choice which would best represent the opinion of the family, if this is possible.

The experimenter then read the item in question saying, roughly:

> Mr. —— said ——, and Mrs. —— said, and (calling the son by his first name) said ——. Talk this over and see if it's possible to agree on one of the choices. When you are finished, call me.

As they began their discussion of the question, the experimenter handed the family a slip on which the item had been duplicated and their responses indicated. He then retired to an adjacent room where the controls for the equipment had been set up. He and the assistant did what they could to keep other children and in-laws from interrupting or overhearing the interaction of mother, father, and adolescent son. Between trials no interpretation was offered, and the experimenter tried not to engage in any very extensive discussion with members of the family.

The recorded interaction over the nine revealed differences took about forty minutes. The members of the experimental team spent, however, on the average, two and a half hours in each subject's home, and collected approximately a hundred attitudinal and informational responses from each family member in addition to the recorded sequence.

The details of the revealed-difference routine were evolved by a series of trial-and-error modifications which may be briefly described. If one contrasts conversations between husbands and wives obtained by concealed recording devices with those obtained by a recorder in full view, one finds no striking differences. Evidently (a) the importance of resolving a difference of opinion with a person with whom one had a solid relationship, and (b) the concurrent requirement of having each member act so that his behavior is consistent with the expectations developed in previous interaction, combine to give a measure which is not greatly influenced by the recording paraphernalia. At the heart of the process is the necessity for "revealing a difference," as has been most clearly demonstrated in a Cornell study by Arthur J. Vidich (*42*). Vidich attempted to have married couples discover and discuss whatever differences they might have about disposing of a legacy. In this he encountered great resistance, with a tendency for couples to be most interested in explaining their respective thinking to the experimenter instead of to one another. Vidich's experience suggests that the group cohesiveness which, when a difference is revealed, creates the motivation for interaction operates to conceal and resist differences when they arise under conditions which the group can control.

In the earlier research with married couples (*39*), we had had the subjects resolve their differences by interpretation of the behavior of three reference couples who were at all times unknown to the experimenter. The questions in the present experiment—involving father, mother, son—were less satisfactory for they dealt with abstract questions of value about which the family might reasonably believe the experimenter to have more authoritative opinions. It was for this reason, we emphasize again, that the experimenter always withdrew to another room and under no circumstances permitted himself to become engaged in the discussions.

To illustrate the experimental procedure concretely, we will quote from the discussion in one Italian home, along with scattered background information. Michael's father, a machinist who stopped attending school just before graduating from high school, conceived of himself as a strict disciplinarian.

I probably should be ashamed to say it, but up to a few months ago I used to beat him, I really let him have it. I still believe that sparing the rod spoils the child. I still do let him have it every so often. I wore out a strap on that boy. You can't overlook badness. It's got to be nipped in the bud.

In his discussion with the interviewers, Michael's father gave this picture of his own discussions with Michael:

Sometimes I feel he keeps quiet when I want him to put up an argument, especially when I look at things the wrong way; maybe I misunderstand the whole situation. I may be wrong, maybe I came home crabby, the kid may have an argument on his hands with me. He may be right; I may be wrong. Well, my tone of voice, my manner makes him keep quiet. Maybe he had all the right in the world in his argument, and he keeps quiet about the whole situation, and then he gets heck from me for not putting up an argument.

Because Michael's father considered himself somewhat of a failure in his own occupation, he was concerned that his son be "not like his old man." He particularly wanted the boy not to have to "punch a clock and work for somebody else all of his life." To correct Michael's inclination to avoid spontaneous exchanges with him, the father deliberately engaged his son in arguments, so as to "sharpen him up." The protocol of their discussion of the first revealed difference question is as follows:

Michael's Family

Experimenter: Two fathers were discussing their boys, one of whom was a brilliant student and the other a promising athlete. Some people believe that one father was more fortunate than the other father. Do you think that the father with the athletic son or the father with the studious son was more fortunate? Michael said that the father with the athletic son was the more fortunate and (the father and mother) said that the father with the brilliant son was more fortunate. We would like you to discuss this.

Father: Why do you say the ah, ah, father of an athlete? (8)[13]

Michael: Because if the son is an athlete he must be getting good marks in order to play sports. (5) He must be getting good marks (6) and—

Father: Not necessarily. (10) Not necessarily. (10)

Mother: While he's out playing, he doesn't get his studies. (5)

Father: No! (10) No! (10) That's not it either. (10) Let's look at it this way. (6) Forget about the school part. (6) Don't attach the athletic life to the school life. (6) Don't make it— Don't make it that the boy in order to be an athlete

[13] The scores in parentheses are Bales' Interaction Process categories (2).

has to have good marks. (6) We know that. (5) But take it as a kid's life; (6) as a guy's life. (6) Would you think that a guy who was a good athlete would get more out of life; (8) get ahead in life more than a kid who was smart in his studies and made every grade just like that? (5)

Michael: Well, the way you're asking the question, you're putting it a little different than the way it reads on the paper, I think. (10)

Father: No! (10) No! (10) I'm not. (10) It means the same thing. (10) It's just that I probably made it a little longer. (5)

Michael: Well, what is the last sentence on the paper exactly? (7)

Father: Look. Do you . . . (sternly) . . . ? (12) I'll read the whole thing. (6)

Michael: (Attempts to protest that rereading is not necessary.) (11)

Father: Two fathers were discussing their boys; (6) one of whom was a brilliant student and the other an athlete of great promise. (6) (continues to read question given above.)

Michael: (inaudible remark) Athletic son . . . (11)

Father: Well. (6) I think if ah, ah, my son were studious and he pursued any vocation at all, (6) Michael (6), I wouldn't worry as much as I would even if I knew he were a brilliant football player. (5) What good is that? ah (8)

Michael: Well, it's like I said before. (10) If he's good in sports, he must be good in marks. (5)

Father: Yes, Michael. (3) What good is being a football player, ah, towards helping you to become something? (8) An engineer or draftsman or something? (6) Football and baseball, there's a limit to it. (5) You've got to live with it and make something out of it. (5)

Michael: I don't know. (10) What do you think, Maw? (8)

Mother: I'd still say the studious type. (5)

Father: Try to make your son understand, Mother, that even if he were a great football or basketball player, after he's 35 or 40 he can't play any more. (4)

Mother: Play any more. (3) That's right, Michael. (5)

Father: What are you going to do then? (8) Live on your laurels? (12)

Michael: No! (3) No! (3) You'd have to quit by then (3) but I mean, I mean you'd have to have good marks before. (10)

Mother: Yes, but– (10)

Father: In other words you agree. (5) You agree you have to be studious first? (8)

All protocols were scored directly from the recordings and were not transcribed. The subsequent processing of the data may be illustrated with Michael's family's protocol. In Table 1 the number of acts by each family member is shown for each decision in each of the three coalition patterns. Previous research (*36*) leads one to expect that persons who talk most should have most power in the sense of winning the most decisions; and that an isolate role, necessitating an explanation of one's position to two others, should also increase participation.

In Michael's family, the differentiation in participation is marked, with the father accounting for more than half of the total acts originated. Even in instances where others are the isolates, he continues to dominate. To anticipate the statistical analysis, the acts originated are converted to percentage values, then transformed to angular readings in this way:

	Father	*Mother*	*Son*
Original acts	432	141	240
Percentage	53%	17%	30%
Arc sine	47	24	33

TABLE 1. ACTS BY PERSON BY DECISION FOR MICHAEL'S FAMILY

Type of Decision	Originator			Total
	Father	Mother	Son	
Fa vs. Mo-So	47 65 76	16 19 23	28 37 41	91 121 140
	188	58	106	352
Mo vs. Fa-So	39 31 52	16 16 39	17 10 43	72 57 134
	122	71	70	263
So vs. Fa-Mo	52 23 47	6 4 2	17 21 26	75 48 75
	122	12	64	198
Total	432	141	240	813

Throughout the statistical analysis and in subsequent tables, arc sine values are used to stabilize the variance.

To form a power score based upon decisions won, it is convenient to assign arbitrary scores, so that winning, or holding one's position when in the minority, is weighted more heavily when one is an isolate than when one is a member of the larger coalition. The conventions are as follows:

Nature of Decision	*Coalition Members*		*Minority Member*
Coalition Wins	1	1	0
Minority Wins	0	0	2
No Decision	.5	.5	1

In Michael's family, the resultant measure of power is markedly differentiated:

	Father	*Mother*	*Son*
Original Score	9.5	5.0	3.5
Percentage	53%	28%	19%
Arc Sine	47	32	26

and it may be noted that Michael's father, who participated most heavily, also demonstrated the highest power. Michael had the second highest participation, but ranked third in power.

Beyond sheer participation, the use of Bales' interaction process categories enables one to create indices of certain qualitative aspects of the deliberation. For example, we utilize jointly the information concerning the originator and target of each act, as well as the category in which it is placed, to form an index which reflects the tendency of a particular actor, number 1, to give positive responses to the attempts at problem solution by another actor, number 2. To arrive at such an index of supportiveness, the sum of the negative acts from person 1 to person 2 is subtracted from the sum of the positive acts and the total divided by the number of acts from person 2 to 1 in the problem-solving categories (4 to 9 in Bales' system). The resulting indices may be summarized in a matrix as follows:

From: \ To:	fa	mo	so
fa	—	–22	00
mo	03	—	07
so	–04	12	—

Inspection of the corresponding cells of the matrix provides a compressed reflection of role relations. The father balanced evenly his negative and positive remarks to the son (00), and the son was slightly more negative than positive to the father (—04). This contrasts with the mother-son relationship in which the highest positive ratios are observed (07 and 12). Between the father and mother there is an interesting asymmetry; the mother is preponderantly positive to the father (03), but the father is sharply negative to her (—22). Michael was quoted in the interviewer's notes as having made the statement, "In my family, it's my mother and I. My sister sides with my daddy." This fragment of information is in agreement with the relations reflected in the interaction process categories.[14]

The three measures, participation, power, and support, are available for each of the 48 families. Before proceeding with the analysis of these findings, however, we need to discuss how the value responses to the questionnaire were treated, so that subsequently we shall be prepared to compare values and interaction within the same family.

The V-Scale and Other Attitudinal Differences

Fifteen items were included in the original screening questionnaire. These items, adapted from research of the Harvard Seminar in Social Mobility,[15] dealt very generally with the types of value differences which have been previously described as characterizing older Italian-Jewish differences. Not all points in the value analysis were covered in the questionnaire. The analysis was completed late in the study, and the questionnaire had been the original device for selecting subjects for the study by the revealed difference technique.

In the first stage of the analysis, we were looking for items which would discriminate at the .05 level between over-achieving and under-achieving students (both Italians and Jews being excluded from this comparison). The original set of 15 items was reduced to 8 (see Table 2). Although in this process items of uneven coverage resulted, it was nonetheless apparent that these scores could be combined (1 for achievement-related responses, 0 for the alternate responses) to provide a moderately efficient discrimination of students receiving above average grades:

V-Score	*Percentage above Average*	*Number*
0	0	2
1	0	6
2	17	46
3	20	82
4	23	146
5	26	207
6	30	226
7	42	220
8	51	76

[14] For a further use of the supportiveness index see Strodtbeck *(40)*.

[15] The assistance of Florence Kluckhohn, Talcott Parsons, and Samuel A. Stouffer, joint directors of this seminar, is gratefully acknowledged.

TABLE 2. V-SCALE ITEMS, FACTOR LOADINGS AND ITALIAN-JEWISH RESPONSE LEVELS

Factor Loading			Percentage Who Disagree	
Factor I "Mastery"	Factor II "Independence of Family"	Items	Jews	Italians
.64	.00	(1) Planning only makes a person unhappy since your plans hardly ever work out anyhow.	90	62
.49	.28	(2) When a man is born, the success he's going to have is already in the cards, so he might as well accept it and not fight against it.	98	85
.58	.15	(3) Nowadays, with world conditions the way they are, the wise person lives for today and lets tomorrow take care of itself.	(80)*	(79)
.04	.60	(4) Even when teen-agers get married, their main loyalty still belongs to their fathers and mothers.	64	46
.21	.60	(5) When the time comes for a boy to take a job, he should stay near his parents, even if it means giving up a good job opportunity.	91	82
.29	.68	(6) Nothing in life is worth the sacrifice of moving away from your parents.	82	59
—.02	.28	(7) The best kind of job to have is one where you are part of an organization all working together even if you don't get individual credit.	54	28
—.05	.00	(8) It's silly for a teen-ager to put money into a car when the money could be used to get started in business or for an education.**	(65)	(63)

* The difference is not significant at the .05 level for pairs of values in parentheses; for the remaining values the differences are significant at the .05 level or greater.

** Per cent "Agree" reported for this item.

Since neither the Italians nor the Jews had been involved in the original computations, Italian-Jewish differences provide an independent check on the distribution of one type of "achievement potential" in the two populations. From inferences made on the basis of status mobility, it was predicted that Jews would have higher achievement-related responses than Italians. Table 2 shows that this prediction was significantly confirmed for six of the eight items, with no differences observed in the other two cases.

A factor analysis reveals that the first three items, relating to a rejection of fate, have a high loading on Factor I (Mastery); and that the next three items, relating to independence of family, have a high loading on Factor II. Item 7, treating of organizational versus individual credit, discriminates between Italians and Jews but is not highly related to the other alternatives. Although Item 8, dealing with postponed gratification, had, like the other seven, discriminated between over- and under-achieving students, it did not discriminate between Italians and Jews, nor did it correlate significantly with other items in the set. The third of the mastery items, Item 3, also failed to discriminate between Italians and Jews. The items dealing with control of one's destiny, separation from the family, and working for a group differentiate between Italians and Jews as predicted in the introductory ethnographic contrasts.

Our practice of using a sum of achievement-related responses of the Likert type to form the V-score would be more clearly indicated if sets of items with common loading had been segregated. While in future studies the components of the scale may be reopened and new items developed, there was no practicable alternative in the present instance to the use of the combined scores, since only eight items were available.

As to the validity of the scale so developed, three bits of evidence are relevant.

(1) The first is based upon the way the fathers responded to the V-items on the questionnaires administered in the home. One assumes that second-generation fathers of higher status have by their own work personally accounted for some appreciable part of their mobility. In terms of such an assumption, one might predict that fathers of higher status would have higher V-scores than those of lower status. These data, presented in Table 3, may be analyzed so that each effect associated with the factorial design (including status) is isolated. The form of the analysis is as follows:

Source of Variation	*Degrees of Freedom*
Corrected Sum of Squares	47
Between Groups	11
1. Linear SES	1
2. Quadratic SES	1
3. Italian (I) v Jews (J)	1
4. (O) v (U) Achievers	1
5. I v J × O v U	1
6. I v J × Linear SES	1
7. I v J × Quadratic SES	1
8. O v U × Linear SES	1
9. O v U × Quadratic SES	1
10. I v J × O v U × Linear SES	1
11. I v J × O v U × Quadratic SES	1
Residual	36

It will be our practice throughout the analysis to examine the variance associated with each degree of freedom. In this instance three significant effects are observed:

Primary Sources of Variation for Fathers' V-scores

Line 1.	Higher SES groups have higher values	$F = 10.85$ $p = < 0.01$
Line 4.	Fathers of over-achievers are higher than fathers of under-achievers	$F = 4.74$ $p = < 0.05$
Line 6.	There is a greater linear SES trend for Jews than for Italians	$F = 4.16$ $p = < 0.05$

Of primary interest is the relation between the father's class position and the V-score. This effect is significant and in keeping with the hypothesis that persons who have achieved higher status have higher V-scores. We must not, of course, lean too heavily upon this finding, because we have not demonstrated that the higher V-scores preceded the attainment of higher status; the opposite might well be the case. But if there had been no relationship, or a reversed relationship, then there would have been less ground for believing that a high V-score in high school would necessarily be associated with status mobility. The observed finding leaves open the possibility that the higher V-scores of the higher-status fathers may have been continuously operative and contributed to the status attained.

From line 6 one learns that there is a greater difference between the V-score of high-status and low-status Jewish fathers than there is between high- and low-status Italian fathers. This finding, which

TABLE 3. FATHERS' V-SCORE BY SES, ETHNICITY, OVER- AND UNDER-ACHIEVEMENT

Socio-economic Status (SES)	Italians		Jews	
	Over-Achievers	Under-Achievers	Over-Achievers	Under-Achievers
High	6	6	8	7
	6	6	8	6
	8	5	8	7
	6	7	8	7
Medium	5	6	6	8
	7	2	7	6
	8	6	8	8
	7	5	7	6
Low	5	5	5	6
	6	8	6	3
	4	5	6	4
	7	6	6	6

in itself appears to be of little consequence, serves merely to draw our attention to the fact that, save for this exception, there were *no* Italian-Jewish differences. That is, the two items—stratification by class and educational achievement of son—remove the Italian-Jewish differences found originally in the school population.

(2) From line 4 one obtains a second, slightly different, validation of the significance of the V-score: fathers of over-achievers have higher V-scores than fathers of under-achievers.

Would the same effects be present for mothers, or is the pattern of their relationship different? To conserve space, the table of actual values for mothers' V-score is omitted, and the results of an analysis of variance examined directly.

Primary Sources of Variation for Mothers' V-scores

Line 3.	Jewish mothers are higher than Italian mothers	$F = 4.46$ $p = <0.05$

In this case, mothers of higher socio-economic status are not differentiated from those of lower socio-economic status. As an after-the-fact speculation, one might say that the status of a family is primarily established by the husband's occupation; therefore there is less reason to believe that higher-status wives personally contributed by extra-familial efforts to the mobility. Hence the lack of SES effects would not controvert the finding in the case of the fathers. Equally interesting is the fact that the mothers of over-achieving boys do not show disproportionately higher V-scores. Again the mother's contribution to a highly achieving son might involve something other than parallel attitudes about the universe, family ties, work relations, and the like. The ethnic difference in the case of the mothers is not removed by the stratification; the expected cultural relationship persists: Jewish women have higher V-scores than Italian women. These data are provocative. Yet the one instance of V-score variation which goes toward validation—that is, the ethnic difference—is counterbalanced by the absence of higher V-scores for mothers of over-achievers.

(3) There remains, of course, the matter of particular interest—the sons' V-scores:

Primary Sources of Variation for Sons' V-scores

Line 4.	Over-achievers have higher V-scores than under-achievers	$F = 5.17$ $p = < 0.05$

For sons, as for fathers, there are, after stratification, no ethnic differences, but over-achieving boys are significantly higher than under-achieving boys. In so far as both Italian and Jewish boys were excluded from the sample at the time the eight items were selected, this finding constitutes, on an independent sub-population, a third instance of validation of the V-scale as a measure of values which are associated with actual achievement. When both parents are in agreement on the positive alternative of the V-score item—or other attitudinal points, for that matter—then the son may be prevented from playing the parents against each other. It is notable that instances of joint V-score agreement in the positive direction are significantly more frequent among Jewish parents than Italian parents.

Primary Sources of Variation for Joint Parental "Achievement Positive" Responses to V-items

Line 1.	Parents from higher SES groups agree more	$F = 9.78$ $p = < 0.01$
Line 3.	Jewish parents agree more than Italians	$F = 13.43$ $p = < 0.01$

Choice of occupation for the son is another point at which the value structure of the family members is obviously apparent. Data on this point were obtained from the questionnaire. All the boys in our high-school sample, as well as the parents of the 48 boys in the intensive sample, were asked whether they would be pleased or disappointed if the sons chose the following occupations (listed by status rank):

1. Doctor, advertising executive
2. Druggist, jewelry store owner
3. Bank teller, bookkeeper
4. Carpenter, auto mechanic
5. Mail carrier, bus driver
6. Night watchman, furniture mover

The results have been reported in full elsewhere (*41*). What is relevant here is that in the total sample, the slope of self-reported pleasure in the occupations by Jewish boys was significantly steeper ($p < .01$) than for Italian boys, meaning that the Jewish boys rejected the occupations of lower status more decidedly. The same result was obtained for the parents; Jewish parents rejected lower-status occupations for their sons more decidedly ($p < .05$) than Italian parents. Finally, there was more agreement among parents and sons ($p < .05$) in the Jewish than in the Italian families.

The difference in emphasis upon education also stands out. For example, the percentage of the respondents in the large sample who "want to" and "expect to" go to college is sharply differentiated between Italians and Jews; but, interestingly enough, Italians are not differentiated from "others."

SES	*Italians*	*Jews*	*Other*
High	(75%)*	83%	77%
Middle	45%	83%	51%
Low	38%	(71%)*	31%

* Values in parentheses are based on low frequencies. See p. 159 *supra*.

Some of the same factors differentiate over- and under-achievers. In cases where boys differed from their parents, the over-achieving boys preferred the higher status occupations significantly more frequently than under-achieving boys ($p < .01$). Also there was more initial consensus among the three family members over all the "revealed differences" in the families of over-achievers. In short, these data support strongly the conclusion based on V-scale results: Jews have values more likely to promote high achievement than Italians do, and there is greater agreement among family members. The additional findings agree with the V-scale also in that they show higher occupational aspiration and greater family consensus among over-achievers than among under-achievers.

n Achievement Scores

A point of articulation between the V-score and prior research arises in connection with the *n* Achievement scores. The scores for each boy in the sample, based on the presence or absence of achievement imagery in the stories written about the pictures shown him, have been analyzed in the manner illustrated with the V-scores.

Primary Sources of Variation for Sons' n Achievement Scores

Line 4.	Over-achievers have higher *n* Achievement than under-achievers	$F = 4.79$ $p =< .05$

In view of previously reported differences between Italians and Jews as to "age of mastery," the absence of an Italian-Jewish difference is surprising, notwithstanding the stratification. The small difference present, an average of 3.2 stories with *n* Achievement imagery for Italians to 3.7 for Jews, is in the expected direction but *not* significant. The difference between over-achievers (3.9) and under-achievers (3.0) *is* significant at the 0.05 level and constitutes an additional confirmation of the relationship of *n* Achievement to high-school grades (*31*).

Family Interaction and Power

Examination of the family patterns of interaction in terms of Bales' interaction process categories showed no significant relationships to socio-economic status, to ethnicity, to over- and under-achievement, to V-scores, or to *n* Achievement. Only two significant effects emerged for the supportiveness index. The first was a greater supportiveness toward their sons by Italian than by Jewish fathers. The interpretation seems to be that there was a tendency for the Italian father to look upon his son as a less mature person; hence it suggests a denial of near-adult status. Second, mothers were more supportive to fathers as the status of the fathers improved.

The point to be emphasized is the very great similarity of Italian and Jewish interaction patterns. If there has been differential achievement—and according to our data this is indeed the case—then one must conclude that ethnic differences in family interaction are not of great relevance in explaining it.

Because the use of power scores is so new, it may be useful to review a little how family discussions of revealed differences actually tended to proceed, what the resolution of such a difference means, and how we may expect Italians and Jews, or people in different status positions, to differ in this respect.

To begin with, what evidence do we have that the resolution of revealed differences is anything more than a chance phenomenon, depending on the particular turn of an argument? Can we assume that such decisions represent family characteristics? Actually, although power scores are assigned to individuals, they are more properly thought of as attributes of an individual's role in the particular group. This we see if we watch the way differences are typically resolved. The analysis is not in terms of what should be done, but rather in such cognitive terms as, "What kind of situation do we have here?" For example, we ask, "Should parents check a 14-year-old boy's homework?" The boy says, "No," and argues, "If a boy is going to college, he should know he has to do his homework." The parents say, "Yes." But it is soon apparent that they all are in agreement on the basic value: "homework must be done." Thus it becomes easy for the boy to shift his answer now that the issue is perceived differently, and there is no loss in family solidarity such as there would have been if the basic values of individual members had really differed.

There is a marked disinclination for families to recognize their differences in the abstract. The arguments soon take the form, "But, son, if you were . . ." or "If mother and I . . ." For this reason it is particularly threatening to an experimenter and awkward to the family when disagreements are squarely joined. One lower-class Italian boy, for example, put the issue boldly: "I know what you want me to agree to, but I won't do it." There were several other instances when a father-son or mother-son coalition put pressure on the third member, and the third member adamantly refused to concur. In more than two-thirds of the families these "blocked" situations were avoided entirely; and in the other families they seemed to involve points of tension which had been previously under discussion within the family. The large majority of all the decisions have a quality which our formal analysis does not communicate; they seem to be brought to the conclusion that "we really never disagreed in the first place."

Obviously, then, the resolution of differences is carried out by families in a way to reflect their consensus on basic values. The outcome of the arguments is thus not a haphazard affair, but determined by stable family characteristics. So too, as in other small groups, particular members have styles of speech which are characterized by great stability of affective tone, burst length, and the like. These styles develop, as it were, in response to the need for communication when differences arise, and they seem not to change much from problem to problem—a fact which again suggests that individual reactions represent long-established roles and mutual expectations within the family.

A more formal way of checking on this matter of basic family characteristics versus chance resolution of arguments would be by test-retest reliability. Though the data are scanty, two types of evidence are available. A recording of one case in which the father had talked more than half of the time was played back to a family, and the heavy participation of the father was so conspicuous that he was moved to say, "Jesus, I talked all of the time." One week later, a repeat session with the same family revealed that, notwithstanding the father's previous insight, his high level of participation (60% of the total) was about the same. In addition to this dramatic instance, it has been shown that participation ranks determined on the first three decisions are consistently in agreement with ranks for the last three decisions (*40*, p. 27).

If family interaction patterns do have the stability reported above, then why not just ask family members directly about their respective roles and eliminate field recordings and the like? Unfortunately such data turn out to be highly fallible. For example, sons who state that their parents "don't take a teen-ager's opinion seriously" (when asked on the questionnaire) have almost as high power scores in winning decisions as sons who believe their parents "regard a teen-ager's opinions almost as important as their own." Also, the son's observation as to whether the father's or mother's opinion is more important does not correspond closely with the experimental results, largely because the son tends to judge his parents as equal in influence, when in fact they are not.

The same tendency to consider parents equal is also present in the way boys in the total sample estimated the power distribution in their families. The results broken down for Italian-Jewish differences, are as follows:

Authority Pattern	*Italians*	*Jews*	*Others*
Fa > Mo	18%	12%	12%
Mo > Fa	13%	9%	6%
Equal	69%	79%	81%
	($n = 211$)	($n = 80$)	($n = 542$)

Note that there is no very great tendency in any of the samples to mention the father more often as more powerful, despite theoretical expectations that he will be. On the contrary, the boys show a marked tendency to say both parents are of equal authority.

Although the differences between the reports of Italian and Jewish boys do not support the ethnographic evidence for the great power of the old-culture Italian father, they do show a smaller expectation of equality between Italian parents—a fact which also is found in ratings made of Italian and Jewish families in Greater Boston by field workers from the Laboratory of Human Development. (See footnote 8, page 153.)

Finally, there is ample evidence from a number of the questionnaire items that sons from Italian homes and from homes of higher socio-economic status perceive parental power to be greater in controlling their behavior. An illustration is the item, "Is there a regular policy in your home for someone to check over your homework every day or almost every day?" The percentage answering "yes" is distributed as follows:

SES	*Italian*	*Jews*	*Other*
High	(29%)	17%	22%
Medium	23%	3%	19%
Low	16%	(0)	16%

Although the frequencies on which this table is based are small for the two values in parentheses, even for these cells the trend is unmistakable: parental control is perceived to be greater in Italian and higher-status families.

Reassured that decision-winning in family arguments should reflect stable family characteristics, and primed as to which power differences to expect, let us look at the empirical findings, presented in full in Table 4. The scores of members of the same family must total 100 (that is, before the arc sine transformation). It is, therefore, to be expected that family members' scores will not be independent but will be negatively correlated. For this reason it is desirable to look at the effects associated with all three family members at the same time.

First it may be noted that in keeping with theoretical expectations (27) (if not with the sons' perception of the situation), the power of fathers is considerably and significantly higher than the power of mothers. The power of mothers is somewhat, but not significantly, higher than that of sons.

TABLE 4. DECISION-WINNING POWER SCORE *
FOR FA-MO-SO IN 48 SAMPLE FAMILIES

	Italians						Jews					
	Over-Achievers			Under-Achievers			Over-Achievers			Under-Achievers		
SES	Fa	Mo	So	Fa	Mo	So	Fa	Mo	So	Fa	Mo	So
High	55	24	24	41	43	24	39	34	34	37	41	26
	39	39	28	35	30	40	43	33	28	45	35	24
	55	27	20	51	29	23	45	30	30	47	32	26
	48	28	28	48	30	27	46	36	22	32	37	35
Medium	33	22	48	39	28	39	33	43	28	34	46	24
	33	45	26	37	34	35	41	35	29	35	40	30
	55	16	30	43	30	32	35	35	35	31	39	36
	46	29	29	24	45	35	33	34	39	29	42	35
Low	33	39	33	48	33	22	37	41	26	35	40	30
	29	46	31	47	32	26	34	46	25	31	31	44
	27	25	51	45	30	30	45	28	32	40	30	35
	24	45	36	28	27	50	35	33	37	40	30	35

* We show the arc sine of the percentage throughout.

Family Role	*Average Power Score*	*p* value
Father	38.85	
	. . .	<.05
Mother	34.31	
		n.s.
Son	31.54	

Now let us break the scores down even further by ethnicity. In keeping with ethnographic expectations, Italian fathers are significantly higher than Italian mothers, but there is no significant difference between Jewish fathers and mothers. Jewish parents, however, are significantly higher than Jewish sons.

Family Role	*Average Power Score*			
	Italians	*p value*	Jews	*p value*
Father	40.1		37.6	
	. . .	<.05		n.s.
Mother	32.3		36.3	
		n.s.	. . .	<.05
Son	32.0		31.0	

The significant trends within the family are as follows:

Primary Sources of Variation in Family Power Scores

Fathers:	Line 1.	Fathers from higher SES groups have higher power scores	$F = 11.82$ $p = <0.01$
	Line 8.	There is a greater linear SES trend for fathers of over-achievers than for fathers of under-achievers	$F = 5.09$ $p = <0.05$
Mothers:	Line 3.	Jewish mothers have higher power scores than Italian mothers	$F = 4.19$ $p = <0.05$
Sons:	Line 1.	Sons from higher SES groups have lower power scores	$F = 6.47$ $p = <0.05$

The higher the status of the families, the less the power of the sons and the greater the power of the fathers (just as the sons had reported). The mothers' power scores do not seem to be influenced by status, but Jewish mothers have more power than Italian mothers. One significant interaction is found; namely, the trend over status is steeper for fathers of over-achievers than for fathers of under-achievers. There were no ethnic differences in fathers' and sons' power scores and no differences in the sons' power scores related to school achievement.

To test the assertions that there were more departures from equality among Italians than Jews, a coefficient was formed by squaring the mean deviations of the power scores within each family. Analysis of this measure by the standard techniques reveals:

Primary Sources of Variation for Coefficient of Dispersion of Family Power (Transformed to Rankits)

Line 3.	Power dispersion is greater in Italian than Jewish families	$F = 3.15$ $p = <0.05$

In short, our data show less equality among the family members in Italian than in Jewish families. This fact agrees with the ratings of power in Jewish-Italian families in the Greater Boston area reported earlier, as well as with the distribution of parental power as reported by Jewish and Italian boys in our own larger sample.

Although participation scores, like the other Bales categories, are not related to any of the variables in this study, they were significantly associated with power scores, as in the author's previous study of husband-wife interaction (39). The residual correlations (after effects of classificatory variables are removed) are for the father .57 ($p <.001$), for the mother .48 ($p <.01$), for the son .56 ($p <.001$). In short, he who talks most wins most.

Interrelationships Among Power, *n* Achievement, and V-Scores

The easiest interrelationships to describe, the sons' *n* Achievement scores, are not significantly related to family power or participation, nor indeed are they very extensively related to V-scores. Note the following residual correlations: *

	Son's *n* Achievement Score	
Father's V-score	.31	$p \sim .06$
Mother's V-score	—.27	
Son's V-score	—.13	

* In these and the following residual correlations, the residual variances and covariances have been used to partial out effects associated with SES, ethnicity, and over- and under-achievement.

Very likely the father's interest in controlling his children's destiny and his willingness to have his son leave home have something to do with the son's *n* Achievement; but oddly enough, the mother's V-score is almost as highly correlated with the son's *n* Achievement in the *negative* direction. This apparent inconsistency with Winterbottom's finding (*24*) that mothers who favor early independence and mastery have sons with higher *n* Achievement is probably due to the fact that the V-scale, unlike Winterbottom's socialization schedule, contains items about leaving the family. These, if accepted by the mother, might well signify a certain coldness in her which, on other grounds, we would not expect to favor the development of *n* Achievement in her son.

Family unity also contributes to son's *n* Achievement. Consensus on the revealed difference items was significantly related to son's *n* Achievement score ($r = .34$, $p < .05$) and also, not too surprisingly, with over- and under-achievement in school ($F = 10.6$, $p < .01$). The fact that the son's V-score and *n* Achievement score are not related is consistent with a large body of data showing that questionnaire measures of achievement values are unrelated to *n* Achievement scores based on fantasy (*24*). Since it was demonstrated in previous sections that both *n* Achievement and V-scores were related to over-achievement in school, their lack of interrelationship suggests that the joint use of these measures would provide a more efficient predictor of over-achievement. The matter will, of course, have to be investigated beyond the present set of data, but the distribution of over-achievers by a cross-tabulation of the measures suggests the possibility of increased prediction (see below), even though the number of cases is small and the results do not differ significantly from chance.

V-score	*n Achievement*	*Percent Over-achievers*
Above Md.	Above Md.	77% ($n = 13$)
Above Md.	Below Md.	46% ($n = 13$)
Below Md.	Above Md.	36% ($n = 11$)
Below Md.	Below Md.	36% ($n = 11$)

The residual correlations among family members' V-scores and power scores are as follows:

	V-scores	*Power Scores*
Father, mother	.21	—.46
Father, son	.02	—.62
Mother, son	.35 $p < .05$	—.28

The intercorrelations of power scores are hard to interpret because the sum of the power scores must equal a constant. Under such conditions negative correlations are expected between pairs of values, and the usual significance levels cannot be used. With these cautions in mind, it is interesing to note that there seems to be a father vs. mother-and-son type of relationship; the correlation between mother and son is less negative than in the other two cases. This suggests either, as Simmel would have predicted, that the two members of the family system with less power more frequently act in unison, or perhaps, as Parsons would have predicted, that the mother more frequently attempts to help the son in an unequal contest. The same mother-son tie appears in the significant correlation between their V-scores ($r = .35$, $p < .05$) and in the pattern of residual correlations between power and V-scores as follows:

	Father's V-score	p	Mother's V-score	p	Son's V-score	p
Father's Power	0.18		—0.36	<.05	—0.44	<.01
Mother's Power	0.06		0.46	<.01	0.31	~.06
Son's Power	—0.36	<.05	0.07		0.17	

That is, the greater the father's power, the less the mother and son subscribe to ideas about controlling destiny and the son's leaving home, and vice versa; the greater the mother's power, the higher are both her V-score and her son's. Oddly enough, the more the father subscribes to achievement values, the less his son's power appears to be—perhaps because the father is himself so energetic that the son assumes a reciprocal, passive role.

The relation between the son's own power and his V-score does not appear important; the correlation is a non-significant 0.17. Rather, it is the relation between the son's power and the balance of power between father and mother which appears to affect the son's V-score. When the mother's power and V-scores are high, the son's V-score is also high. Inspection of the data, however, suggests that an increase of the son's power over the mother while he is still subordinate to the father does not influence the V-score.

In short, the less the mother and son are dominated by the father in the power area, the greater the disposition of both to believe that the world can be rationally mastered and that a son should risk separation from his family. The son's V-score could be accounted for in two ways: by assuming he gets his ideas from his mother, since there is a positive correlation between their V-scores; by seeing in it a product of his power position. Lack of potency in the family might well lead him to infer that he could never control his destiny anywhere and that he had better stay near his parents; if he could not influence his family, how could he be sure that he could influence the larger community? Leaving the family under such conditions would be foolhardy.

These two explanations cannot be proved by the present data, but further light on the question is available from a study by M. L. Sangree (33), who, by the same methods used here, investigated *n* Achievement, V-scale, and power relations in eight middle-class and eight lower-class Japanese-American families in Chicago. She found a residual negative correlation between father's power and son's V-score ($r = -.60$, $p. < .01$) just as here; but the residual relationship between mother's and son's V-scores was *negative* ($r = -.63$, $p < .01$) instead of positive as here. Perhaps, in short, sons are more likely to get ideas about leaving the family and controlling their own destiny, not from their mothers' value system, but from a family situation in which the father has less power (whether because he is inadequate, or because the mother is stronger, or because he believes in democratic methods). The evidence is all the more impressive because the cross-check was carried out in a different language (Japanese). In addition, the strong cultural support for father dominance in Japan might have been expected to take some of the sting out of his power, leaving the son as likely to form one set of values as another. But such is not the case: father's power even here tends to make the son believe more in "fate" and less in leaving home.

Although it is difficult to fit together all the interrelationships noted in this section and unwise to generalize too much on the basis of one especially selected set of families, the best synthesis might run somewhat as follows. The son may be said to go through at least two stages of socialization critical for development of his latent potential. In the first (covering the ages of roughly 4-8) he is exposed to differing amounts of stress upon early mastery, independence, responsibility and the like. This stress, though strongly determined by the values of the mother, stems in part from the parents collectively. When the mother-child relationship is warm and the required acts of independence are slightly beyond the son's level of easy performance, then the child is exposed to the complicated system of rewards which requires him to withdraw from the intimate circle of his mother's activities in order to win the affection which is contingent upon his achievement. The strain of this relationship in which affection has become conditioned upon more mature performance has two effects. First, the more mature achievant behaviors which are rewarded are accepted into the response repertoire with a strength and resistance to extinction which may be likened to traumatic avoidance learning or, at least, the persistence of responses built by certain aperiodic conditioning schedules. Second, this substitute for direct interpersonal gratification creates a relatively greater sense of personal isolation. These tendencies combined result in behavioral dispositions which are captured as expression of *n* Achievement in projective productions and as a disposition to substitute achievant gratifications for interpersonal gratifications in later career crises.

In the second period (lasting from around 8 at least through adolescence) the son tests new limits in which the focus of socialization is not so much his within-home behavior, as it is his beyond-home behavior. Low decision-making power *in* the family, particularly when high V-score consensus of parents is not present, results in a generalization of this inadequacy to matters *outside* the family.

Such a hypothesis must be regarded as circumscribed by cultural values and as highly tentative until confirmed by further research. It is offered merely to suggest directions which such research might take.

Summary

Complicated though the task may be, we must now somehow integrate our empirical findings into the larger theoretical questions which lay behind our original research design. We started with a hypothesis about the American social system—that it contained certain inherent requirements for achievement. These requirements we suspected to have been inherited from the Protestant ethic as described by Weber, Parsons, and others; inherited, but also evolved into new forms. Then, since we could not undertake longitudinal research, we picked sub-cultures which had been conspicuously more and less successful in adapting *as groups* to the American requirements for achievement of high status. Our hope was to search their value systems and family life for clues as to why they differed in the production of achievant individuals in the United States.

It is hoped that no reader will impute an evaluative tone to our comparison of Italians and Jews—the two differentially achieving groups chosen for study. In the first place, status mobility, used as the criterion of "success" in this study, should not be perceived as the only criterion for recognizing activities of social value. There are many alternative philosophies of life which would suggest quite different criteria well worth investigation by the behavioral scientist. Our own choice rests primarily on the fact that status mobility is a societal means of evaluating people which applies to a broad range of social activities in the United States today.

In the second place, we were not primarily interested in studying these sub-cultures *per se,* with the aim of predicting which groups would show the most status mobility from now on. Rather, our interest was in the extent to which each of these "old cultures" was *initially* adaptive to the social setting as we analyzed it. There is considerable evidence in our data, in fact, to support the notion that, whatever differences in values and family interaction originally existed, they are disappearing as both groups are assimilated into American life. For example, using the Bales' categories we found no qualitative differences in family interaction between Italians and Jews and no V-score differences in our stratified sample (with effects of socio-economic status removed). Also, while Jews were more mobility-oriented in their favorable attitudes toward higher education and prestige occupations, there was no evidence that Italians differed from the rest of the population in this respect.

Finally, we know that socio-economic status affects socialization and the power balance in the family, both of which are related to subsequent achievement. But both ethnic groups are changing in socio-economic status. Let us use just one possible effect of this change as an illustration: more Jews are moving into high status where the fathers are more powerful and may therefore, according to our data, tend to produce sons who have values *less* conducive to upward mobility. On the other hand, more Italians may be moving into medium status, where family power may be more conducive to mobility than in the lower status where many of them are now. One might thus predict a reversal of past mobility rates, with a trend toward greater mobility for the Italians in the future. So, lest the analysis be misunderstood, we repeat that our interest in "old-culture" differences is not at all to predict group mobility rates, but to identify clues which might have explained initial differences in adjustment to American life.

To proceed, then, the clues we found consist of the value differences based on ethnographic evidence summarized in the introduction, and whatever further support for them we uncovered in the empirical study. Each of these value differences was selected because, in the first place, it seemed likely to promote status mobility in the United States, and not because it was necessarily the best way of comparing Italian and Jewish sub-cultures. In each case, our expectations were largely confirmed by the data. Three of the five expected value differences turned up in the V-scale, which not only differentiated Italians from Jews, but which reflected differences in *past* status mobility (as represented by higher scores for fathers with higher social status) and probable *future* status mobility (as represented by higher scores for over-achieving sons). There is, then, evidence from three sources that the following three values contained in the V-scale are important for achievement in the United States.

1. *A belief that the world is orderly and amenable to rational mastery; that, therefore, a person can and should make plans which will control his destiny (three items in the V-scale).* The contrary notion, that man is subjugated to a destiny beyond his control, probably impeded Southern Italians in their early adjustment to the United States, just as in this study it impeded boys in school or less successful fathers in their choice of occupations. Unfortunately, we cannot say with any assurance in which direction the curse worked—whether the poor performance of the Italians and of the less successful fathers or sons was the result of their belief in fate, or whether the belief in fate was the result of their poor performances. But since we do know, in the case of the Italians, that the belief was part of their earlier culture and therefore antedated their performance, we may feel justified in concluding that the belief came first so far as the adjustment of Southern Italians to the United States is concerned.

2. *A willingness to leave home to make one's way in life.* Again,

the South Italian stress on "familism," for which we found evidence in the V-scale, may well have interfered with upward mobility and contributed to the lower occupational achievement of Italians as compared with Jews. Family balance of power also affects willingness to leave home, as we shall see in a moment—a fact which demonstrates that one's position in life can produce a value disposition as well as the reverse. But whether the willingness to break up the family comes from an "old culture," from the power balance in the family, or from the father's or son's relative lack of success in job and school, it is certainly a value of importance in the achievement complex.

3. *A preference for individual rather than collective credit for work done.* Because our evidence is based upon only one item of the V-scale, it must be interpreted with caution. We have earlier argued that for achievement to arise from a heightened desire for individual credit, a certain basic competence and discipline within a larger relationship system (i.e., a profession or modern bureaucracy) is required. Familistic organization with emphasis upon collateral rewards has not historically fitted the requirements for achievement of intermediate status in the United States—particularly not as well as more individualistic orientations. Our finding that Jews are more inclined toward individual credit than Italians has positive implications for achievement, but this ethnic difference is less important to our argument than the more general emphasis that individual credit must be sought within a framework of norms which, like the Calvinist's, are pointed toward the betterment both of society and the particular actor.

Beyond the V-scale results, which are impressive because they reflect differential achievement of cultures (Jews versus Italians), of fathers (high versus low SES) and of sons (over- versus under-achievement in school), there are two facts from the larger questionnaire study which relate to a fourth expected value difference between Italians and Jews—namely, the value placed on the *perfectability of man.* The Jews definitely had higher educational and occupational expectations for their sons. Practically speaking, this would mean they believed that man could improve himself by education and that no one should readily submit to fate and accept a lower station in life, the way the Italians were prepared to do.

The fifth and final expected Italian-Jewish value difference had to do with power relationships. From ethnographic reports and other studies, we had been led to believe that Italians would be more concerned than Jews with establishing dominance in face-to-face relationships. Such indeed turned out to be the case. Both in the boys' reports of who was dominant at home and in the actual decision-winning in the homes we studied intensively, the Italians showed greater variations from equality of power than the Jews. While this finding is probably of less importance than those presented above, it nonetheless sharpens our curiosity about the effects of power balance on the son's achievement. Is it perhaps true that when relatively equalitarian relations exist in the home, the son can move to new loyalties for larger systems of relationship, such as those provided by college or a job, without an outright rupture of family controls? Is such an adjustment to new institutions outside the home harder the more the home has tended to be dominated by one parent or the other? Furthermore, what would be the cost to the son of such a rupture—both in performance and in motivation to continue on his own? One wonders, of course, whether the conflict would not be less, the frustration less, when the break came—and consequently the emotional and intellectual adjustment more efficient—if the son had come from a home where controls were already diffuse and equalitarian as they are in many situations in life? The present research involved only a single visit with the families; in subsequent research it is to be hoped that more contact can be arranged as the child is growing up. Thus one could follow the effects of a balance of power on the child's adjustment inside the family and subsequently to life outside it.

So we come back to one of the most persistent and important themes of this study: what have power and the adjustment to power to do with achievement? Let us review the steps of the argument briefly. We held that, to achieve on the American scene, one must adjust to a more or less impersonal, bureaucratic system where power lies not with the individual but with the system, and is used to reward and punish according to the way individuals live up to impersonal specialized standards of performance. In addition, we argued that the family is also a "power system" and that the son's adjustment to it should generalize to his life outside. Of course, the reverse should also be true: performance outside should generalize (at least for the fathers) to performance inside the family. Our data confirm this expectation. Fathers who have adjusted successfully to the American scene (and therefore have high SES in our terms) are significantly more powerful in their homes too. Interestingly enough, the same is not true of sons: those who have done well outside (the over-achievers) do not necessarily have more power at home. This is because the family consists of two adults whose largely complementary roles tend to create a strong coalition working on and for the child; the latter could wield influence only if both the other members were very weak or disunited. The father's occupational success is something else again. He is a key member of the parental coalition; if he fails in his function of "bringing home the bacon"—of adapting successfully outside—his power is reduced at home, too.

But to return to our main concern here—the generalization of the boy's experience with power at home to his possible future achievement—our data on this point are especially striking. They point most clearly to a link between family "democracy" (that is, a relatively powerful mother) and the V-scale. Now, since we have just shown that the V-scale contains values (belief in control of one's destiny, willingness to leave home) related to three types of achievement, we can feel justified in assuming that power balance in the family is of importance in giving a child ideas which will bear on his later success or failure. And oddly enough, it is the power balance that is correlated with the ideas and not whether those same ideas are held by the parents or not. A clear case of the children believing what the parents do and not what they say! For example, a father may have a high V-score and believe that one can control his destiny, as perhaps he himself has done in achieving a high-status occupation. But is his son likely to accept this belief if his father pushes him around all the time? Apparently not, to judge by our data. The son is more likely, at least in this stage of his life, to resign himself to the notion that there are forces beyond his control—in this instance, father.

This analysis immediately suggests the popular notion that there is alternation of generations in the production of great men in a family, or Franz Alexander's analysis of "chronic" achievers as persons who experience guilt for having usurped their father's role.[16]

[16] Franz Alexander, in the *Age of Unreason* (*1*), explains ultra-aggressive, ruthless, and belligerently self-centered personality types produced by impoverished immigrant families in terms of the failure of the parental coalition: "A common solution is that the son usurps the father's place in the mother's affection as well as in economic importance and acquires an inordinate ambition. He wants to justify all his mother's hopes and sacrifices and thus appease his guilty conscience about his father. He can do this only by becoming successful at whatever cost. Success becomes the supreme value and failure the greatest sin because it fails to justify the sacrifice of the father. In consequence of this all other defects such as insincerity in human relationships, unfairness in competition, disloyalty, disregard of others, appear comparatively slight, and the result is a ruthless careerist, obsessed by the one idea of self-promotion, a caricature of the self-made man, and a threat to Western civilization, the principle of which he has reduced to absurdity."

At least it provides a fairly solid ground for such theories to build on: father's power is *inversely* related to V-scale values. It also adds one further item to the growing body of evidence that power relations in the family are an important determinant of personality development. Finally, it provides an interesting example of how the theoretical analysis of family structure, so ably made by Parsons and Bales (27), can be tested by empirical studies of the sort reported here.

In fulfillment of our purpose to break new ground in the study of talent potential, we have focused, both theoretically and empirically, on three fairly novel aspects of the problem: *the requirements of the United States social system for success, the role of values in achievement,* and *family power* as a determinant of the child's most fundamental adjustments to life. If our preceding pages have succeeded by either means—by theoretical argument or empirical fact—in convincing people that these are problems *relevant to talent identification and worthy of further research along the same lines,* our major objective will have been reached.

On the other hand, it would be easy to exaggerate our actual accomplishment within each of these areas. There is still much to be done to satisfy our theoretical curiosity; even more to be done if the results are to have practical consequences. For example, many of the results ought to be replicated in random samples or on ones differently drawn from student, SES, and ethnic populations. The values in the V-scale could be covered with more and different items. The power balance in the family and its precise effects *over time* need to be studied to discover, among other things, *what degree* of power for the mother, in combination with what other variables, is especially conducive to achievement. A wide population of families might be initially screened for power characteristics, and then the effects of extreme power imbalances on children studied. The list of suggestions for further research could easily be extended.

But more than anything else, it is to be hoped that the present study will stimulate research on the actual types of interaction required for successful performance in different achievement-relevant contexts in society. How do successful graduate students relate to their professors? How do successful law-school graduates operate during their first year in a law office? Just what are the self-conceptions and interpersonal relations of successful physicians in a community?

Such studies would have a twofold value. They would, in the first place, provide information on whether power was distributed in the family-like systems of various occupations in ways most likely to maximize the achievement of new members. That is, as Chapter 1 points out, there are "talented" situations as well as talented individuals. Knowing as we do that certain distributions of power in the family are conducive to achievement, we might even speak of certain families as being "talented" in developing their sons—not in terms of the genes they contribute, but in terms of the way they handle power. Likewise, it may be discovered that certain distributions of power in occupational contexts have better chances of producing maximum performance from newcomers. So society may well expend some of its energy looking for the potential talent in situations as well as in persons.

In the second place, such studies in contexts for achievement will give us clues for recognizing a boy's future occupational success while he is still in the later phases of socialization and being oriented to the outer world. Is a democratic home life a good preparation for adjustment to school, perhaps not so good for the first few years as a law clerk, and again good for performances as a law partner? One obviously cannot answer such questions until one has studied the relationship of potential lawyers to others during their school years and at various other stages of their career. Only after such information is available will one know how to look at the behavior of 10- to 15-year olds, and say whether they are preparing well or ill for future success as lawyers.

These suggestions for future research are merely examples of the prospects for talent research which seem to be opened up by concentrating on such points as these: the structural requirements for achievement; values associated with achievement; power relationships in the family, in school, and in peer groups during early adolescence.

References

1. Alexander, F. *Our Age of Unreason.* Philadelphia: Lippincott, 1942.
2. Bales, R. F. *Interaction Process Analysis.* Cambridge: Addison-Wesley Press, 1950.
3. Brown, N. O. *Hermes the Thief.* Madison: Univ. of Wisconsin Press, 1947.
4. D'Alesandre, J. J. Occupational trends of Italians in New York City. *Italy American Monthly,* 1935, *2,* 11-12.
5. Dynes, R. R., Clarke, A. C., and Dinitz, S. Levels of occupational aspiration: some aspects of family experience as a variable. *Amer. sociol. Rev.,* 1956, *21,* 212-215.
6. Eisenstadt, S. N. *From Generation to Generation.* Glencoe, Illinois: Free Press, 1956.
7. Guilds' Committee for Federal Writers Publications. *The Italians of New York.* New York: Random House, 1938.
8. Henry, W. E. The business executive: the psychodynamics of a social role. *Amer. J. Sociol.,* 1949, *54,* 286-291.
9. Hinkle, Gisela J. Review of Irvin G. Wyllie's *The Self-Made Man in America: The Myth of Rags to Riches. Social Forces,* 1956, *34,* 297.
10. Homans, G. C. *The Human Group.* New York: Harcourt, Brace, 1950.
11. Horwitz, M. Psychological needs as a function of social environments. In L. D. White (ed.) *The State of Social Sciences,* Chicago: Univ. of Chicago Press, 1956, 162-183.
12. Inkeles, A., and Levinson, D. J. National Character: the study of model personality and sociocultural systems. In G. Lindzey (ed.) *Handbook of Social Psychology.* Cambridge: Addison-Wesley Press, 1954, 977-1020.
13. Joffe, N. F., The dynamics of benefice among East European Jews, *Social Forces,* 1949, *27,* 239-247.

14. Kardiner, A. *The Individual and His Society.* New York: Columbia Univ. Press, 1939.
15. Kardiner, A. and others. *The Psychological Frontiers of Society.* New York: Columbia Univ. Press, 1945.
16. King, S. H., and Henry, A. F. Aggression and cardiovascular reactions related to parental control over behavior. *J. abnorm. soc. Psychol.*, 1955, *50*, 206-210.
17. Kohn, M. L., and Clausen, J. A. Parental authority behavior and schizophrenia. *Amer. J. Orthopsychiatry*, 1956.
18. Kluckhohn, C. Culture and Behavior. In G. Lindzey (ed.) *Handbook of Social Psychology.* Cambridge: Addison-Wesley Press, 1954, 921-976.
19. Kluckhohn, F., Strodtbeck, F. L., and Roberts, J. *Variations in Value Orientations.* New York: Roe, Petersen, to be published in 1958.
20. Mandelbaum, D. G. *Change and Continuity in Jewish Life.* Glencoe, Illinois: Oscar Hillel Plotkin Library, 1955.
21. Mangione, J. *Mount Allegro.* Boston: Houghton Mifflin, 1942.
22. Mangione, J. *Reunion in Sicily.* Boston: Houghton Mifflin, 1950.
23. Mariano, J. H. *The Second Generation of Italians in New York City.* New York: Christopher, 1921.
24. McClelland, D. C., Atkinson, J. W., Clark, R. A., and Lowell, E. L. *The Achievement Motive.* New York: Appleton-Century-Crofts, 1953.
25. McClelland, D. C., Rindlisbacher, A., and deCharms, R. Religious and other sources of parental attitudes toward independence training. In D. C. McClelland (ed.), *Studies in Motivation.* New York: Appleton-Century-Crofts, 1955, 389-397.
26. Parsons, T. *The Structure of Social Action.* Glencoe, Illinois: Free Press, 1949.
27. Parsons, R., and Bales, R. F. *Family Socialization and Interacting Process.* Glencoe, Illinois: Free Press, 1955.
28. Pellegrini, A. *Immigrant's Return.* New York: Macmillan, 1951.
29. Radin, P. *The Italians of San Francisco: Their Adjustment and Acculturation.* Monographs 1 and 2, S.E.R.A. Project, Cultural Anthropology. San Francisco: 1935.
30. Reissman, L. Levels of aspiration and social class. *Amer. sociol. Rev.*, 1953, *18*, 233-242.
31. Ricciuti, H. N., and Sadacca, R. The prediction of academic grades with a projective test of achievement motivation: II. Cross-Validation at the High School Level. Princeton, N. J.: Educational Testing Service, 1955.
32. Robinowitz, R. Attributes of pupils achieving beyond their level of expectancy. *J. Personality*, 1956, *24*, 308-317.
33. Sangree, M. Lucinda. Expectations and interactions in Nisei families, unpublished Master's Thesis, University of Chicago, 1956.

34. Sangree, W., and Hybleum, M., A study of the people of Middletown of Sicilian extraction with special emphasis on the changes in their values resulting from assimilation into the Middletown community, unpublished Master's Thesis, Wesleyan Univ., 1952.
35. Sartorio, E. C. *Social and Religious Life of Italians in America.* New York: Christopher, 1918.
36. Shannon, J. Early detachment and independence in a study of creativity, unpublished manuscript, Univ. of Chicago, 1957.
37. Snyder, C. R. Culture and sobriety, *Quart. J. Studies on Alcohol,* 1955, *16,* 101-177, 263-289, 504-532; 1956, *17,* 124-143.
38. Stein, M. On the role of the industrial research chemist and its relationship to the problem of creativity, unpublished manuscript, Univ. of Chicago, 1956.
39. Strodtbeck, F. L. Husband-wife interaction over revealed differences. *Amer. sociol. Rev.,* 1951, *16,* 468-473.
40. Strodtbeck, F. L. The family as a three-person group. *Amer. sociol. Rev.,* 1954, *11,* 23-29.
41. Strodtbeck, F. L., McDonald, M. R., and Rosen, B. C. Evaluation of occupations: a step toward explaining Jewish-Italian mobility differences. *Amer. sociol. Rev.,* to be published.
42. Vidich, A. J. Methodological problems in the observations of husband-wife interaction. Unpublished manuscript, Cornell Univ., 1957.
43. Warner, W. L., and Abegglen, J. C. *Big Business Leaders in America.* New York: Harper, 1953.
44. Weber, M. *The Protestant Ethic and the Spirit of Capitalism* (translated by Talcott Parsons). New York: Scribner, 1948.
45. Zborowski, M. Cultural components in responses to pain. *J. social Issues,* 1952, *8,* 16-30.
46. Zborowski, M., and Herzog, E. *Life Is With People.* New York: International Univ. Press, 1952.

V

The Role of an "Ability" Construct in a Theory of Behavior

ALFRED L. BALDWIN

REASONS FOR A THEORETICAL ANALYSIS OF "ABILITY"

WITHIN the general framework of the activities of the Committee on the Identification of Talent, it appeared that a purely logical and theoretical analysis of the concept of ability might well prove to be as fruitful as empirical studies of various problems of talent identification. Two considerations point to the potential value of such a theoretical analysis. The first is the role which theory-building has played in the development of other applied techniques. The second is the existence of two extensive bodies of empirical research which have not yet been brought togther—i.e., research on behavior theory and research on the definition and measurement of primary abilities.

During the early development of a field, it frequently happens that practical knowledge outstrips theoretical explanation. Conant (2) has described how engineers at the time of Galileo knew many facts about pumps which no physicist could explain. They knew, for instance, that the pumps of the period could not be made to lift water more than thirty-two feet in one lift, but they did not know why. Before physics was able to make any important practical contribution to the construction of pumps, it had first to develop an explanation for the facts already known or implicitly assumed in the engineering operations of the period. Once an adequate theory was developed, then the flow of knowledge began to run from pure to applied science rather than the reverse, although at no period of scientific development is the communication entirely a one-way process.

In the development of testing techniques and the identification of talent, we have moved a long distance on the intuitions of early psychometricians like Binet and on the empirical knowledge which has developed from the numerous attempts to predict people's performance in important real-life situations by measurement of their ability and personality. The general dissatisfaction with the slow progress we are presently making in contrast with the rapid advances of thirty years ago suggests that the time may be ripe for attempts to understand the concept of ability in terms of a theory of behavior.

The value of such an attempt is even more strongly indicated when we realize how much research effort has gone into developing behavior theory, without finding an "ability" construct necessary. We have seen the emergence of such concepts as drive, habit, anticipatory goal response, and secondary reinforcement, but not "ability." At the same time a great deal of research has gone into the identification of primary abilities; sophisticated techniques have been developed for the analysis of test intercorrelations without much attempt to understand the way abilities manifest themselves in behavior. For example, how does verbal fluency result in the production of a large number of words beginning with "res" if that is what the test calls for?

For these two reasons, therefore, it seems worth while to study the relation between the concept of ability and a theory of behavior, in the hope that both behavior theory and identification of talent will profit.

Preview of the Discussion

The analysis of ability leads us back to fundamental aspects of behavior theory and will at times seem to be involved in questions which are unrelated to the identification of talent. To give the reader a road map of the discussion, here is a general outline. First, we will distinguish between actual and potential ability, merely in order to eliminate the problems of potential ability from further discussion. Next, we will consider some general problems of behavior theory. Any behavior has three aspects: the performance of an action, the production or causation of an effect on the environment, and the expression of the characteristics of the behaving person. Of these three we will be most concerned with the second, the results of action. Ability will be seen to be a characteristic of the person which permits him to behave adaptively, i.e., to cause the same result even though from time to time the circumstances vary.

We will then turn to the varieties of adaptive behavior which differ as to the process by which the adaptive result is obtained. One distinction is between guided and unguided adaptive behavior, depending upon whether or not there is feedback which keeps the behavioral sequence directed toward some fixed result. A second distinction within the class of guided behavior is between cognitively guided voluntary behavior on the one hand and behavior directly guided by feedback from the external world. We will examine the concept of ability as it relates to each of these different varieties of adaptive behavior, and then turn to the analysis of test scores into primary abilities.

Distinctions Between Actual and Potential Ability

When we speak of identifying talent, we may have two different objectives. One of these is the identification of existing talent. A concert pianist has talent in this sense. He is an accomplished musician; he has musical ability. His ability is actual. On the other hand, we may mean by identification of talent the selection of people who are potentially able and competent. A promising psychologist or a talented teen-age musician does not necessarily have the current ability, but we believe that he can become able; whereas a person without such a potential talent would not develop a high level of ability no matter what we did for him.

The potential talent may require various conditions to become actual. About this process we still know far too little, but we have evidence to demonstrate the importance of time and maturation in the realization of certain kinds of talent. We know that some sorts of ability cannot be effectively taught until after the child is mature enough. We do not know, however, the course of development of many talents. Are child prodigies most likely to be the children who can profit the most from special training? Although on the basis of general experience we suspect so, we do not know.

To become actual, potential talent generally requires special training. That is the reason it is so important to identify potential talent early; we need to know on whom to expend the training necessary to actualize talent. Other environmental factors may also be highly significant in the realization of talent. The importance of family values and other aspects of the family constellation have been discussed by Strodtbeck in the previous chapter.

The problems of identification of potential and of actual talent are quite distinct. Despite the fact that the identification of potential talent is probably more interesting and valuable, certainly more dramatic and difficult, we will limit the discussion in this chapter to the concept of actual ability. We do so because the study of actual talent is logically and strategically prior to the study of potential talent. The problem of the identification of potential talent depends in the final analysis upon an understanding of the process of development. The actualization of a potential ability can be more mundanely described as the increase of ability under the influence of time, training, and other environmental events. The problem of the identification of potential talent is, therefore, the prediction in advance of individual differences in the rate of increase of ability and the maximum attainable level of ability. The problem of talent development is to specify the conditions necessary to maximize the increase in ability and maximum level of ability for each child. At present, we tend to assume that the talented six-year-old pianist will probably become a talented adult pianist. While there is some justification for assuming that high actual talent in childhood is predictive of high potential talent, the evidence is far from conclusive. We cannot logically, therefore, approach this identification of potential talent with a theoretically based procedure of measurement until we have a theory which describes the role of ability in the behavior process and until we have some understanding of the processes of growth and learning of abilities.

These logical considerations, however valid they may be from the point of view of theory-building, should not, of course, be taken as an argument for delaying empirical research on the identification and development of potential talent until the problems of measurement of ability are solved. We must continue using our best judgment and even our intuition about identifying young people with potential talent, and trying as best we can to develop the talent that we suspect is present. It is only because the present discussion is a theoretical one that we must begin with the problem of actual ability and its identification and measurement.

In the next section, therefore, we will consider the meaning of ability in the sense of an already existing quality. In other words, we will be concerned with a theory of action or performance, not with a theory of acquisition or development. We want to know how the skilled violinist achieves a good tone and does so consistently, how he puts his fingers at the proper places on the strings and does so reliably, how his bowing varies with the demands of the music and of his interpretation but is, nevertheless, so controlled that the result is consistent rather than random.

Definition of Ability

The first step in the analysis of ability is a clear behavioral definition of the term. In most discussions of ability the term is used in two senses. The first is a basic definition: the ability of a person reflects what he "can" do. In other words, the definition of ability is reduced to the undefined term, "can." Ability is also used in a much more sophisticated way as "an ability" in the sense of a primary factor. For the moment let us remain with the first of these definitions and try to come to a better understanding of what is tacitly implied in the use of the term "ability." Later we will return to the problem of factoring the entire behavioral repertory into a set of abilities.

The first tacit assumption which seems obviously implied by the use of the term ability, or "can," is that the ability is a necessary but not sufficient condition for actual performance. There is a difference between saying that a person "*can*" run a mile in four minutes and that he "*does*" run a mile in four minutes. The ability is necessary for the performance and the performance is incontrovertible proof of the ability, but a person is not constantly doing all the things he can do. He is not continually displaying all of his abilities. Something more than ability, therefore, is required to predict actual performance.

In many cases the added requirement is a motivational one. If the person can do something and if he wants to, then he will actually do it. In other words, ability is a dispositional construct describable by an "if . . . then" statement. Such constructs are not new in behavior theory. In Hullian theory, for example, both Drive (D) and habit strength (sHr) are dispositional constructs (*4*). Habit strength, for example, describes the strength of a tendency to make a response provided the stimulus is present.

The relation between drive (D) and habit strength (sHr) in Hull's theory resembles in many ways the relation between motive and ability tacitly assumed in everyday use of the terms. The strength of the excitatory potential (sEr), according to Hull, is the product of drive and habit strength. If the drive is strong enough, the habitual response to a stimulus will occur, but if the organism is in a state of low drive, its responsiveness to stimuli will be reduced even though well-established and habitual responses to those stimuli exist.

While the relation between drive and habit resembles the relation between motive and ability, the concept of habit in Hull's theory does not correspond to our usual meaning of ability. Abilities are ordinarily defined in terms of the environmental results of behavior, not in terms of the behavior itself. We talk about a person's ability to hit a target, to make a bookcase, to solve a problem. In most studies, habit is defined in terms of the behavioral acts themselves: eyeblinks, salivation, leg lifting, and the like. If, therefore, we wish to describe abilities in terms of S-R units, we must identify responses by the results they produce.

In the next section we will turn to a general discussion of adaptive behavior and the nature of the mechanisms of adaptive behavior before returning to the problem of how to describe abilities in S-R terms.

Mechanisms of Adaptive Behavior

Three Aspects of Behavior

A performance showing ability is a controlled one that consistently produces the result required of it. The able, competent person consistently produces a certain result. Anybody may accidentally hit a nail head at 100 yards with a rifle; only a marksman can do so consistently and reliably. The marksman's performance is not limited to that object or that distance either. He can make what adjustments are necessary to hit different objects at different distances. The skillful carpenter can make a neat joint almost every time despite all sorts of minor variations in the circumstances that make the do-it-yourself tyro commit errors. Everybody on occasion saws along a line evenly, but most of us cannot do so every time. The saw wiggles, or the lumber is slightly uneven, or something happens which we do not allow for. We are at the mercy of unpredictable events; yet the cabinet maker anticipates or corrects or is unaffected by such minor crises.

We can see that ability is thus related to the results of behavior. A theory of ability is a theory of adaptive behavior and requires us to explain how a person produces a consistent result despite variation in the situation. Adaptive behavior is focused upon one aspect of behavior, its effect on the environment.

But the result of behavior is only one aspect of it. A behavioral act may be described as such, regardless of results. The person raises his hand, closes his eyes, swallows, kicks, etc. We will use the terminology that the person "*performs*" an "*act*" to describe this aspect of behavior.

We can define adaptive or result-oriented behavior as follows: *If, when a person is placed in a variety of different situations, he performs that act in each of them which produces the same result in all of them, we will say that his behavior is adaptive.* If we were to make this definition completely rigorous, we would need to add some qualifications, but for the purposes of this discussion it will suffice. Adaptive behavior is behavior oriented to the consequences of action. We will use the standard terminology—a person "*causes*" a "*result*"—to describe this aspect of his behavior.

A third aspect of any behavior is the information about the behaving person that it contains. An act which causes a benefit to another person usually, although not always, indicates that the behaver likes the person whom he benefits. We will describe this aspect of behavior by saying that it "*expresses*" a "*characteristic.*"

Each behavior then contains all three aspects. The person *performs* an *act, causes* a *result* (or several results), and *expresses* a *characteristic* (or perhaps several of them). When behavioral scientists describe behavior, they sometimes dispute about which aspect of behavior is the proper subject matter of science. Should the observer record the movements or actions as such, should he record the results or achievements of behavior, or should he record the personality traits the actions express?

No problem would arise out of these varying descriptions of behavior if it were not for the fact that the actions, effects, and personal characteristics are not in one-to-one correspondence with each other. The same action does not always cause the same effect, nor does it always express the same characteristic of the behavior. The correspondence between the effect caused and the characteristic expressed is probably closer, but it is by no means perfect.

Although, in our sense, the analysis of behavior in these terms is obvious, it is certainly not obvious where action leaves off and result begins. Actions, because they are the initial events in a causal sequence, may be thought of as a means to an end; but some results are also means to an end. To bowl a bowling ball knocks over the pins. Here the movement of the ball down the alley is certainly an environmental effect, but it is also a means to the goal of scoring a strike. Some environmental effects are described almost as if they were actions, especially when there is nearly a perfect correspondence between the action and the effect. The action of bowling is seldom performed without producing the effect of moving the ball down the alley, and there are few if any alternative actions which are used to produce that same effect. If this correspondence were perfect, there would be no theoretical objection to describing the movement of the ball as an action of the person. When the environmental effect is even closer to the action, as in billiards, we frequently do consider the movement of the cue stick as being the action of the person.

We have seen how external events are sometimes described as actions. On the opposite side of the coin, it is not obvious that a movement of a limb of the body should always be considered as an action rather than the effect of some internal action upon the body as an environmental object. When the recovering polio patient struggles to lift his leg, it certainly seems as if the leg were some heavy environmental object rather than a part of the acting organism.

The fact that actions do not always produce the same results nor express the same personal properties does not, of course, imply any fundamental indeterminism; it merely means that the action is not the sole determiner of the results. The same action in the same situation does always cause the same result. It is variation in situations which requires a person to perform different actions on different occasions if he is to produce a consistent environmental result. When a person does cause a consistent effect even though the situation differs, we have said he is behaving adaptively. Since adaptive behavior is one hallmark of "ability," we want now to see how adaptive behavior might occur.

Varieties of Adaptive Behavior

Guided versus unguided behavior. One of the major technological revolutions of recent times has been the understanding of the mechanisms by which behavior may be guided toward some predetermined result. These principles of self-guidance have been described by Wiener (8) in discussions of cybernetics. The central principle is that of negative feedback. Whenever the consequences of a behavioral act change the stimulus situation; and when there is some aspect of the stimulus situation which indicates the organism's deviation or error from the predetermined result; and when finally this stimulus indication elicits behavior which reduces the error—then we say the system shows a negative feedback and is guided toward the predetermined result.

The commonest illustration of such guided behavior is found in the thermostatic control of a heating system. The heating system raises the temperature of the house. The difference between the temperature in the house and the preset temperature setting on the thermostat determines whether the heating system is turned off or on. If the temperature is below the set value, the system is turned on or kept on; when the temperature reaches the preset value, the system is turned off. Here we see that the result of the heater's operation, the temperature, is a signal which determines whether the heater is allowed to run or not. Thus the appropriateness of the term, feedback.

A thermostat is an effective way to control the temperature, but it is not the only way. We could set the heating system so that it produced the most heat in the morning to heat up the house, the next most in the evening when the outside temperature is likely to be low, some moderate amount during the main part of the day, and relatively little during the night. Such a system would have no guidance through feedback, but it could, nevertheless, do a fair job of keeping a house comfortable. Its effectiveness would be much greater if the weather outside of the house remained reasonably constant from one day to the next. It would be a poor system if there were sudden changes in the weather, whereas the thermostatically controlled system could adjust to weather changes more effectively.

In heating systems we see, therefore, that a predetermined result is possible with both guided and unguided systems; the same is true of the behavior of people. Some adaptive behavior is guided toward the desired result through complicated systems of feedback; while other varieties seem to be fixed and predetermined but still reasonably effective. Let us look at some examples of each.

Wiener gives two instances of guided behavior (8). "If I pick up my cigar, I do not will to move any specific muscles. Indeed, in many cases, I do not know what these muscles are. What I do is turn into action a certain feedback mechanism; namely, a reflex in which the amount by which I have yet failed to pick up the cigar is turned into a new and increased order to the lagging muscles, whichever they may be. In this way a fairly uniform voluntary command will enable the same task to be performed from widely varying initial positions, and irrespective of the decrease of contraction due to fatigue of the muscles. Similarly, when I drive a car, I do not follow out a series of commands dependent simply on a mental image of the road and the task I am doing. If I find the car swerving too much to the right, that causes me to pull it to the left. This depends on the actual performance of the car, and not simply on the road; and it allows me to drive with nearly equal efficiency a light Austin or a heavy truck, without having formed separate habits for the driving of the two."

Without knowing in much more detail just what is the feedback stimulus and how it elicits the appropriate response, we cannot be sure what behavior is guided and what is not, but it seems quite likely that almost all motor skills are accomplished through guided motor behavior. The guidance in the case of planned problem-solving is much more complicated, but here, too, it is obvious that the sequence of attempts toward solution is frequently modified and guided toward the desired result by the perception of the results of one's own actions.

Piaget's observations of the development of behavior during infancy has at places pointed to very explicit guidance processes. In his description of visuo-motor prehension, Piaget describes one stage in the development when the child can reach for a visually perceived object only if his hand and the object are simultaneously in the same visual field (*5*). It seems as if the guidance is strictly visual; later, when the child can move his hand to any spot without looking at his hand, the guidance has become more subtle.

Turning now to unguided adaptive behavior, we find the most striking examples in the instinctive behavior of animals. Numerous investigators have pointed to the "rigidity" of instinctive behavior. By rigidity these investigators mean that the instinctive act is carried out even when in the present instance it is clearly not effective or adaptive. Tinbergen describes how a gull will retrieve an egg that is removed from the nest to the ground nearby. The gull straddles the egg, puts her beak on the far side of it, and backs into the nest rolling the egg along the ground. The unguided character of the behavior is made dramatically evident if the experimenter removes the egg after the gull has begun to retrieve it. The gull does not discontinue the instinctive behavior but follows it through to the bitter end, backing into the nest rolling a non-existent egg (*7*). The behavior pattern is elicited by the appropriate stimulus and is carried through automatically even when the need for it is no longer present and it is no longer appropriate. Nevertheless, such behavior is generally appropriate in the natural habitat and is, on the average, adaptive.

In human behavior automatized habits are not infrequently unguided in that they are automatically elicited and carried out rigidly. William James describes the absent-minded professor who starts to change his clothes for dinner and ends up in his pajamas (*4*). The habitual sequence of actions is carried through even though it is not adaptive in the present instance. On the average, of course, such habitual behavior is adapative; most of the time when we take off our clothes we are going to bed.

Perhaps it is in social behavior that unguided behavior is most frequently adaptive. Consider, for example, the process by which distress elicits sympathy and help. The lost child crying bitterly is behaving in a fixed way. His unhappiness and anxiety lead to tears. His is not guided behavior—he cries just as bitterly when nobody is looking as when help is at hand. The tears serve, however, to bring assistance. His unhappiness elicits sympathy and nurturance in some onlooker, who helps the child find his way home. In this case, the actual lack of guidance is an important aspect of the behavior's effectiveness. If we see the child stop crying when nobody looks, we immediately suspect him of histrionics; we doubt the validity of his distress, and we are less likely to proffer help.

Because of the fact that the same action may have both immediate and remote results, it is possible that behavior which is guided toward some immediate result may at the same time produce a remote adaptive result toward which it is not guided. For example, a person who is easily motivated to be nurturant toward others may, in a variety of situations, help people in trouble. He may give money to a beggar; he may contribute to the Red Cross; he may vote for social security; he may take in lost dogs. Each of these actions is in itself guided toward some immediate result; the remote result, however, may well be to earn him a reputation for kindness and generosity and to generate in others friendliness and gratitude. Here, as in the previous example, it is important for the behavior not to appear to be guided toward the achievement of a good reputation. If that seems to be the intention of the kind action, the remote effect is less surely achieved.

Everyday behavior contains many complex mixtures of guided and unguided adaptive behavior. When the child sees his ball bounce out of sight around a corner, he runs after it. As far as going around the corner is concerned, his behavior is guided, but until he actually sees the ball, the behavior is not guided by stimuli from the ball. If the ball were to be spirited away by some diabolical experimenter, the child would carry out his behavioral act regardless of its unadaptiveness in the present situation. Here, again, we have the behavioral act being guided by one of its results but accomplishing another adaptive result.

In everyday language, however, this last example is quite different from the previous one where the man achieved a reputation for kindness through performing many kind acts. The child's intention in going around the corner was to obtain the ball. The guided behavior was instigated by the presumed presence of the ball. The kind gentleman's benevolences were instigated by the troubles of other people, not by the fact that a fine reputation would be so achieved.

To distinguish between these two examples of adaptive behavior requires a still further differentiation, viz., between cognitively guided behavior and directly or simply guided action. This distinction will be the topic of the next section.

Cognitively guided versus simply guided behavior. This second distinction among the varieties of adaptive behavior is within the class of guided behavior. Any guided behavior can be thought of as a sequence of acts, each of which is determined by the consequences of the previous one. In some cases these component acts are each independent and voluntary, and the organization of the sequence is under intellectual cognitive control. This we will call cognitively guided behavior. In other cases—which can be described as *directly* guided—the entire sequence of guided behavior functions as a unit and the individual components of it are neither independent nor voluntary.

It is clear how, according to this formulation, there is a close relation between voluntary action and cognitive guidance. When the component acts are voluntary, their control and direction are cognitive. What, however, is a voluntary act? The term suggests free will and indeterminism, but it need not do so. Voluntary acts are characterized by two properties: (1) voluntary acts are independent of their goals; (2) voluntary acts are independent of each other.

Independence of acts and goals. One essential feature of voluntary behavior is the independence of the act from its motivation. We assume that each person has a repertory of voluntary acts, which he can use in a wide variety of circumstances and under a wide variety of motivations. He can walk for fun, to get to a place he wants to be, to escape from danger, to show somebody else how to walk, or to exhibit some feature of his gait. A voluntary act is usable in the service of any motive, as a means to any goal, or it may be consummatory behavior.

Let us contrast a voluntary action like walking, closing the hand, lifting the arm, or kicking, with a less voluntary action like crying. We can walk whenever we see that walking is a means to a goal or desirable for any other reason. We cannot cry except when certain feelings or motives are present. A few people, of course—actors among them—can cry voluntarily, that is, they can cry when they do not feel like crying; but for most of us crying cannot be turned off and on at will.

If we consider that a person may have any one of a series of motives and that he has a repertory of voluntary actions, then the important feature of the voluntary system is that any action may occur under any of the possible motives. In other words, in voluntary behavior motivation and action are independent of each other.

This assumption of independence does not mean that in any particular situation a particular action may not be prescribed by a particular goal. If the only way to get money out of the bank is to write a check, then the motive determines the action in that situation. But it is the situation, not the person, which is the source of the restraint. If writing a check is a voluntary act, then in other situations the person can write a check for entirely different reasons; if a different act were established as the means of obtaining one's money from the bank, he could use that act to achieve the same goal.

Independence of voluntary acts from each other. Independence of actions and motives is one characteristic of voluntary action; the independence of two voluntary actions from each other is a second. Voluntary actions may be performed in any sequence. Because writing each letter is a voluntary action (although it may also be part of a larger act as well), we can write C-A-T or A-C-T or T-A-C, one as readily as the other. We can first walk forward and then to the left, or first left and then forward.

Not only may any two voluntary actions be arranged in any sequence, they may be combined into a single action—subject only to the restraints of the external situation. I can extend my arm and open my hand; I can extend my arm and close my hand; I can flex my arm and open my hand; I can flex my arm and close my hand. Closing and opening the hand may be combined with flexing and extending the arm in any way that is suitable to the demands of the occasion. There are, of course, some external limitations on the combination of actions, because two actions like raising and lowering the arm at the same time may be physically incompatible.

When we contrast other sorts of motor skill where the component acts are not voluntary, we can see that the sequence is less flexible. A tennis stroke is a voluntary action, taken as a whole, but the component acts are not. We do not even know what are the exact acts in a tennis stroke. One cannot perform the middle of a stroke independently of the beginning and end with any feeling that the act is the same, in or out of the stroke. We cannot perform the acts of a tennis stroke in reverse order as we can count backwards or retrace our steps back along a pathway. There are many guided actions composed of component movements in which the particular movements vary with the circumstances but in which the individual movements are not independent of each other and cannot be shuffled around in any desired order. This does not mean that they are fixed and rigid, either. The details of a tennis stroke differ from one stroke to another; they depend upon the bounce of the ball, the place where the ball is intended to hit the opposite court, and the direction from which it is approached. All these movements are obviously guided in some complex way to suit the particular situation, but they are not independent units like the words which compose a message or the moves in a chess game.

We have distinguished between guided behavior where the components acts are voluntary and behavior where the individual components are not independent units. Sometimes, of course, the individual units of a cognitive guided sequence of actions are themselves directly guided behavior sequences. The illustration of a chess game is apt. Each move is a bit of guided behavior, moving the piece to a predetermined position. Each move is a voluntary action, taken as a whole, and the sequence of moves is cognitively guided toward checkmating the opponent's king.

Let us pause for a moment to take stock. We have moved ahead in advance of any supporting argument. First, we have defined voluntary behavior in the sense of pointing out certain of its objective properties. If it is a good definition, it should appear plausible to the reader; but, more important, it should have fruitful implications. No one can defend a definition much beyond that.

In addition, we have said that voluntary behavior is cognitively guided rather than directly guided. What are the criteria for these two forms of guidance? Although we cannot, as yet, make these definitions as precise or operational as they should be, we can examine illustrations of the behavioral differences for which we are trying to account.

In visually guided prehension, the distance between the object and the hand could be the feedback stimulus. The organism moves to reduce that distance at every point. We do not know whether this distance is actually the feedback in the usual act of reaching. Probably it is not, but it may be a fair description of the prehension of the young infant or the patient with no proprioceptive feedback. At any rate, this instance would be directly guided behavior.

In guided locomotion to an object not immediately perceivable, the situation is quite different. There is here no actual stimulus from the object which can serve as a feedback stimulus. There is feedback, but it is extremely complex. As the individual moves toward the place where he thinks the object is located, he is continually guided by various landmarks. Although these change from one point to another, the total information from the external world guides the individual where he wants to go. Let us call this behavior "cognitively guided."

Why do we say that such guidance is *cognitive?* The main reason is that perception and cognition are the concepts in behavioral science which are primarily concerned with the interpretation of such complex stimulus inputs and the construction of a representation of the environment on the basis of that input. If we assume that in the mediation of cognitively guided behavior there is a cognitive representation of the person himself and the goal object located in a representation of his environment, then this representation could serve as the guiding stimulus to an individual's behavior. The distance between himself and the goal object in his cognitive map could operate as did the perceived distance between his hand and the object in directly guided visuo-motor prehension. Granted, such a formulation as this solves no problem; it merely passes the buck to research workers in the field of cognition. The distinction between directly guided and cognitively guided behavior becomes identical with the distinction between direct responses to stimuli and responses which are elicited by some mediating stimulus-producing response.

Cognitive representations are not always elicited by stimuli from the external objects represented. Cognitive maps, constructed on the basis of external stimulation, frequently contain representations of aspects of the environment which are not immediately perceptible, like the cognition of the ball that bounced out of sight around the corner. Thus they can guide behavior toward objects which offer no direct guiding stimulus.

A second example of behavior guided by cognition in the absence of direct feedback is a voluntary action carried out in pretense. It seems as if the cognitive representation of the act can guide it even though the stimuli which usually are the bases of that cognition are not present. To pretend to write—when there is no pencil and no paper—might be possible if there were a cognitive representation of the act of writing. Because subjectively we know what it feels like to write our names, we can carry out the action on the basis of proprioceptive feedback alone. Thus, it would seem a likely hypothesis that carrying out such an act in pretense requires a cognitive representation of the act. We know that some brain-injured patients cannot pretend to act, even though in a natural setting they are quite capable of carrying out the action in question. There are, also, certain acts which few of us can carry out in pretense. It is difficult to go through the motions of buttoning a button or tying shoe strings without direct sensory feedback. Other acts like the coordination of clutch and accelerator in an automobile can be carried out only in rough approximation unless the two pedals are actually there. The individual components are not cognitively represented or cognitively guided.

In summary, we have distinguished three varieties of adaptive behavior; cognitively guided, directly guided, and unguided. We have stated the hypothesis that, when voluntary acts are integrated into adaptive behavior, they are cognitively guided. Let us return now at long last to the problem of ability.

The Implications of Adaptive Behavior for Description of Ability

We have argued that ability is a meaningful concept only because it describes the characteristics of a person which contribute to his carrying out adaptive behavior. Since adaptive behavior is described by the consistent invariant result it produces, it might appear that abilities should be described safely in terms of the results which an individual accomplishes.

This implication is not required, however, and we shall see that the most fruitful definition of ability does more than merely specify the result. In the first place, the ability should be a property of the person alone; we want to describe a person by describing his ability. While ability may change, it would be convenient if it did not change as the person moves from one situation to another. We would like to measure swimming ability in such a way that it is the same whether the person is successfully crossing a pool, barely keeping afloat in a storm, or struggling hopelessly in a torrent. In short, we would like the ability to be independent of the difficulty of the particular situation in which that ability is being tested. Yet it is obvious that the result of behavior is not the same in the three situations of different difficulty.

In other words, a person's success or failure at achieving the adaptive result is partly dependent upon his ability and partly upon the demands of the particular situation. In everyday language we tacitly assume a model which postulates two factors: the ability of the person and the difficulty of the situation. The ability of the person remains constant as he moves from one situation to another, and the difficulty of the task remains the same whether it is being coped with by an able person or is overpowering a weak person. The success depends upon the relative value of the ability of the person and the difficulty of the task. If the ability is greater than the difficulty, the person succeeds; if the reverse is true, he fails.

Another way of describing this problem is to recognize that adaptive behavior is not an all-or-none phenomenon. The fact a person can achieve a certain result in a variety of situations does not mean that he can achieve it in every possible situation. While we wish to describe ability so that it accounts for the fact of adaptive behavior, we must recognize that there are limits to ability and that in some situations a person may not achieve the adaptive result.

For a variety of reasons, we tend to think of ability as a one-dimensional description. We speak of batting ability, or tennis ability, or problem-solving ability as if the only difference between the abilities of people was quantitative not qualitative. Probably because past experience develops a system of responses that encompasses a variety of different situations, we may find that the most obvious differences among people is the total number of situations in which they can succeed, and that people of the same ability can succeed at exactly the same tasks. Still we know that there are qualitative differences as well as quantitative. The public may describe a batter in terms of his total batting average, but pitchers know that one batter is a sucker for a low outside ball while another has more trouble with a change of pace.

If we listed for each member of a population all of the situations in which he could achieve a specified adaptive result, we would not find that they made a perfect scale in the Guttman sense (*6*). For some skills, however, we would find that one factor was accounting for a great deal of variability. This is the problem which the factor analysts have worked on so assiduously.

From a purely descriptive point of view, an ability is a system of acts. The different members of this system correspond to the different situations in which the person can cause a particular effect. The invariant feature of such a system is the consistent effect produced by each action.

This definition is extensional, a mere listing of the acts involved in a particular kind of adaptive behavior. It is like defining the strength of a tea cup by listing all the events that do not break it. In the case of tea cups we can do much better than this; we can recognize the equivalence of all events which involve hitting the tea cup with a certain impact and we can scale the impacts so that the strength may be approximately described by a single figure, the maximum impact which does not break the cup.

In behavioral science we are still primitive. We know the sharpshooting ability of a person if we know under which conditions he can hit the target and under which he cannot. Comparing this set of situations among different people, we may find that one or more dimensions are necessary to describe the differences among them. When we have analyzed these individual differences, we may describe them and predict the success of each person in each situation by specifying, first, his ability or abilities, and, second, the difficulty or difficulties of the situations. If the ability is greater than the difficulty, the person succeeds. We will see later that this approach to the description of abilities is not the same as that of the usual factor analysis, although it deals with the same essential problem.

Before getting into the various issues of factor analysis, however, let us look at some of the different problems which the different varieties of adaptive behavior pose for a theory of ability.

Description of Abilities Underlying Cognitively Guided Behavior

We have laid out a program for specifying the abilities underlying some piece of adaptive behavior. Let us consider it concretely for an example of cognitively guided behavior. If a man wants to build a house, there is an amazing confusion of alternative ways of accomplishing such an end. He may construct it himself by hand; he may buy it prefabricated and put it together; he may do the contracting but hire the labor; he may hire a contractor and architect and go to Florida while they supervise the building. If as the first step in describing "house-building ability" we tried to list the variety of situations in which a person would succeed in getting a house built, we would find such a wealth of qualitative differences that we would have no feeling of confidence that two people who faced the same situation and who succeeded had, in fact, employed the same abilities. In other words, there is no hope of finding a single dimension in this set of responses.

All of the examples described in the previous section were relatively simple, directly guided behavior sequences. In each case we tacitly assumed that the same situation posed the same problem to each person who tried to accomplish the same result. The qualitative differences among people could account for the fact that certain situations were easy for some people and difficult for others, but there was no provision for describing alternative ways of meeting the same situation.

Cognitively guided behavior, on the other hand, because it is composed of independent voluntary acts, abounds with examples of alternative means to the same end from the same beginning point. Furthermore, the same act or behavioral sequence may be used to cause very different adaptive results, with essentially the same effectiveness. In fact, the essential feature of cognitively guided behavior is the fact that the person's repertory of voluntary acts and behavioral sequences may be rearranged in various orders or combinations and used to cause any result. It seems clear, therefore, that any attempt to try to label the person's abilities by specifying what results he attains is sure to be misleading if he achieves these results by cognitively guided behavior.

Instead, the description of the abilities involved in cognitively guided behavior might well be approached from two directions. First, there are the voluntary actions which are combined into cognitively guided behavior. Each of these acts may be merely an act or it may itself be a system of directly guided behavior. It is "elemental" in the sense that its components are not separable and independent of each other. The individual's voluntary abilities may be described by describing this repertory of directly guided behavior sequences. In other words, we would describe the elements, each of them a voluntary act or adaptive behavior pattern out of which the cognitively guided behavior must be constructed.

Notice also that our assumption of the independence of these elements is of great significance in testing and training such ability. Since one motive is as good as another for eliciting voluntary behavior, we can employ any convenient motivation for the test or the training session, with the assurance that the action will be available under "real-life" motivation. Usually we test motor skills or intelligence by motivating the subject to please the examiner, to achieve a high score, or to compete with other people. When these motor and intellectual skills come to be used in everyday life, however, the motivation is ordinarily quite different. Yet we assume that the speed of running a race will predict a man's speed in escaping from a bear. If we can do so, we are relieved of the necessity of having to match the test motivation to the criterion motivation.

A second feature of testing voluntary skills is that they need not be tested in the same combination or configuration that they will exhibit in the criterion situation. Because voluntary acts are independent of each other and combinable in many different patterns, the elements can be tested independently; the results of various combinations of these elements can all be predicted reasonably well from the elements themselves. Finally, independence of voluntary acts from motives and from each other can also be used in training skills. If a new voluntary act is learned, it can be employed in a multitude of situations in which other motives are involved. Also, a new voluntary act can be combined with other acts to produce a whole set of new activities.

The repertory of voluntary acts is only one aspect of cognitively guided adaptive behavior. The organization of these acts into adaptive sequences is equally important. In the case of cognitively guided behavior, we assume this organization and planning are cognitive intellectual functions. What abilities underlie cognitive functioning, and how may they be described?

We can do no more than outline briefly some of the relevant abilities underlying cognitive planning. A person's knowledge is one important part of his ability. Knowing the road to town is relevant to the adaptive behavior of driving to the post office. Even if the person does not have the knowledge, he may have well-established acts for obtaining it. Bruner (*1*) has described some of the strategies for attaining a concept from the raw information. In research on insight and problem-solving we have found that there is a problem of recognizing what information is relevant to the problem at hand. How such sifting is achieved is still largely a mystery. There may be, in addition, a true creativity or originality in developing new solutions. In considering cognitively guided behavior, therefore, we have suggested that the abilities underlying its effectiveness may be described by separating the intellectual or *planning* aspects of the behavior from the *executive* aspects. The latter may be thought of as a repertory of elemental behavioral acts or sequences and each member of the repertory may be investigated separately. The intellectual abilities underlying the planning of adaptive behavior reduce to the description of the person's knowledge, his procedures or strategies of acquiring new information, and the much more elusive notion of intellectual creativity.

The Concept of Ability in Directly Guided Behavior

We have already suggested that directly guided behavior lends itself much more readily to the description of ability than does cognitively guided behavior. The relation between the act and the outcome in directly guided behavior is relatively invariant. Rolling a ball down an alley at an object occurs invariably when the objects are ten pins. Certainly there is no other permitted behavior for knocking down the pins. In directly guided behavior, therefore, the ability is frequently described by the adaptive result, as canoeing skill, fly-casting, etc. We have already discussed the problems of defining and describing such skills or abilities.

The fact that these skills are labelled by the particular result does not imply that they are uncorrelated with each other. As the factor analytic studies have shown, there are general factors and group factors in such abilities. Whether such correlation depends upon certain common mechanisms among several skills or whether it implies certain predisposing conditions for learning—such as physical health, athletic interests, or environmental correlations among the agencies which provide training—is unknown. Very possibly both sorts of factors operate, and others as well. For many purposes it is not necessary to understand the basis of the correlation between abilities. We will return to this problem in a later section.

Let us turn for a moment to some of the differences between cognitively guided and directly guided behavior as far as the testing and training of skill are concerned. We have argued that since voluntary actions are independent of each other, they may be tested in isolation from the particular motives and the context in which they will be employed. The situation is quite different for directly guided behavior. Here the responses which make up the system are integrated by the particular feedback stimulus which guides them to the adaptive result. Perhaps, when we know the details of the system, what the feedback is, and how it functions, we will be able to devise isolated testing situations. At present, however, most attempts to test the elemental acts in directly guided behavior do not predict the functioning of the system. The individual acts are not the same when isolated from the system, because part of the stimulus for those actions is the feedback. Voluntary acts, on the other hand, since they are guided cognitively can be more or less faithfully reproduced in isolation.

The Concept of Ability in Unguided Adaptive Behavior

While unguided behavior may unquestionably be adaptive, it seems strange to speak of such personality traits as likeableness or defenselessness as abilities. Yet in many ways each of those traits describes well a pattern of behavior which tends to produce a consistent social response from other people. It is a matter of terminology whether such unguided adaptive behavior patterns should be referred to as abilities. If they are called abilities, it is important to recognize that they are unguided. If, on the other hand, they are not called abilities, it is important not to make unnecessary distinctions between such traits and other unguided adaptive behavior which has more of the appearance of ability. We often hear of the unconscious purposes of behavior. In many cases the behavior pattern that is said to reflect an unconscious purpose is a system of unguided adaptive responses. As soon as we speak of the purpose of unguided adaptive behavior it is natural to distinguish between people who achieve this purpose consistently and those who do not; in other words, the attribution of purpose to behavior suggests the term "ability" to describe effectiveness in achieving that purpose.

It is not within the scope of this chapter to discuss in detail the problem of unconsciously motivated behavior and its effectiveness. Let us merely say that unguided adaptive behavior certainly fits the criteria of unconsciously motivated behavior. It may or may not be necessary to conceive of unconsciously guided behavior. It may even be necessary to recognize unconsciously cognitively guided behavior, and unconsciously directly guided behavior. The only plea here is not to make tacit distinctions which are not necessary.

If we speak of abilities underlying unguided adaptive behavior, the problem of defining and describing those abilities does not appear to be much different from that of describing the sorts of abilities we have already discussed.

We have already seen that one question to be answered before ability can be fruitfully defined is the degree of invariance between the act and the result. If a variety of acts in the same situation may lead to the same result, and if different people do, in fact, use different acts to achieve the same result in the same situation, then it is necessary to define the ability in terms of the acts rather than in terms of the result. This was true for cognitively guided behavior because direct sensory feedback was not an essential part of the performance of the act. In directly guided behavior, the feedback was part of the cause of the act itself.

If the acts are unguided, then the particular feedback which would assure the attainment of the adaptive result is not an effective part of the stimulus which produces the behavior. It might well be, therefore, that the same rigid, unguided response in the same situation would under one set of circumstances lead to one adaptive result but in another circumstance lead to a different adaptive result. It might also happen that different people would respond differently to the same situation, yet both achieve the same result. One person's sociability and good nature may make him lots of friends; another person's sympathy and nurturance may make him the same set of friends.

In the light of these considerations it would seem wise to describe the unguided responses of an individual in terms of their own properties, rather than to label them by the adaptive result they produce. In other words, we consider the elements of a system of unguided responses just as we did the elements of a system of cognitively guided responses. The elements can occur regardless of what result they produce. In cognitively guided behavior these acts are voluntary—selected and organized by cognition to fit the particular demands of the present situation. In unguided behavior the elemental acts may or may not be voluntary; their effectiveness is a matter of how well attuned the organism's responses are to the particular situation. If the response is adaptive, it is because of "preestablished harmony" rather than guidance by feedback.

We said the elements of cognitively guided behavior may be the same as those of unguided behavior. Voluntary guided actions may be part of a system which produces some adaptive result that is irrelevant, as far as the organism is concerned, to the particular adaptive result toward which the behavior is guided. The elements of unguided behavior may, however, be completely involuntary. Blushing, crying, etc., may be part of an adaptive system of unguided response, whereas only voluntary responses make up the system of cognitively guided behavior.

To summarize this discussion of the definition and description of ability in these three areas of adaptive behavior, we have suggested that in directly guided behavior there is such an intimate and interdependent relation among the various responses in the system that the entire system can well be described as a unit. While we need to understand the structure of such a system of responses in order to elucidate the mechanism of directly guided behavior, for purposes of description the unit may be considered as a totality. Many of the specific abilities or skills of everyday life, like ability to hammer in a nail, exemplify such units of directly guided behavior.

In so far as they are under voluntary control, these skills or units may serve as elements in cognitively guided behavior. Other voluntary acts which are not guided toward any consistent result within themselves may also be elements in the repertory of voluntary acts to be combined and organized into cognitively guided adaptive behavior. The new problem we meet in cognitive guided behavior is the description of the cognitive and intellectual abilities underlying the organization of these elements into adaptive behavior.

Unguided adaptive behavior may also be described in terms of the various responses and elements which compose it. The elements of a system of unguided adaptive behavior may also be units of directly guided behavior, provided that the instigation and guidance of the directly guided behavior are irrelevant to the unguided adaptive result which the behavior causes. Elements of unguided adaptive behavior may also be involuntary behavior acts.

Social Skills

With the recognition of the importance of human relations in modern society, we have witnessed recently numerous attempts to describe, analyze and inculcate social and interpersonal skills. In certain important respects, social skills seem to be examples of unguided adaptive behavior. An analysis of some of the problems of describing social skill will therefore illustrate in a significant area the implications of the concepts we have introduced.

We begin with the assumption that the social results of a behavioral act depend largely upon the personal characteristic that act reveals. It is a person in distress who elicits sympathy and nurturance. It is an *intentional* injury that most strongly instigates revenge. It is the friendliness of a person that arouses friendly feelings in others.

There are, to be sure, other effects. The careless driver who kills a pedestrian causes many social effects in the family of the victim; in many ways these effects are the same whether the killing was wilful or accidental, whether it was avoidable or not. But the feedback of these consequences in terms of legal consequences, social opinion, and his own self-evaluation depends largely upon the intention of the driver and his carefulness.

A person who consistently achieves a certain social result like respect, popularity, a good reputation, or love, consistently communicates certain characteristics. It is important, if he is to be liked, that he not only help other people, but do so in a way indicating that he likes them and is helping them for that reason. If he gives the impression that he is acting out of obligation or for some ulterior reason, the friendly act will not evoke a friendly response.

Social Perception

Thus we see that an understanding of adaptive social behavior depends upon an analysis of the way behavior communicates personality characteristics. Our next task, therefore, is a description of some of the conditions for social perception.

Particular perception of motives and feelings. The perception of motives and feelings is not straightforward; the same act, especially if it is voluntary, may be motivated by a variety of different motives and accompanied by various feelings. This fact suggests two different kinds of evidence of motives:

(1) One kind of valid evidence is a fixed involuntary expressive response. To take an earlier example, crying is a reliable indication of distress so long as it is not voluntary or goal-directed. If a child could voluntarily cry, then he might cry in order to arouse sympathy, in which case his weeping might no longer indicate real distress.

If, however, the expressive behavior is involuntary, the relationship between the person's motivation or feeling or emotion and his behavior is such that the behavior is an immediate expression of the motive or feeling. In order to infer the feeling from the behavior, two questions must be answered. First, how many different psychological states may be expressed in the same way? If two different states—e.g., anger and fear—both produce the same expressive behavior, then there will be ambiguity of interpretation. While there may certainly be ambiguity in expressive behavior, it is probably true that there is less than in voluntary behavior. Nevertheless, there is enough to require skillful discernment on the part of the observer.

Is there, in the second place, the possibility of voluntary inhibition of expressive behavior? While it is difficult to cry voluntarily or to look pained convincingly, it is possible to inhibit expressive behavior. The absence of crying is poorer evidence of lack of distress than crying is of the presence of distress.

(2) Voluntary behavior may also be the basis for valid inferences about motives, but the interpretation is more complicated. Since, as we have seen, the same voluntary act may be employed under any motivation, the observer must determine from the circumstances what is the motive for this particular action.

We are habitually wary in interpreting the significance of voluntary behavior. A person can voluntarily say, "I am broke; I need help; please give me a dime, mister." Although such a statement carries some conviction, it is not necessarily accepted at face value. Because language is voluntary, it may or may not tell the truth. Involuntary behavior is more credible.

For just this reason the problem of personality testing is very difficult. We want to put the person in a situation where his behavior will reveal his personality. If we want to know how hostile a person is, we could ask him if he has many fights. His answer is voluntary; he can say "yes" or "no," depending upon what impression he wants to create. Unless we feel sure we can rule out or discern his motive, we mistrust his answer. If he wants a job where hostility is disapproved, then a "yes" answer is accepted as valid, but a "no" answer is not taken at face value. The "yes" answer is accepted because we can't see any reason why he should say "yes" if it were not true. By this same reasoning we have found that adjustment inventories can be generally trusted if the person gets a high neurotic score, but that low neurotic scores are not trustworthy.

Fortunately, the problem of perceiving motives in naturalistic situations is not usually so difficult as inferring them from answers on a test; the instigation of the motive is usually more visible in natural settings. When we see a person fail to return a greeting, we can judge for ourselves whether the greeting was indeed noticeable enough so that he must have seen it and intentionally refused to acknowledge it, or whether he may well not have noticed it at all. Our judgment, of course, is not infallible, and we cannot perceive all the factors. We may not know, for example, that the individual who ignored the greeting was worried and harassed or deeply embedded in thought, and thus less alert than usual to external stimuli. It is true, nevertheless, that in many situations requiring social perception, we are in the position of perceiving both the instigating conditions and the behavioral response. We judge the needs, motives and abilities which are the intervening variables between the two.

In addition to taking note of the instigating conditions—and particularly when they are ambiguous—we may make tacit assumptions about the characteristics of a person. This we do in terms of our general knowledge of people, of the people in this particular culture, and of this person himself. If, for example, a person dives into a rushing flood to rescue a drowning child, we assume that no selfish motive would be strong enough to motivate him. If he had benefitted the child in a minor way, he might conceivably be motivated by desire to obtain a return benefit; but nobody would risk his life for such a selfish reason. Since it must have been genuine altruism, then we hail the rescuer as a hero.

If a person reveals something bad about himself, we can see no reason for his doing so except a strong motivation to be honest. We applaud his truthfulness. We may assume truthfulness, also, when we ask a person about something trivial. We assume that he is telling the truth because we can think of no motive to make him lie. We assume people are honest until proved otherwise.

Finally, we trust a person we know well under circumstances when we would mistrust a stranger. Having established a personality trait through observing behavior in other circumstances, we now assume the trait in cases where the behavior is ambiguous.

In all these cases we see that acceptance of the voluntary behavior at its face value depends upon certain tacit assumptions about the behaving person—either trust in him or some assumption about the probable strength of the alternative motives behind his action.

The Description of Social and Interpersonal Skills

Having seen the conditions which may result in the perception of a personality trait, we can return to the various aspects of social skill. Social skill, as we have said, does not imply a voluntary or intentional communication of a character trait. This talent is one aspect of dramatic ability, but it is not skill in interpersonal relations.

Social skill is, rather, a complex of personality traits which leads to behavior that communicates the appropriate motives, abilities and other traits. We might divide the problem into two parts: first, what characteristics have a general effect on communication of personality traits; and second, what sets of personality traits, if clearly communicated, evoke and maintain a stable social relationship.

Even though such personality traits are part of social skill in the broad sense, the second question goes far beyond the scope of this paper into a general theory of interpersonal relations. Just to illustrate the sort of homeostatic social relationship which can exist, we might look at a friendship. Each person likes the other and knows that he is liked by the other. Each person keeps the other out of difficulty and protects the other from threats and dangers. Each person likes to be in the other's company and by welcoming such opportunities communicates friendly feelings as well as getting personal satisfaction. In the pure case, the whole pattern consists of social responses that satisfy the individual, but, also, satisfy the other and communicate the friendliness, sociability and sympathy that each feels for the other.

To return now to the communication process itself, there are two obvious factors in clear communication of personality traits. One is expressiveness on the part of the actor, and a second is accuracy of social perception on the part of the observer.

We have all known people who feel friendly and altruistic, but who are inexpressive. Through anxiety, shyness, or social isolation, an individual may be so "dead pan" as to provide little information about his feelings and motives. Since unresponsiveness is also a symptom of self-interest, pride and arrogance, inexpressive people are frequently thought to be proud and uninterested in others.

Little need be said here about accuracy of social perception because Chapter II above has been devoted to the topic. One comment might be made about that chapter. Its authors, Bronfenbrenner, Harding, and Gallwey, used a voluntary response—e.g., ratings and verbal expressions of judgment—to indicate perception. Since some of the responses in socially adaptive behavior are not voluntary and not cognitively mediated, it would be possible for a person to be responsive to stimuli which did not modify his ratings. This is a kind of social perception also.

In summary, then, we have analyzed social skill to illustrate particularly the problems of describing ability in the areas of unguided adaptive behavior. Our argument was that adaptive social consequences may be produced (1) by a certain set of traits which (2) are adequately communicated to others. Then we considered two personality characteristics making for clear communication: expressiveness and social sensitivity.

Analysis of Ability Into Factors

To define ability in terms of adaptive behavior, one thinks first of describing abilities corresponding to the various adaptive results which the person can achieve. For some kinds of adaptive behavior this approach turns out to be feasible, especially for directly guided behavior; but not for the patterns of cognitively guided action nor for unguided adaptive behavior. For these, description of the component acts seems more fruitful. All such description of ability, however, stays relatively close to the adaptive results of behavior.

The study of ability has frequently been directed to a more general sort of analysis that attempts to describe a relatively few primary abilities underlying the multitude of specific skills. Thus playing baseball and basketball have different adaptive results, but call for certain common abilities. The search for such basic abilities is the object of much research effort; its idea is the prediction of all a person's skills and ability in terms of a few primary abilities.

Factor Analysis of Test Intercorrelation

One approach to this problem is through factor analysis of test intercorrelation. Usually the tests are not a direct measure of ability to achieve a particular adaptive result in real life, but rather tests which correlate with some criterion of that skill. Thus, there are tests of mathematical skill and achievement; vocabulary, etc. The factor analytic procedure starts with such test scores.

The basic assumption of factor analysis is that a test score can be analyzed into a sum of factors as follows: $S_{ij} = a_{i1}\, x_{1j} + a_{i2}\, x_{2j} + \ldots + a_{in}\, x_{nj}$. S_{ij} is the score of individual i on test j. In other words, the raw data are not items which a person can do, but rather scores on a battery of tests. Scores on tests can, however, be rewritten as items the person can perform.

The formula above says that a person's score can be predicted from the various terms on the right-hand side of the equation. All of the a terms, a_{i1}, a_{i2}, describe the amount of individual i's ability on each factor, 1, 2, 3, etc. The x terms describe the importance of those abilities for test i. If the individual has a great deal of an ability which is important for a test, his score will be greatly increased by that fact—both a and x will be large, and they are multiplied in the formula.

This formula rests on a number of assumptions, both implicitly and explicitly. First, it assumes the substitutability of one ability for another in the individual's performance on a test. Enough of any one ability will compensate for a deficiency in any other. The formula as stated does not admit the possibility that each of two abilities is essential for performance on a test; without either, the individual can do nothing. The formula assumes, furthermore, that these abilities operate in the particular way described by the linear formula.

For a good many tests this assumption is not unreasonable. In examination composed half and half of addition and subtraction, skill on one type of problem would compensate, within limits, for deficiency on the other. Even in division problems where both multiplication and subtraction are required, speed in multiplying would compensate somewhat for slowness in subtracting. It is clear, though, that in other instances one ability cannot substitute for another.

We must remember, however, that one of the important restrictions on the factor analysis of test scores is the limit on the available mathematical and computational methods. This linear assumption is a first approximation, made because it is only for such a formula that the methods of analysis have been well developed. For all that it is ridiculously oversimplified, it has proved to be extremely useful. Yet if we make an assumption general enough to permit a completely realistic description of a performance, we immediately find ourselves in an area of mathematics for which both theory and computational methods are lacking.

A second assumption underlying factor analysis is that of common abilities. In other words, everybody must be assumed to have the same set of abilities and to differ only in the amount of each one. In factor analysis this assumption is contained in the identity of abilities 1, 2, etc., for all of the tests in the battery and for all of the people in the sample. Some people object to such an assumption, but, as we shall see, the whole analysis of test performance into some reduced number of abilities depends upon assuming that every person's abilities can be described in terms of the same set of primary abilities or dimensions. Thus, the assumption of common abilities is firmly at the root of the whole analytic endeavor.

The procedures of factor analysis are well described elsewhere and need not be discussed here. Some discussion of the type of factors to be expected from the application of these procedures will be found in a later section (see p. 229). First, however, let us look at another approach to the analysis of primary abilities based upon Guttman's scale analysis (*6*).

Multidimensional Scaling Procedure

A different approach to the problem of factoring skills may be derived from the basic relation of ability to level of difficulty, along the lines of Guttman scaling technique.

First, we must define two terms, the ability of the person (A_p) and the difficulty of the task (D_t). If the person's ability is greater than the difficulty of the task, he can perform the task. Furthermore, we assume the following rules of operations: If task *a* is more difficult than task *b*, and a person cannot perform task *b*, then he cannot perform task *a*. Conversely, if a person can succeed on task *b* and cannot perform task *a*, then task *a* must be more difficult than task *b*. Because of these rules—which assume that the tasks form a scale—we can define the ability of a person in terms of the difficulty of various tasks he can perform. His ability may be defined as the "upper bound" of the difficulty level of the set of tasks which he can perform. In ordinary English, we can define a person's ability as the difficulty of the most difficult task he can perform. Such a definition enables us to say that if a person's ability is equal to or greater than the difficulty of a task, he can perform the task.

This logical manipulation does not advance us very far in the problem of measurement because we have no measure or definition of the difficulty of a task. It is at this point that we must make some assumptions about the correspondence of the abilities of different people. If we stay entirely within the behavior of a single person, then we can divide the entire population of tasks into two groups: those he can perform and those he cannot perform. We know that the first group is less difficult than the second, but we have no method for ordering the difficulty of tasks within either group. Furthermore we have no method for stating that performance on some tasks requires one kind of ability, whereas performance on other tasks requires a different ability. As long as we are concerned with but a single person, we have no reason for making such a distinction.

It is only when we look at the differences between the tasks that one person can do and those another can do that we may need to discriminate between different abilities. Suppose we find that one person can perform task *a* but not *b*, while another person can perform task *b* but not *a*. Our simple rule about difficulty level is self-contradictory; *a* is more difficult than *b*, and *b* is more difficult than *a*.

In the face of such a problem we may adopt a two-dimensional model. We will define the difficulty of a task in terms of two numbers, D_1 and D_2, rather than one. A task may be difficult in one respect but easy in another. Now we must modify our description of a person also and describe his ability in terms of two dimensions or two numbers, A_x and A_y. These dimensions correspond to D_x and D_y.

If a person with abilities A_x and A_y faces a task with difficulties D_x and D_y, his success depends upon the relation of his abilities to the difficulties. Several assumptions are possible. One possibility is that A_x must equal or exceed D_x, and A_y must equal or exceed D_y for the person to succeed on the task. Such an assumption implies that abilities are not substitutable for each other—just the opposite assumption from factor analysis. If A_x is less than D_x it makes no difference how much A_y exceeds D_y. The individual's ability on one dimension is of no help if ability on another dimension is lacking.

The assumption of complete non-substitutability of abilities is just as questionable as that of complete substitutability. It is not that abilities so defined would be self-contradictory any more than factor analysis is self-contradictory, but that the primary abilities which would be discovered would be different under the two methods of analysis. We will go into this problem in a moment, but first let us follow through the assumption of non-substitutability to extend scale analysis to more than one dimension.

We assume, therefore that if a person with abilities A_x and A_y faces a task with difficulties D_x and D_y, he will succeed if and only if $A_x \geqslant D_x$ and $A_y \geqslant D_y$. This provides us with a measurement of A_x and A_y for a person expressed in terms of D_x and D_y. We find the most difficult task he can perform. The difficulty levels of that task, D_x and D_y, constitute a simultaneous measure of both abilities of the person; if the task were more difficult, either in D_1 or D_2, he would fail.

Now if one person has more ability A_x than A_y, while a second person has more ability A_y than A_x, we can easily find pairs of tasks on which one person will pass one and fail the other, while the other person will do the reverse. Notice that this model, by assuming that the difficulty of all tasks can be defined in terms of the same D_x and D_y, has measured the abilities of the two people in the same terms. We have, therefore, tacitly assumed that the ability of all people may be defined in terms of the same pair of abilities. In other words, we assume common abilities.

When we say that we apply a particular mathematical model, it does not mean that we have a concrete method of determining the actual difficulty of a task. If we are concerned with only two people, however, it is not difficult to see how one might proceed. One merely categorizes the population of tasks into four classes. There are those on which both people fail; there are those which the first person passes, but the second fails; there are those which the first person fails, but the second performs successfully; finally, there are those on which both succeed. Let us represent this situation graphically as in Fig. 1.

Since we have established by definition that a person can perform task *a* only if his ability on *x* is greater than the difficulty of task *a* on *x* and if his ability only is greater than task *a* on *y*, the realm of tasks which P_1 can do must be found in the rectangle of values which are less than x_1 y_1. Similarly for P_2. Now two points have

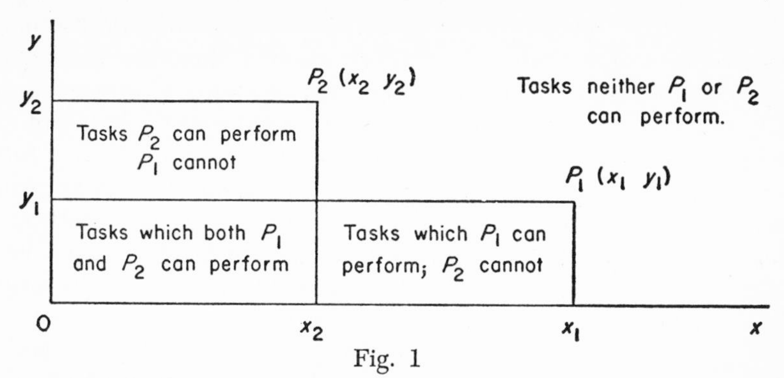

Fig. 1

been established on each axis, x_1 and y_2. With respect to difficulty on x, tasks have been divided into three classes, those which both persons can perform (D_x less than or equal to x_2), and those which only P_1 can perform (D_x greater than x_2 but less than or equal to x_1), and those which neither person can perform (D_x greater than x_1). We have a three-point scale of difficulty on the x dimension and also on y dimension.

If there are more than two people to be compared, we may need to add dimensions to the model. In no case will more dimensions than people (or more dimensions than tasks) be required, and we hope very strongly that we can get along on far fewer dimensions than there are people (or tasks) to be compared. In other words, we hope that some few dozen abilities or less may discriminate everybody.

We can see easily how this might happen by considering a third person in addition to the two described earlier. Suppose we list all the things that the third person can do. We can see the various possibilities in Fig. 2.

The items which individual P_1 can perform must fall within the rectangle between point P_1 and the origin and bounded by the axes. Similarly for P_2. Now if P_3's abilities are describable in terms of the same abilities that P_1 and P_2 already have defined, P_3 must be in some one of the nine positions listed in Figure 2, but nowhere else. This limitation puts certain restrictions on the items P_3 passes and fails. If, for example, P_3 is in the lower left position, then P_3 will pass no items which either P_1 or P_2 fails, but may fail items which P_1 or P_2 or both P_1 and P_2

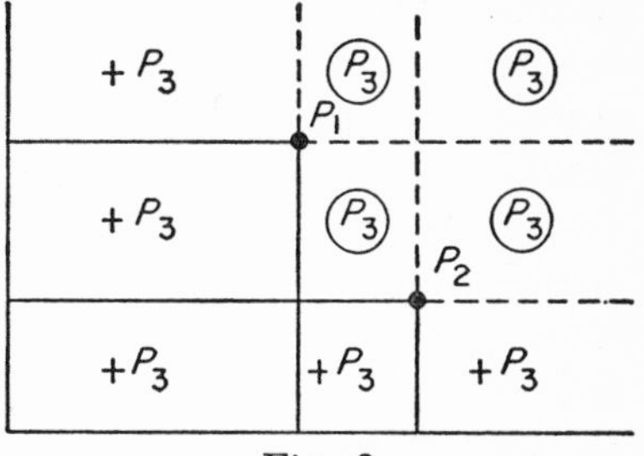

Fig. 2

pass. Similarly, there are certain conditions that must hold for each of nine positions.

Now if P_3 passes some items which both P_1 and P_2 fail (which locates P_3 in one of the four upper right positions marked with a circle in Figure 2) and at the same time fails some items which both P_1 and P_2 pass (which locates P_3 in one of the positions marked by a plus sign in Figure 2), we have a self-contradiction which can be resolved only by adding a third dimension to the mathematical model. This procedure can be extended to indefinitely many dimensions.

As a practical procedure, such a technique presents two serious difficulties. One is technical; for a large sample of people, the task would become prohibitively long. The other is more serious; this procedure, like the Guttman scale analysis, works fine when there is perfect reliability. If a person always passes or always fails an item no matter how often he is tested, then we have no chance variance to deal with and no sampling problem. If, however, there is any unreliability, the effect is to exaggerate the number of dimensions. Perhaps n dimensions would be required by the data, but we suspect that the obtained pattern of passes and failures could be reasonably considered a random deviation from a much simpler pattern requiring only a relatively small number of dimensions. The whole problem of sampling error for Guttman scale analysis has not been satisfactorily solved, although there is no reason to presume it is insoluble.

Sources of Test Intercorrelation

We have looked at two procedures for analyzing into factors or dimensions the behavior of a population of people on a population of tasks. The two procedures differ in several ways, but their basic difference is in the assumptions they make about the relation of one primary ability to another. One assumes that abilities are substitutable for each other; the second assumes the opposite. These are not the only assumptions which could be made; others would probably lead to still further analytic procedures. In this section we want to illustrate the fact that these various assumptions may each be appropriate for certain sorts of analyses. The kinds of basic abilities we discover depend upon the sorts of dimension for which we look.

In the final analysis, all these factor analytic procedures use as their raw data the correlation between tests. While no correlation coefficient is calculated for scale analysis, the conditions which must be fulfilled for two items to be along a single scale are the same that produce a high correlation between the two. The correlation between two tests may stem from the person, the task, or the culture. The appropriate analytic procedures depend upon the source of correlation being analyzed. We can illustrate this position by considering some of the sources of test intercorrelation.

One source of correlation is the presence of identical component acts as elements of the two tests. Subtracting is an element of long division and of extracting the square root. Sawing is a component of making a bookcase and also of making a bird house. Whenever two complex systems of acts have certain identical elements, we would expect a correlation of the two.

The presence of identical components will lead to a correlation most surely if the complex system of adaptive behavior is composed of separable independent components like cognitively guided behavior. Here we feel sure that the component functions well in many different contexts. Two directly guided behavior patterns, on the other hand, may contain common elements but not be correlated because of them. It is possible for the same act to be functional in one pattern but not in another.

Now if the task of analysis is to discover the component acts within a complex skill, we must make assumptions which describe the relation of acts to the systems of which they are part. We cannot expect to discover a "sawing" factor and a "hammering" factor in carpentry if we use a model that assumes substitutability, because the best hammering in the world won't compensate for poor sawing. On the other hand, some acts can substitute for others in complex skills. Use of a square can compensate for a poor "eye" in sawing a board squarely. If a model assuming non-substitutability is employed, it may lead to factors but they will not be substitutable ones. By and large, however, the assumption of non-substitutability seems likely to break down a complex behavior system into the component sub-systems which are independently necessary for the successful operation of the system.

There are other sources of test correlation besides identical component acts in a complex system of actions. Physical strength is required in lifting weights and in putting the shot; yet there are not apparently any common acts in the two behavior patterns. Expressiveness is a characteristic which contributes to making friends and also to campaign oratory, even through actions which are not common to the two sorts of ability.

In a theory of human action we must recognize a multitude of specific habits and stimulus-response relationships, but also many personal characteristics which cannot be readily described in stimulus-response terms. Expressiveness, impulsiveness, cautiousness, etc., are examples. Although we have no adequate theory of the role these characteristics play in the determination of actions, it seems certain that the same characteristic may have its influence upon a wide variety of actions and thus upon a variety of adaptive behavior patterns. The correlation between different abilities may stem from the influence of such general characteristics.

Until we have a better theory of these characteristics or traits, we cannot intelligently decide how such a set of characteristics contributes to the effectiveness of an adaptive behavior system. Since we cannot know to what extent they summate or substitute for each other, we cannot know what analytic procedure is most likely to reveal such characteristics behind the adaptive behavior of the individual.

There is still a third source of correlation between abilities. Both of the first two are operative in the actual behavior itself. There can, however, be correlation among abilities which does not reflect any actual dependence of the abilities on each other, but rather reflects their developmental histories. Such a correlation is a better description of the environment in which abilities develop than it is of the abilities themselves. If in some culture like medieval Europe, Latin and theology were taught by the same institutions, then the people who learned Latin would be likely to learn theology. The result would be a correlation between the two sorts of achievement. It must have been true that skill in mathematics and in Latin were more highly correlated in the 18th century than at present, because they were correlated in the environment. In other words, the correlation is an ecological one and reflects the interdependency of the different aspects of an environmental system.

The intercorrelation among achievement tests might be analyzed as part of a general analysis of the culture in which such achievements exist. If the purpose of analysis were to identify the basic developmental institutions of a culture, the analytic procedure would have to be fashioned to suit that purpose. The contribution of the ecological factor to the correlation would depend upon the extent to which the training influences for one skill affected the same people to the same degree as the training influences for another skill.

These three sources of intercorrelations among skills and abilities do not exhaust all of the possibilities; there are other more problematic bases for intercorrelation. If there are critical periods in the development of abilities, then the ecological factor may be most important during the critical period, and abilities with contemporaneous critical periods may tend to be more highly correlated than abilities with different critical times.

The import of this discussion of the various bases for test correlation is merely to show that the search for basic factors may proceed in quite different directions, depending upon the purpose of the analysis. Certain procedures will allow the appearance of certain sorts of factors, but make it difficult if not impossible for other sorts of factors to be uncovered. The now traditional methods of factor analysis are well suited to some purposes, for which they have proved themselves exceedingly valuable. There are other sources of correlations, however, which they are not designed to reveal.

Summary

This chapter has attempted a theoretical analysis of the concept of ability which might bring together some of the concepts in behavior theory and some of the statistical research on abilities.

If we make the basic assumption that the notion of ability is basically concerned with the effectiveness of adaptive behavior, we find that the description of ability depends upon the mechanism of adaptive behavior. We have suggested three varieties of adaptive behavior: unguided, directly guided, and cognitively guided. Cognitive guidance provides a means of integrating independent voluntary acts or independent voluntary systems of directly guided behavior into an adaptive behavior pattern. Cognition plays two roles here. It provides the feedback from the environment which is essential for guided behavior. Because cognition integrates a multitude of sensory cues, cognitive guidance need not depend upon any single sensory cue for feedback. In addition, cognition provides an internal "schema" of actions which can guide motor acts into a predetermined pattern without any necessity for direct external guiding cues. Presumably, this guidance occurs through cognition of one's own actions and matching them to the cognitive schema.

Directly guided behavior depends upon external sensory feedback. It is thus tied to a concrete external result. Although the actions themselves which are involved in directly guided behavior are not independent or voluntary, an entire system of such behavior may be voluntary and may be integrated into more complex systems of cognitively guided adaptive behavior.

Unguided adaptive behavior depends upon a pre-set behavioral response to a stimulus situation which leads to an adaptive result most of the time. If the environment were entirely constant, unguided behavior could be completely adaptive. Guidance, however, permits adaptive behavior under changing conditions. In social situations, the effect of a behavior pattern may actually depend upon its not appearing to be guided. The social effect depends largely upon the personal characteristics which the behavior communicates; but if it seems to be guided toward such ends as achieving popularity or arousing sympathy, that fact communicates a different personality trait than would behavior that did not look intentional or deliberate. This fact makes the analysis of social skills quite different from that of other sorts of ability.

When we describe abilities, we try to find useful ways of labelling the systems of adaptive behavior which a person may display. It is not sufficient merely to name an adaptive result, because people differ in the circumstances under which they can produce this result. One oversimplification is to arrange all situations in order of difficulty and people in terms of amount of ability, in such a way that a person can succeed on a task if his ability is greater than the difficulty. This plan assumes that the variety of situations all can be arranged on one dimension, difficulty, without doing too much violence to the data. When there are widely different alternative means of producing the same result in the same situation, then the hopes of finding a single difficulty dimension are very small. In cognitively guided behavior and unguided behavior there are frequently so many alternative ways of achieving the same result that it is more useful to describe the various voluntary skills that compose cognitively guided adaptive behavior than to describe the total system.

The process of searching for basic skills can be carried further through attempts to discover the factors underlying quite different abilities. Factor analysis provides one method for analyzing the correlations among different tests. Another method stems from Guttman scale analysis. The suitability of various methods, however, depends upon the purpose of the analysis. There are many possible sources for test correlation; for uncovering some of these bases, but not for others, factor analysis is suitable.

References

1. Bruner, J. S. *A Study of Thinking*, New York: Wiley, 1956.
2. Conant, James B. *On Understanding Science*, New Haven: Yale Univ. Press, 1947.
3. Hull, Clark. *Principles of Behavior*, New York: Appleton-Century, 1943.
4. James, W. *Principles of Psychology*, New York: Holt, 1890.
5. Piaget, Jean. *The Origins of Intelligence in Children* (Trans. by Margaret Cook), Internat. Univ. Press, 1952.
6. Stouffer, S. A., Guttman, L., Suchman, E. A., Lazarsfeld, P. F., Star, S. A., and Claussen, J. A. *Measurement and Prediction*, Volume IV in *Studies in Social Psychology in World War II*, chapter 1.
7. Tinbergen, N. *The Study of Instinct*, Oxford: Clarendon Press, 1951.
8. Wiener, Norbert. *The human use of human beings. Cybernetics and Society*, Boston: Houghton-Mifflin, 1950.

VI

Review and Prospects

DAVID C. MCCLELLAND

How shall the contributions of the Committee be summarized? To a certain extent they cannot be. The task is both difficult and in a sense unnecessary. In the first place, each chapter already contains a detailed summary of research findings that need not be reviewed again here. In the second place, an excellent report on many of its activities and interests by Smith (*16*) has already appeared. In the third place, it is always hazardous and often misleading to select certain aspects of a research program for particular mention in a summary. For the fact is that a new way of looking at a problem or at a particular research finding may make sense only years from now in a quite unexpected way in some other scientist's mind as he is working on similar problems.

In this sense the real significance of the Committee's work will be its net effect on other minds grappling with the problems of identifying talent. And certainly no one who has read earlier chapters in this report would deny that there is plenty of material in them which ought to have an impact on research thinking. Each of the problems tackled turned out to be much more complicated than anticipated, and each required great ingenuity in solving methodological problems. In fact, one could make a case for the position that the Committee's chief contribution lies in its efforts to solve the technical problems that always arise when one starts exploratory research in a new field.

But although we hope that our work will have its effect—perhaps its chief effect—on others doing research on talent, we also feel a responsibility to interpret in a general way what has been accomplished. Have any new perspectives on the problem of talent been achieved? How do the key findings of the research projects fit together? Can we, however tenatively, advance any recommendations for future research or for policy-making, after our several years of study of talent selection? It is to these questions that this chapter is addressed.

A General Point of View

The Committee adopted as its major field of study those aspects of talent which would not ordinarily be classified as "abilities." It concentrated on values and motives—non-academic determinants of achievement—and on social skills and occupational status—non-academic types of achievement. But Baldwin has so clarified the meaning of the term "ability" in the preceding chapter that we can now view our objectives in a new light. He has pointed out that basically ability refers to the adaptiveness of behavior—to the capacity of a response to produce an invariant end-result in the environment. Furthermore, ability may be used to describe adaptive behavior which is unguided by feedback from previous responses (as in instinctive behavior useful for survival), or which is guided by such feedback either simply and directly (as in making a complex muscular coordination) or through cognitive controls.

From this point of view it is clear that abilities as traditionally tested involve usually (though not always) what Baldwin calls cognitively guided behavior—behavior controlled by a cognitive map and consisting largely of *voluntary acts.* By a "cognitive map" he means a schema which is not entirely dependent on sensory input (feedback), and by "voluntary acts" he means acts which can be made in the service of any goal and independently of each other. For example, when a child writes "cat," he is guided by feedback (if his pen is dry and the "c" doesn't appear, he doesn't go on to "a"); the guidance is cognitive as well as perceptual (he could write it even in imagination); the component acts are voluntary and can be put together for any goal (to beat someone at Scrabble, to please the teacher) or substituted for each other in any sequence (c-a-t, t-c-a, a-c-t).

Now it is clear that in this scheme of things the variables with which the Committee concerned itself—values, motives, and social sensitivity—*are not abilities in the sense of cognitively guided skills,* though they may be adaptive either in the unguided or simply guided senses. For example, smiling as the involuntary expression of the motive to be friendly may be adaptive (i.e., it may be considered a kind of talented behavior); but it may be unguided in the sense that the person smiles more or less regardless of the consequences of his smiling; or it may be simply-guided in the sense that the person adapts more or less unconsciously to the way his behavior is received. As soon as it becomes cognitively guided, in the sense of voluntary behavior designed for some ulterior motive (e.g., to gain recognition), we no longer consider it a good index of the motive to be friendly. The same is true of social sensitivity or *n* Achievement, two variables considered elsewhere in this volume. The behavior chacteristic of them either cannot be produced voluntarily (i.e., in the service of any motive) or, if it is, appears to be cognitively guided in a way which is atypical for the variable in question. A person should be able to write c-a-t to please the experimenter, but he may not be able to smile "genuinely" to please the experimenter unless he feels friendly; or he may not be able to learn how to do a task rapidly to please the experimenter unless he has high *n* Achievement.

What are the consequences of this analysis for the identification of talent? When one is dealing with personal characteristics like values and motives, the behavioral expression of which is not under voluntary control, one's general strategy must shift from identifying "talented persons" to *matching persons with certain characteristics to situations in which those characteristics will be most adaptive.* That is, a person's values, motives, and sensitivities lead him to behave in certain ways *whatever the situation.* He develops relatively stable personality characteristics which are not very easily altered, either fundamentally or in their behavioral expression, by different types of feedback. For example, a person's *n* Achievement or belief in family solidarity is presumably not easily changed by information to the effect that neither is appropriate in a particular situation; yet this is exactly what happens with cognitively guided skills. If the child writes t-c-a for "cat," the teacher points out the error, and the child can readily change his behavior. So it makes good practical sense to talk about cognitively guided skills (i.e., most "abilities" in the traditional sense of the term) as being useful in a wide variety of situations: here the "talent" is *in* the person, so to speak. But with characteristics not cognitively guided *the "talent" is in the combination of a particular person with a particular situation.*

The most explicit application of this general point of view appears in Strodtbeck's chapter, where he considers the relative ease with which Jews and Italians have adapted to American values. He first defines the characteristics of the achievement ethic in the United

States and then seeks to discover how closely the traditional Jewish and Italian values matched it. To take a concrete example from his analysis, he argues that a sense of loyalty to a larger collective than the family is part of the American social scene, a sense of loyalty that derives in part from the Calvinist emphasis on God's "master plan" for the whole world and in part from a feeling of increasing interdependency in the modern world. Individuals or groups (like Southern Italians) who have different values—who, for example, put loyalty to the family higher than that to the community—will therefore have difficulty fitting into the American scene. They will be less likely to "show talented behavior" or be successful.

Now to return to Baldwin's distinction, it is clear that high family loyalty is not cognitively guided; it cannot be voluntarily changed in order, for example, to pursue a new goal—namely, better adjustment to American life. It cannot be modified so easily. If it could, as Baldwin points out, it would be more in the nature of an instrumental belief than a fundamental value orientation of the person. Suppose one thinks of high family loyalty as a stable personality characteristic. Then if he tries to assess the probability of its leading to talented performance, he would have to conclude that a person with such a value is not likely to behave in what would be regarded as a talented way in the United States in general, though he very well might in Southern Italy or even in certain specific sub-groups within the United States.

The same general point of view can be applied to Bronfenbrenner's finding that in small discussion groups interpersonal sensitivity depends on the relationship between the sexes. Interpersonal sensitivity is apparently not a cognitively guided characteristic which can function well across social situations. Instead, it seems to be a personality characteristic which is best displayed effectively in a situation where there is some complementarity in the roles played by men and women. In other words, interpersonal sensitivity depends on matching certain people with certain social situations.

Many other examples could be cited from the experimental literature to show that, so far as motives, values, and the like are concerned, *the nature of the situation* is very important in determining the adaptiveness of having a certain characteristic. Sarason, Mandler, and Craighill (*14*), for instance, have shown that subjects with low anxiety perform better (show more "talent") when they are put under pressure to do well, whereas subjects with high anxiety do less well under the same pressure. DeCharms, again, has found

(*4*) that, if talented performance is defined as requiring that a person be susceptible to the opinions of experts, subjects who value achievement highly have a greater talent potential than subjects who do not. For another instance, French (*5*), working with subjects high and low in both *n* Achievement and *n* Affiliation, has discovered that subjects with high *n* Achievement tend to choose experts over friends as working partners, whereas subjects with high *n* Affiliation do the reverse. Hence in choosing teams of experts, one should pick subjects with high *n* Achievement as having more potential talent for such situations, because their "involuntary response systems" would lead them to be more adaptive to the requirements of such a working condition.

The list could easily be extended, but the point should by now be plain enough. If one is working with non-cognitively guided characteristics like values and motives, it is necessary to understand the requirements of the situation in which the talented performance is to be evoked if the knowledge of such characteristics is to be of any assistance in predicting who will perform in a talented way. Knowledge of the situation is also useful, to be sure, when one is dealing with more traditional skills, as Cattell has pointed out (*2*); but it is even more essential here where responses cannot be readily changed to fit new sets of situational requirements.

To make the general point of view clear, we have spoken until now as if the characteristics of a person and the requirements of the situation were both fixed, and as if the problem therefore were to match them as successfully as possible. But, of course, neither is absolutely fixed. The requirements of the situation can be modified to match the characteristics of the person. Similarly, values and motives, which in the first place were learned, may be changed either fundamentally or perhaps merely in the way they express themselves, although the choice of alternative avenues of expression cannot be as much under voluntary control as is the case with cognitively guided skills. A highly anxious person, that is, might have his anxiety reduced at its source or its mode of expression channeled in such a way as to make high-pressure situations less disabling; or subjects with high *n* Affiliation might somehow be trained to select experts rather than friends as work partners—however "unnatural" and difficult such a procedure might be.

But how are such changes to be made? The problem is complicated—certainly more complicated than with cognitively guided skills, where it is often enough simply to make whatever is to be learned as cognitively clear as possible. In relation to changing the situation, for example, the behavioral scientist can indeed analyze its requirements and state the extent to which it fits or fails to fit the characteristics of individuals trying to adapt to it; but whether organizational or institutional changes can be made to modify the situation, and if so how best to make them, may involve major questions of social policy. To shift the whole U.S. social system so that it would encourage "familism" and enable some Southern Italians to adapt better to American life, would be a task in social engineering beyond the resources of almost any group of policy makers—in part because such a change would not be wanted by most Americans. On the other hand, to adjust the power situation in a particular firm—so that a new employee could make his new adjustment in terms of his past experience with power, both in his family and in other parts of the American social system—would be not only feasible, but also probably desired by the company as well as by the employee.

In each case, the monumental and the specific, the behavioral scientist could probably analyze with some accuracy what would have to be done. But in the first instance, real upheaval in the social system would be necessary, requiring fundamental changes in almost every aspect of life. In the second, perhaps relatively minor adjustments in the organization of the firm would do the trick. In both instances, the behavioral scientist provides the information on which policy decisions are based and also on which the methods for carrying them out depend.

Although both are obviously important, to change an individual may seem more appropriate for talent development than to change society. But changing values and motives in individuals requires a vast knowledge—not only of how and when they were formed in childhood, but of how they can be modified later in life. These are problems about which we know very little, and there is not a great deal in our research to shed light on them. We know something definite only in the negative sense that motives, values, and social skills are not to be changed by formal instruction the way cognitively guided skills are. For if we attempt to bring such personality characteristics under cognitive guidance, they turn into something else, just as Baldwin points out. A person can go to a "charm school" and learn to perform in ways associated with friendliness, but whether his basic need for friends or for being friendly has been modified in the process is a real question. Certainly if acts of friendliness become a cognitively guided skill which can be put into the service of any motive, even hate, they lose their capacity to express any basic characteristic of the person.

But perhaps there are ways of subtly changing, by indirect attack, not only the instrumental acts of friendliness, but the basic needs for love and for achievement and the like. Psychotherapy may do just this, though values and motives may be so fixed that even psychotherapy can change only their mode of expression or the way the subject feels about them. These are questions that only further research can decide. Strodtbeck's data, for example, indicate that the balance of power between mother and father in a family is associated with the extent to which the son feels he can control his own destiny. We might feel justified in assuming that the son gets his value orientation toward destiny from the power situation in the family and that such a value is going to influence markedly his subsequent achievement. But how stable is such a characteristic? What do we know about the ease with which it can be changed—if not by formal instruction, then by the power situations in which he finds himself later on, in school, in his first job, or after marriage? The whole theoretical orientation of our times, living as we do under the impact of psychoanalytic thinking, supports the notion that early learning in the family is of key importance and hard to modify by subsequent experiences, certainly by direct conscious teaching. Yet actually we know very little about how subsequent *indirect experiences* may modify basic social skills, motives, and values, presumably laid down irrevocably in early life.

If, then, in pushing beyond cognitively guided skills, we have come to the importance of matching stable personality characteristics with the requirements of social situations, we can also see that this new perspective raises a still further set of questions about how the stable characteristics of the person or requirements of the situation can be modified.

Some Specific Research Contributions

The Committee focussed its attention on non-academic achievement, on non-intellectual characteristics of achieving individuals, and on the sources of those non-intellectual characteristics. What can be said in brief about its discoveries in these areas? Among the non-academic types of achievement, two kinds were studied—skill in social perception and status mobility.

As for social perception, Bronfenbrenner started with a notion that seemed simple enough: that empathy, or the ability to know what other people are thinking and feeling, was a social skill of some importance deserving investigation. What he ran into was a veritable mare's nest of methodological difficulties and of varieties of social sensitivity. In an area of study marked by such technical confusion, it is a very real contribution that his project worked its way through to a careful definition of different ways of measuring social sensitivity.

His project ultimately defined two measures of skill in social perception—one a kind of sensitivity to the social norms of one's own group, "The ability to recognize the typical responses of persons in one's own sub-culture"; the other a "sensitivity to the way other people *differ* in their behavior, perceptions, or feelings." No measure of the former, he found, could be completely purified of the effect of the judge's own adherence to those norms—an effect which might make it easier or harder for him to estimate what others in his group would think. The importance of this factor and the impossibility of erasing it entirely have not generally been recognized in previous research. On the other hand, Bronfenbrenner was able to demonstrate that not all the skill in estimating social norms could be attributed to similarity; that people do differ in their ability to estimate the feeling of a group, even though variations cannot be measured in pure form. From a practical point of view, it may be important to know how to pick out "social barometers," even though they come by their skill in part through similarity to the group.

Bronfenbrenner's other index, the ability to estimate individual differences in other people's feelings, was not contaminated by the similarity factor. When it was used to determine how well a person could differentiate among the attitudes of *others toward himself,* it proved so unreliable as to suggest that, at least in the test situation used by Bronfenbrenner, people were not able to judge what other people were thinking about them. But the index did show that an individual was able to discriminate among the *self-judgments of others* in the group. That is, A could tell how B's attitude toward B differed from C's attitude toward C. For men in the group, this sensitivity to differences in others' feelings toward themselves was a generalized capacity; that is, men who showed it for women were *more* likely to show it for men. But for women it was not generalized. If women were sensitive to differences in the self-perceptions of men in the group, they were *less* likely to be sensitive to the self-perceptions of women in the group. In short, Bronfenbrenner's project found little evidence for a general factor of social sensitivity. For one thing, interpersonal sensitivity was not internally consistent: men showed it for both sexes, but women did not. For another, it was uncorrelated with the other index of social sensitivity he developed—skill in estimating social norms. So it is no longer possible to speak of "empathy" as if it were a unitary characteristic.

The necessity of solving complicated technical problems tended to force the research on social sensitivity into a very simple design, in which a subject was asked to estimate on one questionnaire what other subjects were checking on their questionnaires. Yet the ability to do this, as Bronfenbrenner pointed out, may be quite unrelated to actual social effectiveness, which for many occupations is probably a talent of more importance. In fact, there was some evidence that an individual with general interpersonal perceptiveness was not himself perceived very favorably. Possibly his sensitivity was achieved at a price in terms of realizing his own capacities for creative expression and forthright social behavior. In short, his own good cognitive understanding of what others are thinking may have been developed at the expense of his ability to behave in a way which seems to others to reflect his true feelings. If so, he would be an interesting illustration of Baldwin's point that when expressive behavior (reacting "naturally" to others) is cognitively guided, it tends to appear "unnatural" or instrumental and no longer representative of true inner feelings. In any case, now that methodological problems have been clarified, the next objective would seem to be to study effective interpersonal *performance* in social situations and its relationship to accuracy of perception of what people in the situation are thinking and feeling.

The second type of non-academic achievement studied was status mobility. If one argues, as Strodtbeck does, that a man's occupational and social status in a society is a widely recognized form of achievement, then in a sense those who rise in the status hierarchy and occupy positions of prestige can be considered "over-achievers," while those who perform jobs at lower levels with little pay or recognition can be considered "under-achievers." By this criterion Strodtbeck was able to show that Jews as a group achieved relatively more than Southern Italians, despite the fact that both groups had emigrated to the United States at about the same time and that the Jews had then only a slight edge over Southern Italians in adaptive occupational skills. In his research Strodtbeck located individual families within each of these two groups occupying at the present time different positions in the occupational status hierarchy;

and finally he chose from these families sons who could be classified as over- and under-achievers in school.

An interesting result of this research design is this. Strodtbeck was able to show that the values associated with academic over- and under-achievement are, to a considerable extent, the same as the values associated with greater occupational achievement (as defined by the Jewish-Italian group difference or the difference between fathers high and low in the occupational hierarchy at the present time). Thus, one would have reason to expect school achievement to lead in later life to occupational achievement. Such an expectation has already been shown by much previous research, although seldom in studies which have controlled background factors or investigated the reasons for the association the way Strodtbeck did.

McClelland's research dealt with another aspect of status as a criterion of achievement—namely, its subjective meaning. Here the question was: who are the people generally *perceived* to be achievers in a small community, and what are their objective "stimulus characteristics"? What are they like? Are they the ones who have shown the most status mobility, as would be predicted from Strodtbeck's analysis? A particular effort was made to separate perceived achievement from perceived social status. Yet a case for the independence of the two dimensions could be made only for the most stable of the three towns studied, where inherited social status or "good family" could be distinguished by members of the community from the actual achievement of members of the family in this generation.

By and large, the perceived dimensions of success correspond rather closely to Strodtbeck's analysis of the structural requirements for achievement on the American scene. To begin with, a man's success was judged partly in terms of his occupational mobility, in terms of how many rungs on the occupational ladder he had risen or fallen in relation to his father's position—a fact which supports Strodbeck's contention that occupational mobility is a widely recognized form of achievement. What the study perhaps adds to his notion is that it is not so much occupational level as such which is important for perceived success, but the person's actual occupational movement upwards or downwards. Apparently a man does not get quite so much credit for a high position if he has all the advantages to begin with.

But the most important factor associated with perceived success in small communities was the extent to which the person participated in community enterprises. This second finding fits rather well with Strodtbeck's analysis of the American achievement ethic as including the following elements: (1) man's responsibility to control his own destiny, (2) the importance of loyalty to a larger collective than the family, and (3) the use of a man's actual performance in a large impersonal system as the basis for determining his influence and prestige. Community service fits these requirements in several ways. It gives prestige and power through competence rather than connections; it represents loyalty to a larger community than the family; and it reflects *par excellence* the conviction that man can control his destiny. If Strodtbeck's analysis is correct, therefore, it should hardly be surprising that people who behave as they are supposed to in terms of the achievement ethic—who are active in community service—should be accorded high marks for achievement by their fellow townsmen.

One may argue, of course, that reputation for achievement and actual achievement are two quite different things. It may be this very American demand for community participation that prevents, let us say, our scientists from accomplishing as much in their own chosen fields as they would have been able to if they could have stuck strictly to business. Perhaps so. It is certainly appropriate to judge achievement by different standards for different purposes. But one must also recognize that there *is* a generalized basis for judging a man's achievement in life arising out of the U. S. social system—even if the knowledge is finally used only to protect scientists from being influenced by it.

In addition to such non-academic types of achievement, the Committee turned its attention to the non-intellectual characteristics of the achievers themselves. These may be roughly divided into group and individual characteristics. Among the former must be placed such things as the following: the sex differences Bronfenbrenner found in interpersonal sensitivity; his finding that group differences in knowledge of social norms had an effect on interpersonal sensitivity; Strodtbeck's analysis of differences in occupational mobility among Italians and Jews; and McClelland's finding that various background characteristics such as sex, education, and income were related to perceived achievement. Knowledge of such group influences can, of course, add to one's knowledge of the individual; but they inevitably raise one's curiosity as to factors within the individual which mediate these differences. It is not enough to know that being a Jew is a characteristic often associated with occupational success. One wants to know why.

In this area, the Committee's research projects experimented with several different measuring instruments. Bronfenbrenner used the adjective check-list to determine the "social stimulus value" of people with greater or less skill in social perception. He found that while sensitive men and sensitive women had somewhat different social characteristics and that these characteristics also differed somewhat depending on whether they were sensitive to men or women, the general picture of the sensitive person was of someone who is "perceptive and responsive to others' needs, seldom gives offense, but at the same time, perhaps because of his very sensitivity, tends to be hesitant, restrained, and somewhat colorless." In short, if you want to find someone who is sensitive to others, it would be a good idea to pick someone who is perceived by others as "sensitive" (in a slightly different sense).

If one applied the same finding to occupational achievement, one might expect that the best way to pick a person who is going to be a success later on would be to find someone who is perceived by his peers or superiors as likely to succeed. Although such an approach was not tried in any of the present research projects, previous studies of ratings of school children, checked against their later success or lack of it, would not lead one to expect too much from this method (*17*). Perhaps it would have worked better if adjective check-lists had been used rather than rating scales. Recent research at the California Institute for Personality Assessment by Gough (*6*) and others indicates that more and less successful graduate students have different "social stimulus value" as reflected in adjective check-lists.

Strodtbeck used as measuring instruments a value questionnaire (guided by earlier work of F. R. Kluckhohn (*7*) and others) and a method for scoring *n* Achievement from content analysis of written stories (*8*). The results from the questionnaire were particularly interesting. He was able to find eight items which, when combined into a V-scale, distinguished between three types of over- and under-achievers—namely, Jews versus Italians, fathers of high versus fathers of low socio-economic status, and students doing well versus students doing poorly in school. These items when factor-analyzed yielded two main factors. One seemed to represent the value placed on man's ability to control his own destiny, and the other the value placed on a willingness to leave one's family if necessary to make one's way in the world. A single item suggested that a third value might also be part of this "achievement value complex"

—namely, one placing greater emphasis on individual than on collective rewards for effort expended.

The first value—the belief that man can perfect himself and control his future—was also reflected in other items in the questionnaire which differentiated Jews from Italians. That is, Jews believed more strongly than Italians that higher education was important and that one should not be satisfied with a lower-level occupation "if things turned out that way." These values fit in rather well—in fact, they are partly predicted from—Strodtbeck's analysis of the U. S. achievement ethic, with the possible exception of the one dealing with individual or collective rewards. Here the ethic appears to require loyalty to a larger collective, while the value actually associated with achievement on the American scene involves a preference for individual over collective rewards. The contradiction, however, is more apparent than real. What the American expects, as his emphasis on community service shows, is *individual reward for service to the collective,* which is quite a different thing from collective reward for work for a collective. The particular questionnaire items that Strodtbeck found to make up his value orientations may turn out to be fairly specific to the teen-age population with which he was working; but the theoretical significance of the value patterns he identified goes beyond the items that make them up. In other words, knowing the general character of the values associated with occupational and academic achievement, other investigators can measure them in different, perhaps more appropriate, ways with other populations.

Strodtbeck also confirmed the fact that *n* Achievement is associated with over- and under-achievement in school as reported also by Morgan (*10*), and Ricciuti and Sadacca (*11*). One might expect that since *n* Achievement and V-score are uncorrelated, and since they are both associated with over- and under-achievement in school, a combination of the two measures would yield a good prediction of how well a boy was going to do in school. Strodtbeck did find that 77% of the boys who scored high on both measures were over-achievers as compared with only 36% of those who scored low on both measures, but the sample was too small for the results to be significant.

There is in addition some evidence that *n* Achievement may be an independent factor connected with the occupational achievement with which the V-scale is also associated. Rosen (*13*) has reported that *n* Achievement increases as one goes up the socio-economic scale, so that high *n* Achievement is significantly associated with higher socio-economic status. Furthermore, McClelland and others (9) have reported that Jewish parents express a belief in earlier training for self-reliance than Italians do; and Winterbottom (8) has associated early independence training with higher *n* Achievement. Thus, one might expect it to be highly likely that Jews as a group would have higher *n* Achievement than Italians. Since Jews also show higher occupational achievement, one can argue that an indirect connection has been established between *n* Achievement and occupational achievement. This connection is also backed up by Rosen's findings of higher *n* Achievement at higher socio-economic levels, since boys of such standing will more often turn out to achieve more occupationally. In short, the *n* Achievement score, though independent of the V-scale, is linked just as the V-scale is, though less directly, in three ways to higher achievement—once in school and twice in the occupational world in the differences between Jews and Italians, and between individuals from high and low socio-economic status.

Finally, the Committee devoted some attention, particularly in Strodtbeck's project, to the sources of the non-intellectual characteristics of achievers. Two sources in particular were studied, both related to the family. One was the balance of power among family members, and the other was the value climate of the family as it derived from the religious and cultural background of its members. For example, the Southern Italian's belief in *destino* was traced partly to a Catholic emphasis on man's helplessness before God and partly to old folkways; the Jewish emphasis on schooling was derived from the ancient Jewish tradition of book learning and literacy. Interestingly enough, the values of the parents apparently did not affect their sons in any simple way. There were few if any *consistent* correlations between the V-scores of the parents and either the V-scores or *n* Achievement scores of their sons found either in the original study or a repetition of it with a Japanese-American group. Among the Jews and Italians, the mother's V-score was positively associated with the son's V-score, and the father's V-score with the son's *n* Achievement; but among Japanese-Americans both correlations were significantly negative!

While a case can be made for parental values having their chief effect *indirectly* by the way in which they modify relationships between parents and child rather than directly by modifying the belief system of the child, the safest conclusion is simply that the transmission of values and motives is different in different family types, perhaps because of the other factor Strodtbeck studied—the power balance in the family. Powerful fathers tend to produce sons with low achievement values—with a belief in destiny beyond their control and an unwillingness to leave home. The picture is one of a submissive, obedient son who does not believe in going away from home and conquering the world on his own. On the other hand, if the mother's power is stronger (as reflected in the fact that she wins relatively more decisions), then the son is likely to have higher achievement values. Strodtbeck's interpretation of these findings is that the son's adjustment to the power situation in his family transfers to life outside it. If he lives in an autocratic system, he tends to accept the world as being autocratic, and submits. If he lives in a more democratic system where there is equality between the parents, he has ideas about individuals being able to do things on their own.

It is obvious that interpretations of data on the sources of values and motives in families, like many of the other interpretations of empirical findings in this report, must be regarded as highly tentative until further research data can be collected. It is also obvious that many sources of the non-intellectual characteristics of an achiever—e.g., his peer group, his school, his job—have not been studied. At every point in our research program there are important problems needing further investigation. The attempt throughout has been to interpret as reasonably as possible whatever facts have turned up in our studies; not because the facts are especially secure, but because such interpretations may serve as a source of future research hypotheses.

Prospects

The Committee did not adopt as one of its objectives the formulation of practical recommendations concerning talent identification and development—a task which has fortunately been ably undertaken by Berdie (*1*), Wolfle (*18*), and others. Nevertheless, it is not difficult to see certain policy implications in its findings and general point of view. Since a clear understanding of these implications may be helpful to others whose task it is to shape policy, let us summarize them explicitly.

(1) *The study of what may be referred to as expressive characteristics of the person—his values, motives, skills in social perception —should continue to have a high research priority, as it had for this Committee.* We indeed focussed our attention on them, largely because at that time the study of cognitively guided characteristics— the abilities—seemed to have reached a plateau so far as prediction

was concerned. Now the situation is somewhat different: we have produced additional solid evidence that expressive characteristics are important for achievement or that they are in themselves a kind of achievement valuable in its own right. For example, the values represented in Strodtbeck's V-scale are associated both with academic achievement (after intelligence has been equated for) and with occupational achievement; individual differences in social sensitivity exist and can be measured. Our own efforts to measure such variables have persuaded us that further research along the same lines will pay off.

Such research should be pursued not only because of its potential contribution to the variance in talented performance, but because it will provide information that is essential for identifying potential talent in a democratic way. For the fact of the matter is that background factors like sex, social class, and ethnicity are associated with such large differences in the yield of talented persons that they can be used to improve talent identification; and yet, if we do use them, we are not judging in terms of *individual* merit. There is, for instance, every empirical indication that, in a group of high school boys and girls of equal ability, Jewish students are more likely to be successful, and boys more likely than girls to achieve a successful career. Should we then give preference to Jews and to males in selecting potentially talented individuals? If we did, we would improve our forecasting efficiency—and it is often on just this basis that women are discriminated against in the professions. But to do so violates the fundamental democratic principle that an individual must be judged in terms of his own merits and not in terms of such background characteristics.

Because the temptation is always there to improve one's selection by dipping into group rates—undemocratic though it may be—the only long-run method of handling the problem is to be able to measure the characteristics associated with differential group rates *on an individual basis.* For example, Strodtbeck has begun to measure the value differences which may account for the greater occupational achievement of Jews over Southern Italians. As soon as such values can be measured, they can be located in any boy, whether he is a Jew, an Italian, or a native of Texas. Similarly, Bronfenbrenner has found that men are more likely than women to be sensitive to individual differences in the feelings of both men and women; but since he can measure the sensitivity in question, it is possible to find women who have it too, and it is unnecessary to disqualify a person, just because she is a woman, for a position requiring such a skill. In short, background factors—sex, ethnicity, socio-economic status, religion—are important largely because of their effect on expressive characteristics which we must learn how to measure if we are to assess individuals democratically in terms of their own merit.

There is still a third reason why research on expressive characteristics should be pushed. It is a practical one. The fact that measures of cognitively guided characteristics—the traditional abilities—are so much better developed at present means that when selection is to be made—for admission to college, for awarding fellowships, and so on—the judges have a precise measure of one set of factors, the abilities, and no measure at all of the others: values, motives, social skills. What they have instead is a vague knowledge of actuarial rates of talent production in various groups (e.g., Jews are more likely to succeed than some other groups, men are less likely to drop out than women, boys from "better families" often turn out better than their school performance would lead one to expect), and some impressions of personality characteristics based on interviews and perhaps tests of personal adjustment. Judges dislike using the first kind of knowledge because it is undemocratic, and the second kind because it is imprecise. So in the end the selection comes to be based largely on the precise *and* democratic measures of the traditional abilities. The difficulty with this solution is that it tends to ignore altogether the contribution of personality factors to achievement and causes some talent loss by screening out individuals whose cognitively guided skills may not be unusually high but whose other characteristics may suit them admirably for success in college or later life. So to correct the errors that arise from increasing reliance for talent selection on precise measures of only one set of factors, it is highly desirable to push the measurement of characteristics like motives, values, and social skills. And this is true, no matter how difficult the task may prove to be to find methods as precise and as free from distortion through faking as those developed for measuring the traditional abilities.

(2) *The structural requirements of the social situation in which talented performance occurs should be subjected to thorough study.* If it is true, as we have contended, that emphasis on stable personal characteristics means a greater emphasis on *matching* individuals with situations whose requirements are such as to make them most likely to adapt successfully, then those requirements must be known in advance. Strodtbeck's analysis of the requirements for achievement in the American scene is a case in point, but much more detailed knowledge is necessary. Just what are the role requirements

of being a doctor, an engineer, a musician, a TV star, a mother in the United States in our time? The question is not simply one of asking members of these occupational roles or others what they perceive the nature of the role to be. It is much more one of actually observing how they spend their time, what kinds of persons and situations they have to meet, what kinds of decisions they make and why. By way of illustration, Strodtbeck demonstrated that perception of parental roles was not always accurate as measured against role performance. One of the chief methodological advances his study makes is to stress the importance of measuring the actual interaction of parents or others in various role situations. For unless we know the performance requirements of social roles, how can we fit individuals with stable personality characteristics into the role which is most likely to call forth from them a "talented response"?

Of special importance is a study of the role of being a student in our society, because nearly all talent selection nowadays is done via the school system. Although there was a time when a man could become President or attain some other considerable achievement without going to college, it is becoming increasingly difficult. Unless a man succeeds in some way in school, he is handicapped for all kinds of subsequent achievement. But what are the requirements for achievement in the school situation? Is the power or reward system such, for example, that individuals with certain stable characteristics cannot adapt successfully to it, even though they might adapt quite well to the power and reward systems in jobs for which *success in school is a prerequisite?* The point is that, if schools and colleges are to serve increasingly as a screening device for all sorts of subsequent achievement, they must be subjected to close scrutiny *as social systems.* We need to know to what extent the role requirements of being a student are the same as or different from those of various other status systems in later life.

(3) *Ways of modifying stable characteristics of persons and of situations should be investigated.* If we know little about how to measure values and motives, and less about the requirements of social systems, we know perhaps least of all about ways of changing either the one or the other. The one thing we do know, as has been pointed out already, is that direct conscious teaching is not likely to change needs and values fundamentally, although it may change the way they are expressed.

But this does not exhaust the possibilities. It is true that both our research and our theoretical orientation have convinced us that early learning in the home is a main source of such characteristics.

It is also true that some individuals of high ability will undoubtedly not have the desirable kind of home background. Is there anything that can be done for them? Can school or peer-group social systems make up for such deficiencies? If a boy comes from an authoritarian home in which one parent makes all the decisions, he may very well, according to Strodtbeck's findings, have developed values not conducive to most types of achievement in the United States. But would it be possible to change those values by exposing him to an especially democratic teacher-pupil relationship in school? Take the case of a boy whose *n* Achievement is low presumably because his parents are not interested in standards of excellence and do not encourage him to do things well by himself; could such a boy develop more *n* Achievement by a series of indirectly controlled achievement experiences in school or in the peer group? Can social sensitivity be increased by repeated exposure to varieties of human experience, or perhaps through a personal psychoanalysis? The answers to such questions can only be given by further research. And since the normal methods of producing changes in behavior by conscious instruction do not seem applicable here, indirect methods of changing basic personality characteristics deserve special research attention.

(4) *At the practical level of stopping talent loss, our research suggests that offering increased scholarship aid is not by itself going to be sufficient*—a conclusion also reached by others who have done research in this area (*1, 3, 18*). Many of the talented individuals in our society who decide not to go on toward a higher education, do so because of their values and motives—their interest in other things. While the offer of scholarships may put college on a level to compete successfully with other interests, there are always the disadvantages that it will do so for only a minority (only 12% mentioned lack of money as the most important reason for not going to college (*3*)); that even for the minority, scholarship aid may help only for a limited time; and that individuals whose interest in education has to be subsidized or "bid up" in competition with other desires are not particularly good bets in the long pull anyway. The real problem is to develop interests, values, and motives that will be more favorable to achievement in the American scene.

As Berdie (*1*) and Wolfle (*18*) point out, the general method of solving the problem involves improvements in the school system and in counselling services available for parents and children, preferably in the seventh to ninth grades when career choices are being made. The Committee's research helps focus attention on the general objectives of such improved services—on the kind of values, motives, and sensitivities that are likely to need developing and on the factors in the home that are likely to block their development. As an experiment it might be worth picking out, at the seventh or eighth grade level, in a given school system the 50% of the top 27% in grades and ability who do not plan to go to college (*18*, p. 248). Through tests and interviews their values and motives, and those of their parents, could be assessed and compared with those of college preparatory students and with Strodtbeck's findings. Presumably the potential "drop-outs" would have less confidence in such beliefs as man's ability to control his destiny or the wisdom of leaving home to make one's own way; would show a motive pattern less conducive to achievement; and would perhaps have an abnormal reaction to power (whether over-compliance or rebellion) based on an authoritarian balance of power in the home. Then they and their parents could be exposed to counselling procedures designed to change their values. If the home influence were too negative to overcome, scholarships could be used to send the students to special summer camps or boarding schools, where they would live in an atmosphere more favorable to developing their achievement potential. At the end of a trial period one could estimate how many potential "drop-outs" had been saved for higher achievement as compared with control schools where nothing special had been done.

To a certain extent several current research projects, such as the Quincy Youth Development Commission under the general direction of Dr. Robert Havighurst, are already designed to achieve part of such an objective—to measure the effects of special counselling and instruction within the school system on the development of talent. What our analysis does is to suggest additional lines for such research to take. In particular, it focuses attention on the kinds of values, motives, and sensitivities that need developing, on ways of measuring them, and on the possible importance of giving some children a living experience outside the home to set over against negative effects of early experiences in the family.

For those who are interested in doing something practical about the problem of talent loss, an experimental program aimed at changing some of the stable personality characteristics of able 13- to 15-year-olds through summer camps or boarding schools has much to recommend it. At least it would be attacking the problem at a more fundamental level than is done simply by providing more scholarships for those who are not really interested in a higher education or who do not have the values and motives likely to succeed in terms of our achievement ethic anyway.

Trying to engineer a solution to the problem of talent loss raises certain ultimate questions. Is there a danger that talent will be too effectively identified—that too many people will go to college, perhaps? The arguments for such a danger run all the way from a contention that there are not enough jobs at the top to take care of all the talented people, to a fear that removing all the talented people from the bottom would disrupt society. The first argument has been discussed by Wolfle, who feels that the market in many fields of specialization can handle an increased supply in the foreseeable future and that, in any case, "there are never enough people of the highest quality in any field" (*18*, p. 266).

It may be worth pursuing the second argument for a moment—the contention that society would be disrupted. Suppose that as a result of research we could put a stop to "talent loss" and see to it that all individuals of high ability and appropriate personality characteristics were fitted into high-level occupations which would maximize their potential. Indeed, knowledge leading to such an outcome would appear to be the ultimate objective of research on identification of talent. Would this mean that there would be no able people left to do jobs such as bricklaying, carpentering, or the operating of machines?

Riesman points out that in the modern factory a man may often show initiative, even in carrying out orders, because he realizes that the higher-ups may not know all the practical requirements of the job in hand. "William F. Whyte of Cornell tells the story of the workmen in an oil-cracking plant in Oklahoma who got angry because, in a collective bargaining session, the management had referred to them as semi-skilled. They proceeded to carry out literally the instructions of the chemist, instructions which they had previously treated as a good chef will treat a recipe—soon bringing the plant to a halt." Riesman also refers to "the important role workmen play in modifying a customer's requirements for accuracy according to their own knowledge of what is actually needed, thereby minimizing the number of rejected pieces" (*12*, p. 292). To construct an "overprint over a blueprint" like this obviously requires some intelligence, some achievement motivation, and a belief that the individual should take initiative. What would happen if the selection system were so good that all people with characteristics favorable to good performance were in higher level jobs? At the very least, the factory would have to be organized differently.

Fortunately in the present stage of society and of our knowledge of talent, such ultimate questions are not pressing. In the first place, the present methods of talent identification are so inadequate that the problem is how to correct a bad situation rather than how to avoid making it too perfect. In the second place, the characteristics making up the talent potential are by no means perfectly correlated. So, for example, there may be plenty of people with high motivation for achievement who lack the intelligence to be high-level executives. Such people may be just the ones to take the initiative in modifying the customers' blueprints, in Riesman's example. Different characteristics may lead to "talented responses" in different situations.

In the third place, in a democratic society the long-range problem may not be one of a better distribution of a limited supply of talent, but one of increasing the over-all supply because of the growing demands that all types of occupations place on people. As Schwartz (*15*) has pointed out, an "open" society, with its heavy demands on the individual, frequently has a talent deficit because there are not enough able people to go around to fill the large number of jobs which are really demanding. In contrast, a "closed" society, which may be as highly organized as an ant-hill, requires less talent of most of its individual members except for the very few at the top, and so is likely to develop a talent surplus.

Ultimately, then, questions of the supply and distribution of talent are related to the type of society involved. As far as a democracy is concerned, the problem is one of increasing the supply in order to handle the many existing jobs of responsibility and improving the distribution so that each individual gets a chance to reach his own highest level of potential achievement. If the supply is increased, then improvement in distribution is not likely to result in a dearth of talented individuals to fill jobs lower in the occupational scale.

(5) *Research on basic theoretical problems in talent identification and development should receive additional strong support.* Americans have frequently been criticized for being too much concerned with practical, engineering problems in the physical sciences rather than with the basic theoretical questions which must be answered before technology can advance. Whether or not the criticism is justified in the main, it has a considerable basis in fact so far as the situation of talent is concerned. We know something about measuring abilities, and we know that, in the past, financial handicaps have prevented people from going to school. So the

pressure is always to apply this knowledge on a grander scale—to measure abilities of more people more precisely, to provide more scholarships for more people. There is nothing wrong with such objectives in themselves *unless they divert attention and resources away from other theoretical problems that must be solved.* In our rush to give every potentially talented child a break or to beat the Russians in the production of engineers, let us not forget that the quota of basic knowledge on how to solve such problems is not very large. It was the task of this Committee to try to explore ways of increasing such basic knowledge. We believe that our results, at the very least, justify further efforts directed at the same objective. Research to improve selection for a specific criterion by known methods will always be supported by those who have a direct stake in the results. What is needed is more long-range, venture capital to develop new theoretical resources—capital of the sort with which this Committee was provided.

References

1. Berdie, R. F. *After High School, What?* Minneapolis: Univ. Minnesota Press, 1954.
2. Cattell, R. B. Personality and motivation theory based on structural measurement. In J. L. McCary (ed.) *Psychology of Personality.* New York: Logos Press, 1956.
3. Cole, C. C. Current loss of talent from high school to college: summary of a report. *Higher Education,* 1955, *12,* 35-38.
4. DeCharms, R., Morrison, H. W., Reitman, R., and McClelland, D. C. Behavioral correlates of directly and indirectly measured achievement motivation. In D. C. McClelland (ed.) *Studies in Motivation.* New York: Appleton-Century-Crofts, 1955, pp. 414-423.
5. French, E. G. Motivation as a variable in work-partner selection. *J. abnorm. soc. Psychol.,* 1956, *53,* 96-99.
6. Gough, H. *Predicting Success in Graduate Training: A Progress Report.* Berkeley: Univ. Calif. Institute of Personality Assessment and Research, 1950. (Mimeographed)
7. Kluckhohn, F. R. Dominant and substitute profiles of cultural orientations. *Social Forces,* 1950, *28,* 376-393.
8. McClelland, D. C., Atkinson, J. W., Clark, R. A., and Lowell, E. L. *The Achievement Motive.* New York: Appleton-Century-Crofts, 1953.
9. McClelland, D. C., Rindlisbacher, A., and deCharms, R. Religious and other sources of parental attitudes toward independence training. In D. C. McClelland (ed.), *Studies in Motivation.* New York: Appleton-Century-Crofts, 1955, pp. 389-397.
10. Morgan, H. H. A psychometric comparison of achieving and nonachieving college students of high ability. *J. consult. Psychol.,* 1952, *16,* 292-298.
11. Ricciuti, H. N. and Sadacca, R. The prediction of academic grades with a projective test of achievement motivation: II. Cross-validation at the high school level. Princeton, N. J.: Educational Testing Service, 1955.

12. Riesman, D. *Individualism Reconsidered.* Glencoe, Ill.: The Free Press, 1954.
13. Rosen, B. The achievement syndrome. *Amer. sociol. Rev.*, 1956, *21*, 203-211.
14. Sarason, S., Mandler, G., and Craighill, P. G. The effects of differential instructions on anxiety and learning. *J. abnorm. soc. Psychol.*, 1952, *47*, 561-565.
15. Schwartz, R. D. Functional alternatives to inequality. *Amer. sociol. Rev.*, 1955, *20*, 424-431.
16. Smith, M. B. Conference on non-intellective determinants of achievement. *Items,* 1953, *7*, 13-18. New York: Social Science Research Council.
17. Terman, L. M. Scientists and non-scientists in a group of 800 gifted men. *Psychol. Monogr.*, 1954, *68,* No. 378.
18. Wolfle, D. *America's Resources of Specialized Talent.* New York: Harper, 1954.

Appendix

Jewish and Italian Immigration and Subsequent Status Mobility

BY FRED. L. STRODTBECK

JEWISH AND ITALIAN IMMIGRATION

THE chronological patterns of immigration for Jews and Italians to the United States are generally similar, if care is taken to distinguish between Northern and Southern Italians, as well as between German and East-European Jews (*7,* pp. 143-146, 158-165, 107-114; *11,* pp. 113-120; *19,* pp. 230-231, 387-390). Both Northern Italian and German Jewish immigrants comprised a proportionately small segment of the total number of immigrants in their respective ethnic groups. German Jewish immigration started in 1815; it moved slowly, was never very large, and reached its peak in the early 1800's (*7,* pp. 215-216). After 1880 it virtually stopped (*14,* p. 1220), until the victims of Nazi persecution came again in large numbers to this country in the 1930's. The total immigration of German Jews during the nineteenth century has been estimated at 150,000 (*14,* p. 1218).

Beginning in the 1880's, the mass migration of Jews from Eastern Europe, on the other hand, reached its peak between 1901 and 1914 (*11,* pp. 113-120; *19,* p. 389). From 1880 to 1942 it is estimated that 2,601,690 Jews, almost exclusively of East European origin, entered the United States (*14,* p. 1216). In 1950 the estimated Jewish popu-

[1] The original draft of this appendix was a hundred-page document prepared by Florence Sultan. Bernard C. Rosen supervised Miss Sultan's work and subsequently condensed the first version. Mr. Rosen's version was in turn rewritten by Fred L. Strodtbeck and Hava Eve Bonné.

lation of the United States, combining persons of both German and East European Jewish ancestry, was given as five million (*1*, p. 248).

Northern Italians began migrating here in the 1820's and came in gradually increasing numbers. Numerically this group was never very large and has been estimated at 81,000 (*7*, p. 114). From 1880 to 1900 a larger wave of about one million Italian immigrants entered America; and of these, the majority were Northern Italians (*7*, pp. 111-112, 114). In 1900 the emigration center shifted radically from Northern to Southern Italy. From 1900 to 1930 a total of 4,569,918 Italians arrived in this country, the vast majority of whom came from Southern Italy. By 1925 the Southern Italians numbered more than four-fifths of all the Italians in the United States (*19*, p. 235). The greatest period of Italian immigration was from 1901 to 1910, with the peak year occurring in 1913 (compared to the 1906 peak year for the Jews) (*4*, p. 9). It has been estimated that by 1940 there were approximately six million Italians in the United States (*19*, p. 231).

Similarity in the economic and occupational characteristics of Jewish and Italian immigrants is much greater than is usually recognized. Contrary to widespread belief, Jewish immigration to this country was not entirely a movement of the merchant class, as the term is ordinarily understood. The overwhelming proportion of Jews arrived in this country without capital; indeed, most of them were impoverished. Like the Italians, they had endured great economic deprivation in Europe and were little prepared to enter typical American middle-class occupations.

An excellent source of information regarding detailed occupational distribution of Jewish immigrants in their countries of origin is the Reports of the Commissioner-General of Immigration, which have been summarized by Joseph (*11*, p. 187). These are based on a sample of 590,000 persons reporting occupations in the period from 1899 to 1910. The figures reveal that about two-thirds of Jewish immigrants were skilled laborers. Within this category the leading types of specialization were tailoring, carpentry, dressmaking, shoe repairing, clerical work, painting, and butchering. The second and third most frequent occupations were unskilled labor (12 per cent) and domestic service (11 per cent). Only 5 per cent of these Jewish immigrants were classified as merchants and dealers, and this latter category consisted largely of peddlers and petty storekeepers. It is worth noting that the number of farm workers among the Jewish immigrants (2 per cent) was at least as great as that of the Jewish professional immigrants (1.3 per cent), and both were negligible proportions. The majority of the professionals were teachers and musicians.

Between 1900 and 1925, the occupational distribution of Jewish immigrants remained similar to the above pattern (*14*, p. 1230). Almost two-thirds of the 992,000 gainfully occupied Jewish immigrants admitted during this period belonged to the industrial class of craftsmen and artisans. Merchants comprised 10 per cent of this group, an increase over the percentage reported for the earlier immigrants. The proportion of unskilled laborers and house servants remained almost identical (10.4 per cent and 12.4 per cent, respectively). Again, the number of agricultural workers slightly exceeded that from the professions (2.4 per cent, compared to 2 per cent).

Estimates of the proportion of Italian immigrants in the agricultural category range from 65 per cent to as high as 85 per cent (see Brown, *4*, p. 262; Schermerhorn, *19*, p. 232; Williams, *23*, p. 17; and Covello, *6*, p. 438). In Joseph's summary of the period from 1899 to 1910, the occupational category second in numerical importance was unskilled labor; 14.6 per cent of the immigrants were classified in that group (*11*, p. 190). Foerster states that the leading types of skilled workers were (in order of their frequency) stone-cutters, mechanics, mariners, masons, barbers, seamstresses, and shoe-makers (*9*, p. 333). Williams says that fishing was the second leading occupation after farming (*23*, pp. 17, 25), but this is not stressed by Foerster. Only 0.4 per cent of the Italians were in the professions.

Jewish and Italian Mobility

Although the intervening steps may not be clear in all cases, it is an established fact that at the present time Jews occupy to an unusual degree the higher positions in the status hierarchy. There is no exception to this conclusion in more than twenty-five available studies (*2*, pp. 266-269; *3*, pp. 180-199; *5*, p. 57; *8*, pp. 320-323; *12*, 207-216; *15*, pp. 408-409; 413-415; *17*, pp. 1243-1246, 1255-1256; *18*, pp. 13, 31, 32, 37, 38, 46, 51, 183-184; *20*, pp. 26-33; *21*, pp. 26-28, 31). American Jews are concentrated in four vocational categories: commerce, the professions, white-collar work, and industry. Only a small proportion can be found in the occupational areas of public service, domestic and personal service, transportation and communication, agriculture, capital goods manufacturing, and construction. In terms of the socio-economic status of their occupations, Jews are heavily represented in the upper strata of professionals, semi-professionals, and white-collar workers. Correspondingly, they are greatly under-represented at the working-class level; only a small percentage of them is employed as skilled, semi-skilled, or unskilled workers. Our knowledge is imprecise in detail because of the inherent difficulty of determining accurately the occupational characteristics of a religious group. For the fourteen studies in which Florence Sultan made a comparison of the occupational distribution of Jews with the occupational distribution within a given city, there were no instances in which an index, determined in the manner illustrated in Table 1, did not indicate a clear concentration of Jews in the upper-status categories. The comparison between the median values for Jews and the distribution of all gainfully employed urban males in Table 1 satisfactorily reflects the individual Jewish occupational studies and strongly confirms the higher status of Jews in comparison with the total urban population.

TABLE 1. JEWISH OCCUPATIONAL DISTRIBUTION (MALE) FROM FOURTEEN COMMUNITY STUDIES COMPARED WITH GAINFULLY EMPLOYED URBAN MALES, 1940

Occupational Class	Jews		U.S. Urban %	Index
	Range %	Median %		
Professional and Semi-Professional	8 to 19	13	7	186
Proprietors, Managers, Executives	11 to 58	35	13	269
Clerical, Sales	21 to 56	36	19	189
Foremen, highly-skilled workers	3 to 16	7	19	37
Machine operators	0 to 18	5	30	17
Protective service	0 to 4	1	2	50
Service (excluding protective)	0 to 4	1	7	14
Laborers	0 to 4	1	10	10

Source: Studies of Buffalo (1938), Camden (1948), Charleston (1948), Detroit (1935), Erie (1940), Grand Rapids (1944), Indianapolis (1948), Jacksonville (1945), Miami (1949), Newark (1948), Pittsburgh (1938), Portland, Oregon (1947), San Francisco (1938), and Utica (1948) found in the *American Jewish Year Book, 1950* (*1*).

The comparison of the occupational patterns of immigrant and native-born Jews constitutes an interesting developmental study of Jewish occupational mobility. What appears as a fairly characteristic occupational pattern for immigrant Jews after arrival in the United

States is presented in the 1900 census data. The sample consisted of 143,337 gainfully employed persons classified as "Russians," virtually all of whom were Jewish, living in seven large American cities (*5,* p. 56). The majority were employed in manufacturing (60.6 per cent). Next in order of numerical importance were the categories of trade (19.9 per cent) and the professions (2.6 per cent). The great bulk of the Jews in industry were wage workers engaged in the apparel, tobacco, and metal-work industries.

The mobility path for many of these immigrant Jews led them, after several years as workmen in industry, to leave the workshop and enter the area of trade. To a much less extent, they entered clerical work and the professions.

Studies made of Jewish occupational distribution in the years 1924-25 reflect the shift of Jews from industry into trade, the professions, and clerical occupations (*10,* pp. 162-166). A survey of thirty-six cities made at the time revealed that the relative number of Jews in manufacturing and in domestic and personal service decreased, while the relative number of those in trade, the professions, and clerical work increased. The larger number of Jews in America in 1925 were foreign-born, but a sizable portion of the native-born was included in the 1924-25 study. This trend toward increase in representation in trade, clerical work, and the professions has continued through World War II for American Jews. Quite recently, the proportion of Jews in trade has declined somewhat, perhaps suggesting that native-born Jews show less inclination toward this vocational area (*10,* pp. 263-266; *17,* pp. 1243-1250; *20,* pp. 58-59).

The occupational divergence between immigrant fathers and their American-born sons is illustrated in the 1940 study of Baltimore Jewish youth that is summarized by Reich (*17*). While only 5 per cent of the fathers were engaged in professional or technical work, 13 per cent of the sons were engaged in, and about 50 per cent aspired to, professional careers. An indication of the decline of interest in trade among the native-born appears in the finding that, although 46 per cent of the fathers were engaged in trade, only 5 per cent of the sons were working in, and only 6 per cent aspired to, this career. The growth of interest in white-collar work is shown by the fact that, whereas 7 per cent of the fathers were employed in office and sales work, 53 per cent of the sons were engaged in, and 26 per cent aspired to, this work. Significant also is the trend away from skilled labor. A third of the fathers were employed in this area, but only 2 per cent of the sons were engaged in, and only 7 per cent showed preference for, skilled labor.

The occupational distribution of Jewish women differs significantly from the distribution of all United States female workers. The proportion of Jewish women employed in the higher-status occupations of clerical and sales work and in the professions is greater than the national average of women workers so employed. Correspondingly, the proportion of Jewish females working in skilled, semi-skilled, and unskilled categories is smaller than that of all female workers.

The occupational pattern of American Jews, then, may be summarized as follows: (a) Certain occupational patterns differentiate native-born and foreign-born Jews. A greater proportion of the native-, as compared to the foreign-born, are employed in the professions, white-collar jobs, and public service. The proportion of foreign-born employed in trade, industry, and skilled, semi-skilled, and unskilled labor exceeds that of natives. (b) There are slight differentiations in the occupational patterns of Jews in large cities in contrast with those in smaller towns and cities. Jews in large cities are more heavily represented in industry, public service, and working-class occupations, and less represented in the professions and trade than are Jews in smaller cities. (c) Working Jewish women are more frequently found in higher-status occupations and less frequently in low-status occupations in comparison to the national averages of female workers.

Turning to the Italian occupational distribution, it seems that, unlike Jews, few Italians have been interested in the study of their countrymen's jobs. The documentation is very light, but quite consistent. Schermerhorn estimates that only 15 per cent of the Italians entered rural areas and farming (*19*, pp. 230-231, 387-390), and Brown states that the proportion of Italians working in agriculture is smaller than for any other nationality group except Greeks (*4*, p. 263); that is, despite their preponderant agricultural background, they shifted to other types of activities in their occupational adaptation.

Italian immigrants who settled in urban areas started predominantly as unskilled laborers. They were employed particularly in construction work, where they played a leading part in the building and maintenance of public works, the construction of plants, skyscrapers, roads, bridges, subways. Typical occupations of first-generation Southern Italians included work as street cleaners, excavators, surfacers and graders in street paving, sewer diggers, and other non-skilled construction jobs. For the second generation there was a marked increase in the number of small independent businessmen and a slight increase in the number of professionals. Despite these increases in higher-status occupations, as late as 1930 the leading occupation for Italians was still reported to be "unskilled labor."

Fortunately, a few studies deal with the comparison between Italian and Jewish occupational mobility. For example, Warner and Srole investigated the ethnic groups in Yankee City (22). The indices of occupational status, residential status, and class status that were computed in this study provide excellent comparative data. Warner and Srole report that the two ethnic groups settled in Yankee City during the 1890's (*22*, pp. 61, 67, 98; see especially Chapters I-V). The Jews, whose status was first measured in 1913, showed an index of 3.10 even in that year. This value surpassed that for all other groups—even the natives of the city—in 1913. In the decade from 1913-1923, the Jews moved further upward and continued to surpass other groups of the city. During the next decade, through 1933, the last year for which the indices were computed, the Jews, with an index of 3.32, achieved their highest occupational status. That this status index was higher than that for all other groups is particularly meaningful in view of the fact that one-third of the native-born Jews had left Yankee City during the latter decade for the brighter opportunities to be found in larger cities.

Employed Italians were too few to be shown in the Yankee City tables before 1923. When first reported, they showed an *occupational* status index of 2.32, a level between skilled factory and skilled crafts work. After reaching this level, Italians exhibited no further occupational mobility. In fact, by 1933 their index had declined to 2.28. Koenig's and Myers' studies in New Haven confirm the Yankee City findings in all but one respect (*12*, pp. 138 ff.; *13*, pp. 193 ff.; *16*, pp. 175-182). They find that after 1930, Italians in New Haven did show marked gains in status.

There is no way in which one can make an accurate allowance for the Italian handicap of applying peasant skills in an industrial setting. That the status positions of Jews are high cannot be denied, and that their status advantage over the Italians has increased since their arrival in this country is also highly probable. It would be a mistake, however, to think of the Southern Italians as nonmobile, for their occupational status has risen steadily, even if less spectacularly than that of the Jews.

In summary, only a small percentage of either the Jewish or Italian immigrants were in the professions, but the percentage of Jews was higher. There were also more Jews in commerce, but even in the latter periods of immigration this occupational group did not exceed 10 per cent of the total. At least two-thirds of each group was in the category of laborers, but here again the Jews had skills with greater relevance to urban occupations than the Italians, who in many instances lost their skilled status as florists or vinegrafters and became in this country common laborers.

The popular belief that the largest proportion of the Jewish immigrants were merchants is clearly refuted by these data. Both groups came to this country in great numbers within the same decade, but the Jews came a little earlier. While the occupational structure of both groups at the time of immigration reflects a much closer likeness than was formerly recognized, Jews hold a slight but consistent advantage. The argument that Jews have shown greater mobility than the Southern Italians must take account of the original advantage of the Jews and demonstrate that the gap between the groups has been widened. There can be little doubt that, in fact, Jews now have a status distribution well above the average, and that the Southern Italians are still somewhat below.

References

1. *American Jewish Yearbook, 1950, 51.* Philadelphia: Jewish Publication Society of America, 1950.
2. Bernard, J. Biculturality: A study in social schizophrenia. In Graeber, I., and Britt, S. H. (Eds.) *Jews in a Gentile World.* New York: Macmillan, 1924.
3. Bloom, L. The Jews of Buna. In Graeber, I., and Britt, S. H., *Jews in a Gentile World.* New York: Macmillan, 1924.
4. Brown, F. J. Italian Americans. In Brown, F. J., and Roucek, J. S. (Eds.), *One America.* New York: Prentice Hall, 1945.
5. Cohen, E. Economic status and occupational structure. In *American Jewish Yearbook, 1950,* Vol. 51.
6. Covello, L. The social background of the Italo-American school child: A study of the Southern Italian mores and their effects on the school situation in Italy and America. Unpublished doctoral dissertation, New York University, 1944.
7. Davie, M. R. *World Immigration.* New York: Macmillan, 1949.
8. Flowerman, S. Should Jews change their occupations? *Commentary,* 1947, *3.*
9. Foerster, R. F. *The Italian Emigration of Our Time.* Cambridge: Harvard Univ. Press, 1919.
10. Goldberg, N. Occupational patterns of American Jews. *The Jewish Review,* 1954-55, *3.*
11. Joseph, S. Jewish immigration to the United States from 1881 to 1910. *Columbia Univ. Studies in History, Economics, and Public Law,* 1914, 59, No. 4.
12. Koenig, S. The socio-economic structure of an American Jewish community. In Graeber, I., and Britt, S. H. (Eds.), *Jews in a Gentile World.* New York: Macmillan, 1924.
13. Koenig, S. Ethnic factors in the economic life of urban Connecticut. *Amer. sociol. Rev.,* 1943, *8.*

14. Lestschinsky, J. Jewish Migrations, 1840-1946. In Finkelstein, L. (Ed.), *The Jews: Their History, Culture, and Religion,* Vol. II. New York: Harper, 1949.
15. Lestschinsky, J. The position of Jews in the economic life of America. In Graeber, I., and Britt, S. H. (Eds.), *Jews in a Gentile World.* New York: Macmillan, 1924.
16. Myers, J. K. Assimilation in the political community. *Sociology and Social Research,* 1951, 35.
17. Reich, N. Economic structure of modern Jewry. In Finkelstein, L. (Ed.), *The Jews,* Vol. II. New York: Harper, 1949.
18. Robinson, S. M. (Ed.), *Jewish Population Studies.* New York: Conference on Jewish Relations, 1943.
19. Schermerhorn, R. A. *These Our People.* Boston: Heath, 1949.
20. Seligman, B. B. The American Jew: Some demographic features, in *American Jewish Yearbook, 1950,* Vol. *51.*
21. Sklare, M. *Conservative Judaism.* Glencoe, Ill.: The Free Press, 1955.
22. Warner, W. L., and Srole, L. *The Social Systems of American Ethnic Groups.* New Haven: Yale Univ. Press, 1945.
23. Williams, P. H. *South Italian Folkways in Europe and America.* New Haven: Yale University Press, 1938.

Index